Blacks Facts

~

An Ultimate Primer to the Historical and the Hysterical

It was a warm late-spring Minnesota evening on that fateful day… May 25, 2020. At 8:19 pm the sun was beginning to set on the city of Minneapolis, as well as the life of George Floyd. A scant nine minutes and twenty-nine seconds later he would be dead, murdered by a city policeman in what became a galvanizing moment.

The mantra "Black Lives Matter" had first entered the lexicon in the aftermath of the Trayvon Martin murder of 2012. So this was not outrage-original, but it did seem to become a crescendo of outrage-intensified. And it also served as an indirect impetus of inspiration for this book. We wanted to write a rallying cry, so prepare for some screaming stories.

We've got . . .

the comedian/activist who refused to buy a lifetime membership in the NAACP for fear he'd wake up one morning and the country would be integrated, thus squandering his lifetime investment.

the American who became a French WW II spy smuggling maps and documents all over Europe in her sexy underwear.

the girl who was the most highly paid child star on the planet in 1929 but was completely off the radar after 1934. No one knows what happened to her, when she died, or where she's buried.

the comedienne whose star first shone as her high school's "Conquistador" mascot where her drawing power actually exceeded that of the football team, enabling her to bribe the principal for a cut of the profits from the concession sales.

the W. Kamau Bell story where he conveys his exasperation in response to Hulk Hogan's use of the "n" word saying to him, "Come on man! People are dying, Hulk, so we gotta let that one go. I'm afraid the best we can do for you is put you in the Black Rage Waiting Room over here."

BLACKS FACTS

An Ultimate Primer to

the Historical and the Hysterical

by

Tim & Deb Smith

Pandamensional Solutions, Inc.

Mendon, New York

This book contains both original and previously published work. Some material contained herein represents the opinions of the individuals quoted and not necessarily the opinion of the authors or the publisher. In some cases, for metaphorical purposes, this work contains fiction. In such circumstances, names, characters, places and incidents are either the product of the authors' imagination or are used fictitiously. Any resemblance to actual events or locales or persons, living or dead, is entirely coincidental.

Limit of Liability/Disclaimer of Warranty: While the publisher and the authors have used their best efforts in preparing this book, they make no representations or warranties with respect to the accuracy or completeness of the contents of this book and specifically disclaim any implied warranties or merchantability or fitness for any particular purpose. No warranty may be created or extended by sales representatives or written sales materials. Neither the publisher nor author shall be liable for any loss of profit or any other commercial damages, including but not limited to special, incidental, consequential or other damages.

COPYRIGHT © 2022 BY TIM & DEB SMITH

Published by Pandamensional Solutions, Inc., Mendon, NY

Cover art by Varvara Gorbash

ALL RIGHTS RESERVED

INCLUDING THE RIGHT OF REPRODUCTION

IN WHOLE OR IN PART IN ANY FORM

ISBN-10: 1-938465-14-8
ISBN-13: 978-1-938465-14-7

What others are saying about Tim & Deb Smith's

Blacks Facts

"I am honored to be included in this inspirational, informative, entertaining, and often hilarious study – can't wait to give autographed copies to the favorite people on my list! Best wishes for the success of this project."
- Dr. Daryl Cumber Dance, current professor at the University of Richmond and former advisory editor of the Black American Literary Forum

Thanks again for taking time to gather and provide this information on the History and Humor of Black people in America. Having grown up on the sister continent – Africa, in the country of Kenya, we learned a lot about the history of White people but little about Black people in America.

I also attended a predominantly White Christian college (Roberts Wesleyan in Rochester, NY) and later HBCU North Carolina A & T (where he developed a communications chip for NASA) and they all have their own cultures. This book provides a clear picture of the journey in all aspects of life that Black Americans have gone through and brought to the table. Looking forward to the book becoming the one-stop source for February Black History Month awareness education. Forever grateful!
- Kennedy Cheruiyot, IBM Electrical Engineer

From the city of *North Star* publisher Frederick Douglass, this delightful survey of Black accomplishments also reminds us that humor has helped African Americans survive 400 years of oppression. I can see that the book will be very helpful for students, teachers and families in particular.
- Jennifer Leonard, President & CEO,
Rochester Area Community Foundation

[Your book *Black Facts*] sounds like a wonderful resource. Thanks for sharing.
- Dr. La TaSha Levy, Black Studies scholar currently serving in the Department of American Ethnic Studies at the University of Washington

What a great read. *Blacks Facts* educates and entertains. As a history teacher, it reacquainted me with the famous, and also educated me on significant storylines and fascinating lesser-known historical and entertainment figures. The research done for this book was obviously daunting. In typical Tim and Deb fashion, their writing is hysterical and informative. I particularly liked how they ranked the different personalities into unique categories. *Black Facts* is a must for your home library, both for a reference and entertainment.

~ Bob Caulkins, New York State history teacher

This is great! Your story on Madame C.J. Walker brought back great memories. I did a report on her when I was in 4th grade; I was so proud of that report. Thanks for bringing me back to that time.

~ Arianna Horton, Syracuse University Department of
 Broadcasting and Digital Journalism

I very much look forward to reading *Blacks Facts*.

~ Professor Danielle Morgan who specializes in
 African American literature in the 20th and 21st centuries
 at the University of California at Santa Clara

I'm sure others will write passionately about all aspects of this wonderful book. I, however, at the risk of being exposed as a woman with a very narrow focus, feel myself inclined to tackle the timelines. Never before had I found myself experiencing the feeling of "I can't put this down" while reading a timeline and there are two of them here. I finished the sports timeline thinking the next one couldn't be any better and then the general timeline turned out to be equally rewarding.

~ Entrepreneur, Katherine M. Gonyea

Very interesting work you've been doing. I can't imagine how many hours you've spent on research! You have certainly leveraged your professional expertise as educators.

~ Elizabeth Murray, Director of Community Engagement,
 Causewave Community Partners, Rochester, NY

We appreciate the support and best of luck with your book.

~ The Phoebe Robinson Team (Robinson is a writer, comedienne
 and actress)

Thank you for sharing the great information. You will have great success with your work [on *Blacks Facts*].
> ~ Linda Reed, African American Studies Chairperson, University of Houston

All best regards, I also want to join in congratulating you! I wish you great success with *Blacks Facts*.
> ~ Tshepo Masango Chery, South African scholar specializing in African history, with a focus on racial formation at the University of Houston

It's the beauty and the balance of the blending that raises *Blacks Facts* to the forefront of nonfiction. You could read a funny book about Black humor or you could read an informative book about Black history, and they're certainly out there. The aspect of this book which sets it apart is how adeptly it delves into both components of the Black experience.
> ~ Historian, Mike McGory

One of our most passionate topics in this book is Paul Mooney, a statement which can be verified by the fact that we chose to make him the last chapter, the grand finale, the big enchilada. Then as we were finishing up this book in the summer of 2021, we were devastated by the news that Paul Mooney had passed. It was the first time we ever had to go through a book chapter perfunctorily changing the verb "is" to "was." It was a tearful operation. After finishing the book, we began to send out feelers to some of the websites of people we'd written about and certainly a zenith in the process was when we heard back from the Mooney World Legacy Team which is handling his affairs. This led to a series of correspondences in which the Mooney Team expressed an appreciation for our work and further led to his children volunteering additional comments to our project. Before moving on, here's a nutshell summary of Mooney's career; he was Richard Pryor's go-to writer as well as a writer and performer on both the Wayans Brothers *In Living Color* and *Chappelle's Show*.

Mooney's children wanted to offer the following additional thoughts on their father…

Spring Mooney, his daughter, wrote about the book, "I'm with it! Look's cool!" and about her father wrote, "He was the recipe to comedy not just the cake. Fearless in his delivery while giving you precious ingredients!! Cut from a different cloth indeed."

Daryl Mooney, his son, wrote, "Paul Mooney was not only a comic he was an educator. He taught the world through humor about racism and Black Greatness."

Dwayne Mooney, his son, wrote, "Paul Mooney gave comedians courage to speak their truth".

The Paul Mooney World Legacy Team collectively wrote, "Thanks again for everything! It's a beautiful tribute. Thank you! Would love to see links of the TV show interviews when done. Chat soon."

~ Mooney World Legacy Team

Dedication

With this book, we will be giving birth
To a work, which we hope bares the worth
Of expanding our goals
Unifying the souls
That will bring to the world peace on Earth

It Takes All Of Us

Table of Contents

1 ~ CHAPTER 1 ~ STORYLINE SAMPLER

12 ~ CHAPTER 2 ~ SALUTE TO THE KING

CHAPTER 3 ~ THIS ONE IS FOR THE "GOAT"S
15 ~ Dave Chappelle
17 ~ Redd Foxx
19 ~ Bill Cosby
21 ~ Eddie Murphy
23 ~ Chris Rock
27 ~ Richard Pryor

CHAPTER 4 ~ FIVE FEMALES WHO BROKE BARRIERS IN ENTERTAINMENT
31 ~ Josephine Baker
37 ~ Esther Jones & Betty Boop
41 ~ Gladys Bentley
42 ~ Hattie McDaniel
44 ~ Nichelle Nichols

CHAPTER 5 ~ FOUR FEMALES WHO BROKE BARRIERS IN MODERN COMEDY
48 ~ Tiffany Haddish
53 ~ Issa Rae
54 ~ Amber Ruffin
57 ~ Phoebe Robinson

CHAPTER 6 ~ FROM SITTING ON A BUS TO SITTING IN THE WHITE HOUSE
63 ~ Claudette Colvin
64 ~ Bayard Rustin
66 ~ Shirley Chisholm
68 ~ Barack Obama

CHAPTER 7 ~ THE MALE COMEDY ROLL CALL FROM THE MODERN ERA
72 ~ Jamie Foxx
74 ~ Kevin Hart
77 ~ Martin Lawrence
78 ~ Tracy Morgan
79 ~ Trevor Noah
82 ~ Wayans Clan
83 ~ W. Kamau Bell

CHAPTER 8 ~ SOME BELOW-THE-RADAR BLACK SPORTS HISTORY
87 ~ Jack Johnson
89 ~ John Baxter Taylor
90 ~ Mack Robinson
91 ~ New York Renaissance
93 ~ Satchel Paige
96 ~ Muhammad Ali

CHAPTER 9 ~ THE GATEWAY FROM THE CHITLIN' CIRCUIT TO THE MAINSTREAM
98 ~ Pigmeat Markham
100 ~ Slappy White
101 ~ Nipsey Russell
103 ~ Flip Wilson
105 ~ Dick Gregory

CHAPTER 10 ~ NOTEWORTHY CONCEPTS & EVENTS
107 ~ Interracial Marriage
108 ~ The Quakers and the Jews
111 ~ Juneteenth
113 ~ The Wiz
114 ~ Motown 25
116 ~ We Are the World

CHAPTER 11 - THE ORIGINAL LADIES OF BLACK COMEDY
117 - Bertice Berry
117 - Daryl Cumber Dance
119 - LaWanda Page
120 - Moms Mabley

CHAPTER 12 - WAR IS HELL
123 - Cathay Williams
125 - 6888th Central Battalion
127 - Harlem Hellfighters
128 - Tuskegee Airmen

CHAPTER 13 - THE ORIGINAL WAVE OF BLACK COMEDIANS
132 - Bert Williams
135 - The Tutt Brothers
136 - Butterbeans and Susie
138 - Stepin Fetchit
140 - Mantan Moreland
141 - Willie Best

CHAPTER 14 - SETTING THE WAYBACK MACHINE FOR SOME VINTAGE STORIES
143 - Onesimus
144 - Phillis Wheatley
146 - Bass Reeves
149 - Bill Pickett
151 - Matthew Henson
153 - C.J. Walker
154 - Bessie Coleman
157 - The Scottsboro Boys

CHAPTER 15 - SAVING THE "X" FOR LAST
164 - Kings of Comedy
165 - Cedric the Entertainer
167 - Steve Harvey
168 - Bernie Mac
169 - D.L. Hughley
170 - Whoopi Goldberg
172 - Paul Mooney

177 - **ADDENDUM 1 - THE SCOTTSBORO BOYS**

182 - **ADDENDUM 2 - SPORTS TIMELINE**

215 - **ADDENDUM 3 - HISTORICAL TIMELINE**

FOREWORD

By Amir Campbell

A masterful and lovingly written look into the history of Black lives. As a Black man I appreciate how Deb and Tim shed light on many of the unknown moments and lives that have contributed to the lifting up of society. From the content to the cover, you can feel their love, respect and appreciation for every one of the stories portrayed throughout.

I consider myself very well-read in terms of Black literature and I even went online to confirm what I pretty much already knew to be true; there is just not another book like this anywhere out there. There are books on Black humor and there are books on Black history, but no one has ever attempted to merge those two threads into the eye of a single needle. And the Smiths have accomplished this with pinpoint precision.

Just when you have laughed so hard that you need a little break, they throw the history book right back at you. Next, you find yourself reading an incredible story about some Black person that you've never heard of before, and by the end of it, you're thinking, "Why have I never heard of this dude? Thank you, Tim and Deb, not only for having brought this story to my attention, but also for bringing it to the forefront for all those who make it a priority to stay well-read in terms of any pertinent new material woven into the fabric of the Black consciousness."

The breadth and depth of the research that went into this book is totally astonishing. No stone has been left unturned. From the comedy perspective, the reader is provided with a comprehensive review of the entire gamut of Black humor from the late 1800's through the modern-day. The historical component dates back even further with the earliest entry on the timeline going all the way back to the late 1400's. Which brings me to the topic of timelines…

There are two of them included amongst the addenda. A general comment that could accurately be applied to both would be to say that they manage to add an unexpected air of creativity and entertainment. In my mind, any writers who can put pizzaz into a timeline have me solidly in their literary corner, and the Smiths have managed to do that here.

Leading off, pun intended, is the sports timeline. This one is written in past tense and is based upon the premise of "firsts." They do a great job of using the concept of "firsts" to incorporate all of the great Black athletes and, in some cases, they have to take an interesting stretch to get to the "firsts." Let me use Muhammad Ali to exemplify. Ali was perhaps the greatest Black athlete of all time, but when you examine his career, his most significant "first" does not drop out of the sky and hit you in the head like an anvil.

Running through his most milestone achievements, Ali was **not** the first Black to win an Olympic Gold Medal, he was **not** the first Black to win the heavyweight championship, and he was certainly **not** the first Black to avoid the draft, so the Smiths skillfully scan his career legacy and land upon the fact that he **was** the first man (Black or White) to win the heavyweight championship on three separate occasions. So, they seize upon that moment to incorporate the entire Ali story into their timeline.

Their general timeline of Black history is written in present tense serving to convey a spontaneous feeling as if it's all happening right now. Some of the events included will be ones you may know but, for the most part, it's a revealing magic carpet ride through twisting tunnels of time where treasures will be revealed regarding the first Blacks to make a million dollars, appear on a postage stamp, and score a #1 song and album. Of course, those are just a sampling of the 500 gold nuggets to be found in this treasure chest.

My heritage has been blessed by their thoroughness and so has society's. In the heart of the book, you will be blessed by gal-pal stories such as the first Black woman to publish a book (a 12-year-old slave), enlist in the Army (passing the physical while posing as a male), and serve as a WW II spy (before Coretta Scott King asked her to head the civil rights movement after MLK's assassination). For the he-men, stories are shared about the first Black rodeo star (his secret was to bite the steer's lip), the Wild West's most maniacal marshal (inspiration for the Lone Ranger), and the oldest musical artist to score a Top 40 hit. (remember "Here Come Da Judge"?)

Let me finish up with a tagline I would like to serve as my closing statement. This book should be in every home across America.

Acknowledgements

This whole thing got started one morning when we simply went out to get the mail. We live in the downtown section of a small town in Upstate New York with a population of about a thousand. The office of our local newspaper happens to be right next door to us and we love to tell stories. That can be a dangerous combination.

On the morning in question, we crossed paths with the newspaper publisher and shared our rather unique personal back story. That prompted the response that, "You should share that story in the paper." A week later we hit the presses for the first time and the essence of that story can be enjoyed in the "About the Authors" segment in the back of this book.

Soon thereafter we had taken over the back page for a weekly *Sentinel Lifestyles* feature called "Life With the (Word)Smiths." In general, our feature covers an eclectic variety of topics including entertainment, sports, travel, history and human interest. "We're all over the place" is a comment that ironically can be applied to both our writing for the paper and our approach to this book which you are about to read.

So, our writing has expanded to the point where we are currently composing three columns a week for the paper and this is our fourth book we've published. We have much more in the pipeline and we're hoping you'll join us to have some fun along the way

After launching our newspaper career, our publisher Chris Carosa, began encouraging us to write a book. The stars, for us, aligned in the beginning of 2019 when we connected the dots on some historical events and came to realize that occurring within a 30-day period that coming summer would be the 50th anniversaries of First Man on the Moon, Chappaquiddick, the Manson Murders, Woodstock and one other thing… it also happened to be the 50th anniversary of the day we met.

We were waiting for a sign from God and this seemed to be thrust down upon us like a lightning bolt hurled here from Heaven. We needed to pick one of those 50th anniversary events, take it by its literary horns and run with it. That led to the composition of our first book, *The Beatles, The Bible & Manson: Reflecting Back with 50 Years of Perspective*.

So what to do for a follow up? The answer that just kind of fell into our laps was a thematic compilation of all the material we had generated for the paper which we titled, *Tit For Tat Exchanges - Tim & Deb's Greatest Hits*. The first half of the title is a reference to the single line we wrote that generated the greatest response from our readers.

At one point we did a story on Easter Island which is a territory of Chile located off the western coast of South America in the Pacific Ocean. One part of our Easter Island coverage featured a dispute between the territory of Easter Island and its mother country of Chile which was described as a tit-for-tat exchange.

We love to analyze and play with words and that storyline gave us pause to ponder… isn't "tit-for-tat" such an interesting little colloquialism? Does not that pause to ponder give one cause to wonder, "What exactly is tat? How do I get some? And where can I turn it in for the other thing?"

We followed up *Tit For Tat* with a tome called *What's in a Name? - Your Geography Hall of Fame*. In that book we combined our love for historical geography and penchant for storytelling to compose a compilation of the places on the planet that have the funniest and/or most bizarre place names.

We spent a few years researching this project and the storylines that made this book basically had to satisfy two criteria. To even achieve consideration the place needed a unique name, but in order to make the cut, it also needed to be accompanied by a story worthy of sharing and one that lent itself to our irreverent writing style.

That brings us to the point where we are now going public with our testimonial to *Blacks Facts - An Ultimate Primer to the Historical and the Hysterical*, the book you are currently holding in your hands. We plan to engage and entertain you on multiple levels as we make you laugh and make you think. Let's kick start this soiree and get down to some *Blacks Facts*.

Tim & Deb Smith
Mendon, New York
December 1, 2021

INTRODUCTION

As we mentioned earlier, the murder of George Floyd on May 25, 2020 seemed to bring a new level of energy to the national debate regarding racial inequality. Ground Zero of The Black Lives Matter movement can be traced back to the 2012 killing of Trayvon Martin, so it's not like that piece was new, but the murder of George Floyd had somehow managed to push the volume of the movement to an all-encompassing crescendo it had never before achieved. And while that reality frightened some people, if you're reading this book you probably agree with us that it was a fear that needed to be instilled.

The sultry summer of 2020 sizzled and not at all surreptitiously. It was unavoidable, the coalescent cacophony of racial unrest playing out amidst the somber backdrop of a pandemic. That summer sucked and shocked in ways no one could have previously imagined and this whole crazy mess was covered with a coating of Covid.

We wanted to do something… anything, that could possibly contribute to an initiative to get our society moving in a positive direction. The most effective of our possible outlets seemed obvious. Since retiring from decades of teaching, we've undertaken second careers as writers.

We've written a weekly feature for our local paper in Rochester, New York since 2015 and this is our 4th published book. So, once that write-a-book decision had been made, the project needed to be conceptualized.

We write nonfiction, so that was a given, and we had the notion that we wanted it to be purposeful rather than preachy. We felt that the most impactful approach was to broaden the spectrum as wide as we possibly could. It was this approach that led to our use of the word "primer" in our title.

Words of praise that we have often heard regarding our work are that readers appreciate our ability to inform as well as entertain. Seizing upon that, we chose the two-prong approach that characterizes this book and its title. Therefore, (Inform = Historical) + (Entertain = Hysterical) was an equation we thought we could run with. And those are the two concepts we weave throughout this book.

People like to laugh and they like to learn things. For our laughter component we surveyed the entire spectrum of Black comedy and basically functioned in the role of research editors serving up the best of the brightest and most brilliant Black comedic minds off all time. How can anybody not love that? You'll get to read them all here. Prepare yourself for some rolling in the aisles.

Regarding the historical component of this book, we felt the most effective focus should be upon the line from the previous paragraph which reads that people "like to learn things." To that end we sought out what we felt were the most interesting Black stories that were a little off the beaten path. There are highs (Obama elected) and lows (King assassinated) about which most everyone knows, and we made a conscious effort to **not** dwell upon those in our book. In our historical sections, we have taken strides to weave some tales of topics atypical.

LINGUISTICS LOGISTICS ~ Recent years have seen an ongoing debate regarding the capitalization of the "B" in Black when referring to race. Because that word has been used to identify race for so long, one might think that the accepted usage would have become standardized long ago. But alas, that is not the case as various media organizations which dictate the edicts of language usage such as the AP Stylebook and the Center for the Study of Social Policy have reflected a fairly recent shift with more organizations moving in the direction of now capitalizing the "B." The racial identification that had traditionally been "black" is now solidly trending toward "Black."

And that's the way we're going to punctuate this book. We also have some related thoughts on the topic. The prevailing logic that seems most compelling to us would be the fact that if other racial identities such as Asian, Latino and Native American are capitalized, Black should also be when used to identify a race rather than a color.

This of course leads to the question of whether "White" should be capitalized when referring to race. It traditionally has not, but that too seems to be a growing subject of change. We agree with the sentiment that to not capitalize White is actually a practice that is inherently anti-

Black. To not capitalize White is to imply that it is somehow accepted as the norm, or the standard, with everyone else falling into some kind of "other" category. So we will also capitalize White throughout this book anytime it is referring to a race, rather than a color.

The capitalization of White inadvertently achieves a mutually symbiotic goal. It also serves to cancel out a racially motivated tactic employed by many White supremacist groups who have traditionally capitalized White in their literature. When nobody was capitalizing White, their doing so achieved a self-aggrandizing purpose. If everybody capitalizes White, their gesture is rendered meaningless.

CHITLIN' CIRCUIT ~ One term that comes up frequently, especially with the earlier waves of Black entertainers, is the "Chitlin' Circuit" so let's take a moment to provide the necessary background to put that concept in context when it appears in this book. Basically stated, the Chitlin' Circuit was a consortium of venues, mostly east of the Mississippi River that catered to Black performers and audiences.

The dates can be subject to debate, but the Chitlin' Circuit existed in one form or another from the late 1800's through the 1960's. Prior to the advent of the motion picture, the primary avenue of entertainment for both Blacks and Whites was vaudeville, so let's toss in a quick summary of that medium.

Vaudeville acts of both races toured the country presenting live shows featuring some combination of both comedy and music. Because the venues were segregated, the early Black vaudeville circuit was essentially the Chitlin' Circuit of its day, even though the first documented use of the term Chitlin' Circuit did not occur until 1917.

The earliest touring Black show we will cover in this book will be that of the Tutt Brothers who first hit the road in the late 1800's and were a major factor in Black entertainment through the 1940's. Their career spanned vaudeville, Broadway and the movies and when someone first dropped the term Chitlin' Circuit in 1917 it did not change what they were doing even one iota. So, it should be noted that Chitlin' Circuit is a very unofficial designation thrown out as a type of umbrella covering the general concept of live Black entertainment during that specified era.

Let's finish with a touch on the etymology. Chitlins were short for chitterlings which were boiled pig intestines. This would have been a dining destination arrived at by necessity rather than choice. It was a culinary concoction that actually dates back to medieval Europe where it was a dietary staple of the poor. When chitlins entered the mainstream of the Black American diet the nuance was added that they were usually boiled, then fried.

Never let it be said that the Smiths can't whet your literary appetite and set the table with the most delicious delicacies of culinary cuisine. Now it's on to the main course where we hope every chapter will leave you hungry for more. More chapters that is, not more chitlins.

Chapter 1
STORYLINE SAMPLER

The concept of Chapter 1 assuming the responsibility of providing an overview of *Blacks Facts* is one that we've employed in each of the four books we've published. Since raucous reviews have resonated, we're rockin' on with that same strategy. By the end of this chapter, you will have a solid flight plan outlining the key destinations which will comprise the itinerary of this journey.

Our "Blacks Facts Ultimate Primer" will weave two threads throughout this endeavor on our part to both inform and entertain. That's where the "Historical and Hysterical" kicks in. Our chapters will alternate between historic Black tales that are a little bit off the beaten path and a comprehensive review of the history of Black humor which will provide you with a riotous tour down very well-beaten paths of laughter that, we assure you, will stir some great old memories while creating some even greater new ones.

THIS DUDE LEADS OFF FOR A REASON ~ There was one man who, as we write about later, seemed to line-straddle between comedian and activist more than any other. If we were to share with you that, other than civil rights, his greatest activist cause was the anti-Vietnam War movement, could you name that comedian? Here's one of our favorite lines of his… *They asked me to buy a lifetime membership in the NAACP, but I told them I'd pay a week at a time. Hell of a thing to buy a lifetime membership, wake up one morning and find the country's been integrated!*

BLACK ICE ~ Google "Who first reached the North Pole?" and the big-black-block-letter flash-up you'll get is "Robert Peary." Well, we're here to tell ya that you can't believe everything you read. The dude who actually flagpole-rammed the Stars & Stripes into the Arctic ice was Black and we have his story.

A CHARMING CHAP ~ Current comic legend Dave Chappelle had one line that predates some of the more recent atrocities. Several years ago he went on record saying, "Every group of brothers should have at least one White guy in it. I'm serious, for safety, cuz when the shit goes down someone is gonna need to talk to the police."[1]

THE GAY SWAY TO MLK ~ How many of you would be surprised if we were to tell you that the following bullet points could all be found on the same man's résumé.

* Openly gay
* Worked on human rights movements in multiple countries
* Taught MLK the principle of non-violent resistance
* Primary influence in MLK giving up his guns
* Lead planner of event where MLK delivered "Dream" speech
* Received Presidential Medal of Freedom from Obama in 2013

Yep, all of these descriptors apply to the same guy who we promise to make into one of the great behind-the-scenes stories of the civil rights movement.

BLUESY SUSIE ~ If you've never heard of Butterbeans and Susie you're gonna want to order a bowlful-big of these guys. They were a life-for-real husband and wife team who toured the Chitlin' Circuit, doing the envelope-push on sexuality. Susie's occasional expressions of sex deprivation were paradoxically juxtaposed by Butterbean's blustery boasts to the contrary.

Their comedy act was musically sex-craze driven and we will hold out temporarily on the dirty-down details of "I Want a Hot Dog for My Roll" but we will share with you now a little ditty called "New Jelly Roll Blues" where Butterbeans seems ready to deliver the goods, so to speak, or at least he's talkin' a good game.

Jelly roll, jelly roll, ain't so hard to find
There's a baker shop in town bakes it brown like mine
I got sweet jelly, a lovin' sweet jelly roll
If you taste my jelly, it'll satisfy your soul

PROPHESIES OF PHILLIS FULFILLED ~ You will absolutely love the story of the first Black, male or female, to have a book published on planet Earth. Hitting the presses in 1773, it features some fascinating nuances. Undoubtedly, the most fascinating of these would be the fact that it was written by a 12-year-old slave.

Phillis Wheatley's book of poetry included one called "To His Excellency, George Washington," clearly picture-painting Wheatley as a poet ahead of her time. Take a minute to date-process this one. Not only was Washington not yet president, the Revolutionary War hadn't even begun. What was "His Excellency's" response to the prophetic poetry? Washington arranged a meeting with her at his headquarters!

TIMELY TRIBUTE ~ Do you remember the following two catch phrases from the early 1970's?

* "What you see is what you get!"
* "The Devil made me do it!"

Well, you will absolutely flip when we tell you the man who was behind those lines. In January of 1972 *Time* magazine featured him in a cover story boasting the headline "TV's First Black Superstar."

SEEKING SATCHEL ~ Perhaps our favorite sports story of this book is the component on baseball pitcher Satchel Paige. He dominated the Negro Leagues when he was in his 20's & 30's and then, after the race barrier was broken, he shockingly dominated Major League Baseball in his 40's. He was characterized by his ability to perennially lead the league in wins, strike outs, and one-liners. It was a triple threat that made him legendary.

With the Cleveland Indians, Paige deflected questions regarding whether he was married or not. When the team noticed that different women were picking up tickets being left for "Mrs. Paige" every day, he was questioned. "Well, it's like this," Satch said, "I'm not married, but I am in great demand."

ACCOLADES ATTRIBUTED ~ In researching the comedic thread of this book we conducted what we will refer to as our "poll of polls." We sought out and saved every respectable source poll of best (Black) comedians of all time and averaged them to compile a consensus poll of polls. The "(Black)" in the prior sentence was to convey the fact that several, actually most, of these polls were straightforward rankings of the greatest comedians of all time, regardless of race.

Those polls we shook through our sifter, extracting only the Black performers, to compile a list that would be purpose-pertinent to this project. For example, *Rolling Stone* magazine's feature on "50 Best Stand-Up Comics of All Time" we honed down to come up with *Rolling Stone's* list of the top 13 Black comics.

So now that we've established our protocol, how 'bout we offer up our next interactive experience of the book. Your challenge is to guess who was ranked as the #1 Black comedian of all time in our poll of polls and we are going to give you three colleague quotes as clues. About him the following opinions were shared.

DAVE CHAPPELLE ~ You know those evolution charts of man? He was the dude walking upright. He was the highest evolution of comedy.
BILL COSBY ~ He drew the line between comedy and tragedy as thin as one could possibly paint it.
BOB NEWHART ~ He was the seminal comedian of the last 50 years.

As we continue to identify some of the motifs we will employ in this book, please allow us to progress from our poll of polls to our poetry. This piece of literature will be limerick-laced and here's our first, which was written from the perspective of our aforementioned #1 comedian. Check it out below.

I grew up in a world full of crime
In that world made a Hell of a climb
As the great ones would tell
From Newhart to Chappelle
I am simply the best of all time

BETTY & THE RANGER ~ Next, we have one example of how two totally unconnected people have somewhat similar storylines. There are two fictional-figure-famous folks in American media who most everyone always thought were White, but turns out they were Black, sort of. We're dishin' on one dude and one chick in this component, and we're prepared to pour on the paradox. How 'bout we go from a male, most-macho, to a female, fabulously feminine? We have the storyline on how Wild West hero the Lone Ranger and voluptuous cartoon character Betty Boop were both Black.

GREGARIOUS GALS ~ We are gonna downright-do some lady-lovin', especially the new wave of Black comediennes including Tiffany Haddish, Amber Ruffin, Phoebe Robinson and Issa Rae. But, going back a generation, we'll close this segment with a teaser.

Can you guess the famous Black comedienne who absolutely told it like it was with the following assessment of White America in the 1980's when she said, "When Rock Hudson came out as gay, it was like John Wayne fucked his horse." Who would have been honest enough to do that kind of layin' it on the line?

HELLFIGHTING RATTLERS ~ We have a WW I story about perhaps the most efficient American military brigade in the war, the Harlem Hellfighters or, as they were also known, the Black Rattlers. Curiously, they fought for the French Army rather than the U.S. Army. We'll tell you how in the world that strange juxtaposition came to be.

COLOR US RED ~ The Black comedian who comes in at #5 in our poll of polls was best known for his starring role in a classic 1970's sitcom which, depending on your age, may or may not be enough of a clue to figure out who he is. Here's one of his better stories.

As a note of explanation, the Black scientists he references in the following joke are Charles Richard Drew for the blood work and George Washington Carver for the peanut butter.

You must utilize every Black brain in America to make our country strong. We had great Black scientists. One started the first blood bank and researched blood plasma; another Black scientist crossed some peanut butter with a mule. Got a sandwich with long ears and a piece of ass that sticks to the roof of your mouth. We need that Black genius working in America![2]

M & M's ~ We have a couple shooting stars whose storylines seem to magic-mirror one another in multiple manifestations. First of all, there's the cool-groove nicknames you're sure to feast upon when we identify the subjects of this soiree as Moms Mabley and Pigmeat Markham. And in our alphabetical-order working draft of this book, it was hard to slip-slide a piece of paper in between the pair's last names.

In terms of career storylines, you have two performers who were both early-1900's born, did teeth-cutting performances on the Chitlin' Circuit in the 1920's, enjoyed lengthy Black-audiences-only careers, and wound up enjoying the most successful decade of their lives during the 1960's when they were able to master the mixed-race mainstream audience crossover dance.

Oh, and they were also able to share one more similar experience, and this is perhaps the quirkiest fun fact of all. In the late 1960's they each had Top 40 hit songs, within a year of each other, becoming the oldest two artists to ever attain that **geriatric gyration** on the *Billboard* charts.

We'll close with one final crime story. We highly suspect one of them stole a little something from the other. In exploring famous quotes from each we found the following, but we were unable to lie detector-down the date debuts of either delivery. Moms Mabley once said, "Outside of malt, men and manna, I have no vices." Pigmeat Markham's equivalent was, "Outside of booze, broads and bread, I have no vices." Obviously it was a shared sentiment.

COAT OF MANY COLORS ~ Of all the deep-dive delving we did in the research process for this book, here's one piece that really popped. How 'bout a woman whose robust résumé includes these ten tantalizing tidbits…

* First married at the age of 13
* Ten serious romantic relationships; six with men, four with women
* Achieved fame dancing nude except for string of fake bananas around her waist
* First Black woman to appear in a feature film
* Was an undercover spy during WW II
* Bought and lived in a castle
* Adopted twelve kids from different nationalities and religions
* Only female opening speaker at MLK's "I Have a Dream" Speech
* NAACP Woman of the Year
* Coretta Scott King asked her to lead civil rights movement after MLK's death

Look forward to having us dot-connect those 10 tittilators into a single storyline.

TUBMAN & TRUTH – Rosa Parks was famous for the fact that it was her Supreme Court case that led to the desegregation of bus transportation in the United States. But the Rosa Parks bus seat story actually comes with an asterisk-outright. Before there was Rosa, there was Claudette Colvin. While the Rosa Parks incident occurred on December 1, 1955, it was on March 2 of that year, nine months earlier, that the 15-year-old Colvin refused to move to the back of a Montgomery bus. For her efforts, she was arrested and thrown in jail.

We will not only share the whys and wheretofores regarding how Rosa Parks emerged as the female face of the bus boycott, this is also the source of one of our favorite quotes in the book. The words are what Colvin said was going through her mind when she was asked to give up her seat. She said, "I felt like Sojourner Truth was pushing down on one shoulder and Harriet Tubman was pushing down on the other. I was glued to my seat."

My girl Sojourner Truth spoke to me
Harriet Tubman was loud as could be
Sit back down on your throne
And world, let it be known
That before Rosa Parks there was me

R.O.C.K. IN THE U.S.A. – In our poll of polls, Chris Rock was rated the #2 Black comedian of all time. If there's one thing that clearly characterizes Rock's work in general, it's a flair for telling it just like it is. That attribute is aptly displayed in the following samples…

* So you gotta look at OJ's situation. He's payin' $25,000 a month in alimony, got another man drivin' around in his car and fuckin' his wife, in a house he's still payin' the mortgage on. Now I'm not sayin' he shoulda killed her… but I understand.[3]

* (during the early-2000's administration of Bush 43) You know the world is going crazy when the best rapper is a White guy, the best golfer is a Black guy, the tallest guy in the NBA is Chinese, the Swiss hold the America's Cup, France is accusing the U.S. of arrogance, Germany

doesn't want to go to war, and the three most powerful men in America are named "Bush", "Dick", and "Colon." Need I say more?[4]

WEDDING BELL BLUES - How many of you knew that interracial marriage was illegal in all, or parts, of the 13 colonies/United States for 303 years? That is one long-ass run that didn't go up in smoke until 1967 when a couple from Virginia, where interracial marriage was still illegal, went to Washington D.C. to knot-tie their nuptials.

That "Virginia Is For Lovers" advertising pitch notwithstanding, the Old Dominion State had a whimsically wistful "congratulations and welcome home" present for them. They were arrested and convicted for the offense of dragging one of those nasty interracial marriages back onto their home turf. Ironically, that actually turns out to be a good thing for reasons which we'll fill you in on soon.

NOAH'S ARC LARK - Perhaps you go to bed too early to have noticed, but America does have its first Black South African late night talk show host who we'll be sure to tell you about later, but right now we'll share one of his pithier comments regarding his South African origins. He said, *"You have to work a bit harder to offend me because I'm from the home of some of the best racism in the world. I'm a snob when it comes to racism. I never thought I'd be more afraid of police in America than in South Africa. It kind of makes me a little nostalgic for the old days back home."*[5]

VACCINATION FASCINATION - Here is our nomination for the wildest WTF? in the book. Would it surprise you to be told that the first vaccination against disease in America was performed by an African slave in Boston? Now for a bonus "Say What?" we'll tack on the fact that within the next decade, vaccinations had become a standard procedure in both Colonial America and England. All because of what a man named Onesimus had learned in his hometown back in sunny sub-Saharan West Africa.

ROYAL ENTOURAGE - One of the great comedy tours of all-time hit the road between 1997 and 2000. Billing themselves as the Kings of Comedy, this 4-man show featured Steve Harvey, Bernie Mac, Cedric the Entertainer and D.L. Hughley. The latter espouses the theory that Black folks don't have to look for dangerous distractions because just being Black is dangerous enough. But White folks, not so much. Here's Hughley's take on the subject…

Stuff happens to White folks, don't happen to nobody else. I live in Southern California and two people were mauled by mountain lions. I knew right away they wasn't Black people, cause we don't hike. Turns out, there's only one way a mountain lion could get a Black person and Hughley will give us the line on the lion when we hand him the mic a little later.

Here's Steve Harvey sharing a story from his "my-ass-be-strugglin'" younger days. "Bill collectors were always callin' me," Harvey said. "They call so much I developed routines. They say, 'When can we expect payment?'"

I say, "You can **expect** it anytime you want, **gettin'** it is gonna be your problem."

WILD WEST WACKINESS ~ One resounding résumé we'll share is that of Bill Pickett, the legendary Black cowboy, rodeo star and Wild West show performer. He will be the only person in our book whose ability to bite live animals proves to be an integral part of his success. We hope you'll like our limerick on this one which is written from the perspective of the rodeo steer.

While it's rarely my style to complain
That Black cowboy is truly insane
There's his legs on my hip
Then that bite on my lip
Which I must say I truly disdain

EDIFYING EDDIE ~ Effervescent Eddie Murphy mans up at #3 in our comedy poll of polls and here's his take on the convergence of finances, figures and fingers…

Every bad decision I've made has been based on money. I grew up in the projects and you don't turn down money there. You take it, because you never know when it's all going to end. I made [Beverly Hills] Cop III because they offered me $15 million. That $15 million was worth having [film critic] Roger Ebert's thumb up my ass.[6]

BLACK RENAISSANCE ~ Did you know the first Black inductees into the Basketball Hall of Fame were actually a team called the New

York Renaissance and they were the greatest team you've never heard of. You'll love their storyline which includes the 1932-33 season during which the aka-Rens compiled a record of 120 wins and 8 losses, including a winning streak of 88 games, a record never matched in pro basketball history. In 1939 the first "World Professional Basketball Tournament" was organized and the Rens defeated the Harlem Globetrotters, advancing to the finals. There they defeated an all-White team to win what is considered to be the first world title in pro basketball.

BERT, BABY, BERT ~ In researching this book, truly one of the greatest treasures we unsurfaced was the story of the Black man who could lay claim to three amazing accolades in the first quarter of the 20th century. During that era he was the consensus choice as to being the funniest Black comedian, he sold more records than anyone else, and he also made the most money. Let's have a laugh, cue up a tune, and take it to the bank with Bert Williams.

In the early 1900's, when racial stereotyping was common place, Williams managed to envelope-push in multiple areas. In 1902 he became the first Black to assume the lead role in a Broadway play, in 1914 he became the first to land the lead in a film. He was referred to as "one of the great comedians of the world" by the *New York Dramatic Mirror* in 1918.

FRENCH FEMALE FLIGHT ~ Just after WW I, there was an employee at a Chicago hair salon who was totally fascinated by the stories of Army fighter pilots returning from the war and that employee became aviation-avocation-allured. Okay, noble dream and all, but how much of a deck-stacked dilemma is hovering over our hair-to-air heroine?

Sure, people have overcome obstacles to achieve success, but how about the stigma-triple facing this person… Our "hair-to-air" candidate is part Black, part American Indian, and all-woman. Fortunately she was not a baseball player because, despite already being in three-strike-status, Bessie Coleman was definitely not out. We promise you'll be moved by her story.

TRANSGENDER TRAILS ~ If we told you we had a good story about a Black woman recruited to help the Union Army efforts during the Civil War you might say, "Sounds interesting, you've got my attention, tell me more." How 'bout if we were to add the caveat that this same woman would later disguise herself as a man and succeed in completing the entire enlistment process, including the physical, to become the first woman to ever enlist in the U.S. Army.

Hopefully you'd be saying, "No freakin' way, can't wait to read this, bring it on." If that's your reaction, the news is good; we're here for you. The lady who stars in this story is one Cathay Williams or, as she becomes known in the second half of the story when she flip-flops her name as part of her enlistment ruse, William Cathay.

When this whole sex change put-on began
Getting sick wasn't part of my plan
'Cause I had to concede
That as soon as I peed
The doctor would know I'm no man

SPACE, THE FINAL FRONTIER - Is the name Nichelle Nichols a bell-ringer for you? Well, it rang a bell for Martin Luther King Jr. One of our stories here takes place at an NAACP convention in 1967 where King seeks this actress out and imparts upon her advice that will change the direction of her career.

PUNCH AND LAND IT - The 1960's also took on an unusual storyline combining Stepin Fetchit and Muhammad Ali. On some levels the two men may seem to rest at opposite ends of the spectrum of Blackness. During the same decade, while Fetchit was being criticized by some in the civil rights movement for the stereotypical Black roles he had played in movies decades ago, Muhammad Ali had come to represent the face of a newly defiant Black America which was making its most forceful statements ever in the drive for equal rights.

So what was it that brought these two men together? In 1964 Muhammad Ali (fighting as Cassius Clay) had won the heavyweight championship by knocking out Sonny Liston. After changing his name, Ali's next fight, his first title defense, was a rematch with Liston. During his training for this fight, Ali summoned Fetchit to his training camp for an extended period of time. We guarantee you're going to be knocked out when we tell you the reason why!

Chapter 2

Salute to the King

Martin Luther King Jr. (1929-1968)

Obviously the Martin Luther King Jr. story could fill volumes and that's really not our goal with this project. We're taking the broad-spectrum approach here and obviously the MLK thread runs through many of our stories. That being said, we still wanted to bless this acknowledged leader of the cause with a short chapter of his own, featuring a couple jokes and stories.

The story that we picked was a behind-the-scenes look at the "I Have a Dream" speech as there are a few notable nuances regarding how that one went down. On Tuesday, August 27, 1963 which was "I Have a Dream" Eve, King had gathered with a group of his advisors at the Willard Hotel in Washington D.C. to go over notes for the speech. When Team-King turned in for the night, they had landed on a plan for the speech to be more political and less historical than the direction to which King would choose to divert the next day.

Resetting the table, the speech which is delivered on the steps of the Lincoln Memorial is the culmination of the March on Washington. A crowd of 250,000 has gathered by the time King takes to the podium. During the early portion of the speech Mahalia Jackson is standing on the wings of the Memorial repeating the phrase, "Tell 'em about the dream, Martin."

So that oratorical concept is clearly one that King's close friends and advisors know he has in his arsenal. Whether Martin reacted to Mahalia's cue was never definitively documented, but this much we do know. After saying, "We are not satisfied, and we will not be satisfied until justice rolls down like waters, and righteousness like a mighty stream," King shoves his notes aside and goes off script.

Some of the most immortal words ever spoken on the face of the planet would follow: *Even though we face the difficulties of today and tomorrow, I still have a dream. It is a dream deeply rooted in the American dream. I have a dream that one day this nation will rise up and live out the true meaning of its creed: "We hold these truths to be self-evident, that all men are created equal."*

[I have a dream that one day] little Black boys and Black girls will be able to join hands with little White boys and White girls as sisters and brothers. I have a dream today! I have a dream that one day every valley shall be exalted, and every hill and mountain shall be made low, the rough places will be made plain, and the crooked places will be made straight; and the glory of the Lord shall be revealed and all flesh shall see it together.

And, of course, the grand finale is when he closes with: *When we allow freedom to ring, when we let it ring from every village and every hamlet, from every state and every city, we will be able to speed up that day when all of God's children, Black men and White men, Jews and Gentiles, Protestants and Catholics, will be able to join hands and sing in the words of the old Negro spiritual:*

> *Free at last! Free at last!*
> *Thank God Almighty, we are free at last!*[1]

HAVE A LAUGH ~ We'll close our King component with some keen comedy. Once when Johnny Carson went on vacation from *The Tonight Show* for a week in 1968, he turned over the guest hosting chores to Harry Belafonte. During his week, Belafonte was able to book his own guests and he chose to take an approach that was very Black-oriented. One of the guests he had was MLK who shared the following funny story.

I flew out of Washington this afternoon and as soon as we started out, they notified us that the plane had mechanical difficulties and that kept us on the ground for a good while. Finally, we took off and landed. Whenever I land after mechanical difficulties I'm always very happy, and I don't want to give you the impression that as a Baptist preacher I don't have faith in God in the air. It's simply that I've had more experience with him on the ground.[2]

JOHN LEWIS ~ In one interview we watched, the late Georgia Representative John Lewis (1940-2020) spoke about what a funny man King was. On the way to one of their marches King spotted a small hole-in-the-wall diner in a town they were passing through. King said, "Why don't we stop in and get a bite?"

Lewis replied, "Why in the world would you want to stop here?"

What was King's response? "Well, at least if we get arrested, we can go to jail with a full stomach."[3]

GAYLE KING ~ Here's a final funny MLK story. It comes from *The Late Show with Stephen Colbert* and his guest on this particular show was Oprah Winfrey's close friend and *CBS This Morning* host Gayle King.

Gayle said... *You guys will like this [story.] There was a time when Martin Luther King Jr. was on the cover of* Time *magazine and, you know, I'm a little kid. I was, like, in fourth grade, and they said something about Martin Luther King and I said, "Oh, my uncle Marty!"*

The teacher said, "Martin Luther King Jr. is your uncle?"

And I said "Yes!"

So when my parents came for the parent-teacher conference, my teacher said, "Oh my god, Mr. King it's an honor to meet you. The work your brother is doing...

And my father is going, "Beauregard and Jerome?"

My teacher then said, "No, Martin Luther King Jr."

My parents just sat there in stunned silence. Of course, I got in trouble. That was my first introduction to the concept that it's not good to tell a lie![4]

CHAPTER 3

THIS ONE IS FOR THE "GOAT"S

The acronym GOAT has recently come in vogue to designate the "<u>G</u>reatest <u>O</u>f <u>A</u>ll <u>T</u>ime" in various categories which seem deserving of such ratings. So following our Storyline Sampler, where we gave you a little taste of everything on the menu, and our "Salute to the King," we're going to hit you with our best shot next.

In Chapter 1 we explained our "poll of polls" concept which we used to establish some overall ratings for the greatest Black comedians of all time. We took a dozen different polls from sources such as *TV Guide*, *Rolling Stone* and Comedy Central and averaged them together to come up with a consensus ranking of the best the Black Laugh Meter has to offer.

Right now we're going to throw a half dozen heavyweights at you and, just to create a little drama, we're going to start with #6 and countdown to #1. Coming in at that #6 spot we have…

#6 ~ DAVE CHAPPELLE (1973 -)

Dave Chappelle's initial television appearance occurred on September 13, 1990 and it was actually about as low profile as you can get while appearing on what was actually network TV. In the pilot episode of ABC's *America's Funniest People*, there was a component featuring a montage of random "people on the street" each telling one joke and Chappelle was one of the jokesters. Wasn't much, but it was a start.

His breakthrough moment was his 1992 appearance on HBO's *Def Comedy Jam*, which led to multiple late night talk show appearances. Chappelle's film career kicked off with 1993's *Robin Hood: Men in Tights*. While his popularity continued to grow throughout that decade, it was the satirical sketch comedy series *Chappelle's Show* that high-hurled him onto the top of the comedy heap. That show ran on Comedy

Central from 2003-2006 with the network and the comedian parting on contentious terms. Chappelle walked away from a $50 million deal.[1]

His subsequent stand-up career has flourished and in 2015 he signed a deal with Netflix whereby he would be paid $20 million each, for a series of comedy specials.[2]

Here's a sampling of Chappelle comments and comedy…

* The biggest enemy of an artist is apathy… A kid gets killed by the police and I buy a T-shirt and before I can wear that one, there's another kid [killed] and I'm running out of closet space.[3]

* Like, see, I'd never vote for George Bush Junior, but I don't know anything about his politics. All I know about George Bush Junior is that the guy sniffed cocaine. That's right. Now, listen, we can't have that shit in the White House. That may be fine for a mayor; but goddammit, not the White House![4]

* Chivalry died when women started readin' the shit in all them magazines. They got too much advice about men from other women. And they don't know what the fuck they're talkin' about. I see them in the grocery store, says on the cover "100 Ways to Please Your Man" by some lady. Come on, man. Ain't no 100 ways. That list is only four things long.[5]

* You can't get unfamous. You can get infamous, but you can't get unfamous. (The example Chappelle uses to illustrate this is perfect as he jokes about Rick James going from a crack musical performer to a crack addict.) I'm Rick James, bitch. Is this the 5:00 Free Crack Giveaway?[6]

* Have you ever watched, like, a cartoon that you used to watch when you were little, as an adult? I was sittin' there with my nephew. I turned on *Sesame Street*. And I was, like, "Oh, good. *Sesame Street*. Now he'll learn how to count and spell." But now I'm watching it as an adult and I realize that *Sesame Street* teaches kids other things.

It teaches kids how to judge people and label people. That's right. They got this one character named Oscar. They treat this guy like shit the entire show. They judge him right to his face. "Oscar, you are so mean. Isn't he, kids? Yeah. Oscar, you're a grouch!"

He's, like, "Bitch, I live in a fuckin' trash can! I'm the poorest motherfucker on Sesame Street. Nobody's helpin' me."

Now you wonder why your kids grow up and step over homeless people, like, "Get it together, grouch. Get a job, grouch."[7]

Here's our limerick on this, from the perspective of Oscar.

> *My Sesame Street gang is a brash clan*
> *They share with me no fuckin' cash man*
> *Not a dime will they spare*
> *They sure seem not to care*
> *That I live in a damn fuckin' trash can*

#5 - REDD FOXX (1922-1991)

Born John Elroy Sanford, Redd Foxx was a comedian who achieved his greatest fame playing the lead character in the 1972-1977 NBC sitcom *Sanford and Son*. But there were significant aspects of his storyline that went down both before and after.

Foxx first became a star performing his X-rated nightclub act on the Chitlin' Circuit during the 1950's and 1960's. That paved the way for his landing the 1970's sitcom that, while dialed down from the nightclub routine, still managed to serve as cutting edge television in that pre-cable era. (Note: A full explanation of the Chitlin' Circuit was presented in the Introduction.)

In *Sanford and Son*, Foxx played Fred G. Sanford who along with his son, played by Demond Wilson, ran a junk/salvage store in the poor section of Los Angeles. Their less-than-ideal lot in life provided the backdrop for the racial humor that characterized the comedy of the series.

After a contract dispute, Foxx left the series to host a variety show for ABC. That series, however, was canceled halfway through the season and Foxx returned to the club circuit wowing audiences with his stand-up routine. In 2004 when Comedy Central aired its *100 Greatest Stand-ups of All Time* special, Redd Foxx was ranked at #24 overall and #5 amongst Black comedians.[8]

Here's one of our favorite Redd Foxx stories and it features Carl Stokes, the Black mayor of Cleveland and a respected Democratic politician during the 1960's, along with Lyndon Johnson who was then-President of the U.S. ...

President Johnson and Carl Stokes, you know, the brother, they were in the restroom in Washington and President Johnson looked over at Carl to speak to him. And being a little taller than Carl, he had to look down and he happened to glance into Carl's bowl. He said, "Goddamn, fellow American, how'd you get that?"

Carl say, "Well, Mr. President, just before I have sex, I beat it on the bedpost four times."

President Johnson said, "Well, hell, I'ma try that tonight when I get home." President got home, took a shower, walks in the bedroom and beat it on the bedpost four times.

Lady Bird Johnson woke up and said, "Is that you, Carl?" [9]

If it didn't click when you started this segment, it was Foxx who had the joke about the piece of ass that sticks to the roof of your mouth which we shared with you in the Storyline Sampler and here is a sampling of some more of Foxx's humor...

* I smoke and I drink. Some of y'all fanatics out there fussin' over your diet and avoidin' alcohol and tobacco. You health nuts are going to feel stupid someday, lyin' in hospitals, dyin' of nothing.[10]

* What's the difference between a Northern girl and a Southern girl? A Northern girl say you can, and a Southern girl say y'all can.[11]

* Where do cousins come from... aunt holes.[12]

* What's the difference between a peeping Tom and a pickpocket? A pickpocket snatches watches.[13]

* Beauty may be skin deep, but ugly goes clear to the bone.[14]

* Do you realize that if the pilgrims have been chasing bobcats instead of turkeys... we'd all be eating pussy on Thanksgiving?![15]

* There were two good buddies, and one was a practical joker. This guy buys one of those life-size rubber dolls, sex toys like they sell at porno

stores... Maybe you got one. You blow her up, slide some grease in and she's ready to go. So the guy greases her up, puts her in his bed and pulls the cover over her. Then he calls his buddy and say, "Man I got a chick over here, she's too much for me, I can't handle her by myself, hurry on over here."

Before he can hang up the phone, his buddy's comin' through the door sayin', "Where is she?"

Guy say, "She's in the bedroom."

His buddy goes in. He's in the bedroom about one minute, then he comes back outside and say, "Man where'd you meet her? God damn!"

Guy say, "What happened?"

Buddy say, "Man, what a freak, I bit her on the neck and she farted and floated out the window."[16]

* Hey, let me tell you about this chick. She had sneezes. You know, almost like when you have hiccups, three or four in a row, she had sneezes terrible. And every time she went to the doctor she say, "Doc, I have these sneezes. And every time I sneeze I have a climax."

He say, "Well, what are you doin' for it?"

She say, "Sniffin' pepper."[17]

> *Your next date... question is, how to prep her*
> *Your spice rack, it could be your next step sure*
> *Her sex juices do flow*
> *And at least now you know*
> *All the reasons a girl might sniff pepper*

#4 ~ BILL COSBY (1937-)

Obviously the sexual misconduct debacle was not the ending Bill Cosby was hoping for, but he absolutely has to be celebrated in any thorough review of Black humor and history. So let's cue up the Cos. His career began on the nightclub circuit during the 1960's which paved the way for his success in television.

In 1965 Cosby became the first Black to score a lead role in a dramatic TV series. Co-starring with Robert Culp, *I Spy* ran for three seasons on NBC. In this series the pair spanned the globe as U.S. intelligence agents who also dabbled in tennis, cars and beautiful women.

Cosby next played a phys ed teacher in the first eponymous Black comedy series, *The Bill Cosby Show*, which ran on NBC from 1969 to 1971. In a unique display of diversity, his next project, the animated *Fat Albert and the Cosby Kids*, would run on CBS from 1972-1984.

And of course his most impactful television effort would be the iconic *The Cosby Show* which ran on the NBC network from 1984-1992, accumulating some incredible accolades along the way. It was the #1 show in the country for five consecutive years, joining *All in the Family* as the only other sitcom to match that achievement.

It finished in the Top 20 during all eight seasons. On May 13, 2002, *TV Guide's 50 Best Shows of All Time* feature ranked *The Cosby Show* as #28 and Cosby's character, Dr. Cliff Huxtable was named the "Greatest Television Dad" ever.[18] Here's a sampling of Cosby's comedy...

* A word to the wise ain't necessary, it's the stupid ones who need advice.[19]

* I said to a guy, "Tell me, what is it about cocaine that makes it so wonderful." And he said, "Because it intensifies your personality." I said, "Yes, but what if you're an asshole?"[20]

* I guess the real reason that my wife and I had children is the same reason that Napoleon had for invading Russia: it seemed like a good idea at the time.[21]

* Don't worry about senility. When it hits you, you won't know it.[22]

* I wasn't always Black... There was this freckle, and it got bigger and bigger.[23]

* Did you ever see the customers in health-food stores? They are pale, skinny people who look half dead. In a steak house, you see robust, ruddy people. They're dying, of course, but they look terrific.[24]

My career on TV climbed so high
Dr. Cliff was a hell of a guy
That damn gynecology
Led to how I got to be
In the cell where I did play "I Spy"

#3 - EDDIE MURPHY (1961 -)

Saturday Night Live provided the breakthrough for Eddie Murphy who was a regular on the show from 1980-1984. He parlayed that success into his movie career which began with *48 Hrs.* in 1982, *Trading Places* in 1983, and *Beverly Hills Cop* in 1984. He then went on to become one of the most popular stand-up comedians of all time. Here's his story…

Eddie Murphy was born in Brooklyn in 1961. His father died when he was eight and he split his youth living in foster homes and living with his mother and stepfather. He cites Richard Pryor's 1974 album *That Nigger's Crazy* as the definitive moment in his decision to become a comedian. Also included among his early influences were Bill Cosby and Redd Foxx.

When Murphy debuted on *SNL* in 1980, he was only 19 and over the next four years he was generally credited with the rejuvenation of the show. Included among the characters he introduced was a sullenly cynical parody of Gumby whose line, "I'm Gumby, damn it!" became a national catch phrase. Then there was his parody of the kids' show *Mister Rogers' Neighborhood* where the iconic lead character was turned into a streetwise Mr. Robinson.

Finally, his version of Buckwheat from the old *Little Rascals/Our Gang* series never failed to bring the house down. Actually, so many houses came down that it was driving Murphy crazy because fan shout-outs for him to do Buckwheat were becoming annoyingly numerous.

Murphy subsequently came up with an appropriately sensational strategy to retire the character. What did he do? On the streets of New York, Buckwheat was gunned down on live television right outside the *SNL* studio. Yep, in an unlikely reunion of 1930's greats, Buckwheat got Al Caponed right there at Rockefeller Center.

Reiterating Eddie Murphy's importance to the *SNL* franchise, a *Rolling Stone* rating of every *SNL* cast member ever, polls Murphy as #2, behind only John Belushi.[25] His success with *SNL* and the movies led to two of the most popular stand-up specials of the 1980's, *Delirious* in 1983 and *Eddie Murphy Raw* in 1987. These were both very edgy, profanity-laced, and fantastically funny.

Proving his diversity, Murphy bridged the spectrum from X-rated storyteller to cartoon hero, emerging as a major player in the world of animation as a voice artist in family films. This trend began with Disney's *Mulan* in 1998 and continued through the run of Dreamworks' *Shrek* films where he played Donkey.

Eddie Murphy reunited with *Saturday Night Live* in February of 2015 when he was honored at the 40th anniversary special. Then in December of 2019 he returned as *SNL* host for the first time since 1984. This show turned out to be the highest rated since 2008 when Tina Fey was killing it with her run of Sarah Palin impersonations. In the 2019 show, Murphy reprised his aforementioned roles as Mr. Robinson, Gumby and Buckwheat (for the first time in 35 years).

> *Mr. Rogers' show I will revive*
> *Damn it Gumby, I'll bring you alive*
> *This shit brings me to tears*
> *When it comes down to years*
> *To do Buckwheat, I'll need 35*

In comedy, as in life, give it time and things will eventually do the come-around. Coming up next is our sampling of Murphy's snippets…

* A bear and a rabbit were taking a shit in the woods. And the bear turns to the rabbit and says, "Excuse me, do you have problems with shit sticking to your fur?" And the rabbit says, "No." So the bear wiped his ass with the rabbit.[26]

* I been seeing newspapers every Sunday morning, White dudes be in there in their drawers, never having no bulge in those drawers. Smilin' atcha. I know one thing, if I ain't have no bulge, I damn sure wouldn't be smilin'![27]

* There's something about the ice cream truck that makes kids lose it. And they can hear that shit from ten blocks away. They don't hear their mothers callin' but they can hear that motherfuckin' ice cream truck.[28]

MOVIE EXCERPTS ~ In addition to his stand-up comedy, Eddie Murphy has a film career including about 55 movies. We've worn out our DVD player looking to isolate his funniest lines and here's where we've landed.

(from *48 Hrs.*)
Eddie Murphy (Reggie): *Jack... Tell me a story.*
Nick Nolte (Jack): *Fuck you!*
Eddie Murphy (Reggie): *Oh, that's one of my favorites.*

(from *Vampire in Brooklyn* - 1995)
Kadeem Hardison (Julius Jones): *Hey, man, my pops always said the quickest way to a woman's heart [is] the church.*
Eddie Murphy (Maximillian): *It's actually through the ribcage, but that's a bit messy.*

(from *Life* - 1999)
Eddie Murphy (Ray Gibson): I've been in prison for three years. My dick gets hard if the wind blows.

#2 ~ CHRIS ROCK (1965 -)

Talk about some big bang for your buck, in 2017 Chris Rock signed a lavishly lucrative deal when Netflix agreed to pay him $40 million for two stand-up specials.[29] While that amount stands stunning, Netflix hasn't achieved its status in the entertainment world by making poor financial decisions. After launching his career on *Saturday Night Live*, Rock has gone on to achieve an avalanche of accolades including being named the funniest person in America by *Entertainment Weekly*.[30]

Rock has won four Emmy Awards and three Grammys. In 2008 he set the record for drawing the largest audience ever to a live comedy show when almost 16,000 people saw him perform at the O_2 Arena in London.[31] He hosted the Academy Awards in both 2005 and 2016 and is ranked as the #1 Black comic of all-time at the website of *Biography*.[32]

THE BACKSTORY - Chris Rock was born in South Carolina in 1965 and shortly thereafter his parents moved to Brooklyn. He made his stand-up comedy debut at New York City's Catch a Rising Star in 1984. In addition to Eddie Murphy, whose storyline we will pick up in the next paragraph, Rock's early comedy influences include Dick Gregory, Redd Foxx, Bill Cosby, Flip Wilson, and Richard Pryor.

As his fame increased, he earned bit roles in minor movies and TV shows, but the big break for Chris Rock occurred when Eddie Murphy happened to catch his act at The Comic Strip in New York City. An analogy that clicks for us is that for Eddie Murphy it had to be like seeing himself in the mirror a decade earlier. Murphy sought Rock out after the show, introduced himself, and in a moment of reality rather than analogy, Chris Rock was, out-of-the-blue, face-to-face with his comedy idol. Murphy would go on to serve as a mentor for Rock and also provided him with his first major film role in *Beverly Hills Cop II*.

Following up on that decade analogy from the previous paragraph, Chris Rock made his *SNL* debut in 1990, with his 1990-1993 run basically mirroring Murphy's 1980-1984 stint. He also has hosted three *SNL* shows, those being in 1996, 2014 and 2020.

In addition to the many aforementioned accolades, one we have not touched upon yet would be that Rock is perhaps the best talk show guest ever. Please allow us to share a couple of examples to make our case.

Chris Rock on *Late Night with Dave Letterman*…

Dave: You and Oprah are friends; I know you've traveled with Oprah as a matter of fact.
Chris: I went to the opening of her school.
Dave: South Africa?
Chris: Yes. (pauses, then sarcastically) I noticed you weren't there Dave.
Dave: No. But I'll tell you something. I love Oprah and I'd like to weasel my way in and get closer to her.
Chris: Oprah is an amazing person. She's close to being a superhero. Almost, you know what I mean? 'Cause she can get away with things that a normal human being could never get away with. Like Oprah's got

her own magazine, called *Oprah* magazine and she's on the cover every month.

Dave: Every month.

Chris: I couldn't get away with such an act. If I had a *Chris Rock* magazine and I was on the cover every month people would be going, "Who the hell does he think he is?" And I love it, I look forward to it. I love the magazine. I read it every month and I look forward to the picture because she always has a different pose. It's like Oprah playin' football (does Heisman Trophy pose), Oprah ridin' a horse (makes galloping pose), Oprah poppin' a wheelie (grabs pretend handlebars). You know I love it so much that if somebody else is on the cover I get mad. Like even if Martin Luther King Jr. was on the cover, I'd go, "What the hell has he done to be on the cover of *Oprah* magazine?" That Dream was a long time ago, Dave, right?" That's what I'd say.

Dave: You're pretty sure people have your email address, right?[33]

Chris Rock on *Jimmy Kimmel Live!*...

On the eve of the 2012 presidential election between Barack Obama and Mitt Romney, a truly memorable segment was aired on the *Jimmy Kimmel Live!* show. Kimmel introduced a film prerecorded by comedian Chris Rock.

Kimmel introduced the bit by saying, *"As you know the presidential election is on Tuesday and according to the polls Obama and Romney are still neck and neck. Both campaigns made their final push today. Romney has a strong lead among White voters but some prominent Obama supporters are looking to chip into that and my friend Chris Rock is one of them. Chris Rock is here tonight and he's recorded a special message targeted specifically at undecided voters of the Caucasian variety."*

Just to set you up for the Rock monologue, the theme is that, despite actually being Black, Barack Obama is one of the Whitest guys you know, and all of you Caucasian skeptics should get onboard the Barack bandwagon. Here is our transcript of the Rock film:

"Hi, I'm Chris Rock with a special message for White people. In times like these you need a White president you can trust. And that White president's name is Barack Obama. Let's take a look at the facts. For the first

two-thirds of his life, Barack Obama was known as Barry, which is the third Whitest name on earth. Right after Cody and Jeff.

After college, Barry went into Black neighborhoods in Chicago to try to organize people. How White is that? Black people don't go into Black communities. We don't have to; we're already there.

Look at him, (in the following sequence a picture appears on screen showing Obama doing each of the things Rock is describing) *playin' golf, body surfin', wearin' mom jeans, dancin' with Ellen. Barack Obama supports gay marriage. Most Black men don't support straight marriage.*

President Obama has a dog. But is it a pitbull? Is it a Rottweiler? No, it's a Portuguese water dog and he named him Bo, after The Dukes of Hazard.

If you want a White president I've got a polo-wearin', Hawaii-livin', home-beer-brewin', league-bowlin' guy for you. Barry Obama. He's juuuuuuuuust WHITE." [34]

Here's some more Chris Rock humor...

* I had a cop pull me over the other day, scared me so bad, made me think I stole my own car. "Get out of the car, get out of the fuckin' car! You stole this car!" I was like, "God damn, maybe I did!"[35]

* Charlie Brown is such a loser. He wasn't even the star of his own Halloween special. [and then bemoaning the plight of Franklin, the only Black cast member in the Peanuts gang...] You ever see Franklin? 25 years, not one line. Nothin'. 25 years, man. Everybody on Charlie Brown got their own little character, and it's all thought out, you know, Linus got the blanket, Lucy's a bitch, Schroeder plays the piano, Peppermint Patty is a lesbian, everybody got their thing except Franklin. Give him something, damn. Give him a Jamaican accent or something. They don't even invite him to the parties. But Pigpen's in the house and Snoopy's there, dancin' his ass off.[36]

* We got so much food in America we're allergic to food. Allergic to food! Hungry people ain't allergic to shit. You think anyone in Rwanda's got a fuckin' lactose intolerance?![37]

#1 ~ RICHARD PRYOR (1940-2005)

It would be difficult to identify another man on the planet whose life story could contain the range of highs and lows that characterized Richard Pryor's. Let's get the lows out of the way. There's an old cliché that goes, "Will it play in Peoria?" In this cliché, Peoria is meant to represent the most stereotypical Midwestern town you could pinpoint-pick on the map of America. In other words, if it will work there, it'll work anywhere. Why do we bring this up? Richard Pryor was born in Peoria so his roots are about as Middle America as you can get. Or so you might think… but not so fast.

Richard Pryor's Peoria playbook was not so typical. Let's review. He was born in a brothel. It was owned by his grandmother. His mother was the brothel's most prized employee. And oh, by the way, Mom was also an alcoholic. Everyone needs a regimen to prepare for work.

Dad, when he was in the picture, supported himself as a conman and hustler. So much for the lowlights of his early years.

After ascending to heavenly heights, which we'll outline a few paragraphs down the road, Pryor's one-of-a-kind career cataclysmically collapses, cocaine not coincidentally contributing to the calamity. Here's the scoop…

LOW TIDE ~ On June 9, 1980 he is in the midst of free-basing cocaine, while binging on 151 rum. Because, as we all know, sometimes 150-proof just isn't quite enough to get the job done. As one might suspect, that combo was probably not the perfect pairing of Pryor's party practices.

In the category of "shit happens" the next thing you know, Richard Pryor finds himself engulfed in flames and sprinting down the street of his Northridge, California home. He's looking for what… a fire hydrant with a screw-off cap? Why is it that you can never find one of those mofos when you need one?

A 911 call from a woman reporting a flaming ghost floating past her house prompts a rapid response from the Northridge PD. When the police ghostbusters arrive, they quickly douse the flames, call an ambulance, and know that somewhere down the road Pryor's gonna have some serious 'splainin' to do. Explanations can often be damn difficult, but this one certainly ascends rapidly up of the rungs of the ladder-laborious.

Then the double whammy concludes with Pryor's August 1986 diagnosis of Muscular Sclerosis. Obviously the game would never be quite the same for him again. But neither of these tragic turns can strip the sheen from the career that manages the following accolades…

HIGH TIMES ~ If we had to pick the two most resoundingly respectful examples which sing Pryor's praises to the loftiest heights here's what we'd go with. He was ranked #1 on the following lists, both of which were released in 2017.

* Comedy Central's 100 Greatest Stand-ups of All Time[38]
* *Rolling Stone's* 50 Best Stand-up Comics of All Time[39]

In our poll of polls that we used to come up with the rankings we've used in this book, Richard Pryor is the consensus #1 Black comedian of all time. Congrats, Richard!, and here's the backstory…

It was 1963 when Richard Pryor left Illinois for the Big Apple where he was a hit on the club circuit performing with the likes of Lenny Bruce and Woody Allen. That success led to multiple TV appearances including *The Tonight Show Starring Johnny Carson* and *The Ed Sullivan Show*. In 1975 Pryor became the first Black guest host on *Saturday Night Live*.

During the early 1970's he became a sought after writer, working for TV series such as *The Flip Wilson Show* and *Sanford and Son*. He won an Emmy Award for his work on Lily Tomlin's self-titled 1973 TV special. After conquering TV, his next conquests would be comedy albums and movies. He strung together an impressive run of three consecutive Grammy Awards for Best Comedy Album as listed below.

* 1974 ~ *That Nigger's Crazy*
* 1975 ~ *… Is It Something I Said?*
* 1976 ~ *Bicentennial Nigger*

In addition to hosting the Academy Awards twice, Pryor also appeared in dozens of movies including the list which follows…

* Lady Sings the Blues (1972)
* The Bingo Long Traveling All-Stars and Motor Kings (1976)
* Car Wash (1976)
* Which Way is Up? (1977)
* The Wiz (1978)

ACCOLADES ~ As you might suspect, high praise has been afforded Richard Pryor by many of his contemporaries. Next we will add to and reshare the favorites which were included in our Storyline Sampler…

DAVE CHAPPELLE ~ You know those evolution charts of man? He was the dude walking upright. Richard was the highest evolution of comedy.[40]

JERRY SEINFELD ~ Richard Pryor was the Picasso of our profession.[41]

BILL COSBY ~ Richard Pryor drew the line between comedy and tragedy as thin as one could possibly paint it.[42]

BOB NEWHART ~ Richard was the seminal comedian of the last 50 years.[43]

I grew up in a world full of crime
In that world made a Hell of a climb
As the great ones would tell
From Newhart to Chappelle
I am simply the best of all time

Here's a sampling of Pryor's humor…

* I'm not addicted to cocaine. I just like the way it smells.[44]

* I went to Zimbabwe. I know how White people feel in America now; relaxed! 'Cause when I heard the police car, I knew they weren't coming' after me![45]

* I had to stop drinkin', cuz I got tired of wakin' up in my car drivin' ninety.[46]

* Let me tell you what really happened… Every night before I go to bed, I have milk and cookies. One night I mixed some low-fat milk and some pasteurized, then I dipped my cookie in and the shit blew up.[47]

* When that fire hit your ass, it will sober your ass up quick! I saw somethin', I went, "Well, that's a pretty blue. You know what? That looks like... FIRE!"[48]

* When you're runnin' down the street on fire, people get out of your way![49]

* I'd like to die like my father died... My father died fuckin'. My father was 57 when he died. The woman was 18. My father came and went at the same time.[50]

Upon the occasion of his death, fellow comedian Paul Mooney wrote, "The king of comedy is dead. Richard Pryor was the king of comedy. The rest of them are the king of copycats."[51]

CHAPTER 4

FIVE FEMALES WHO BROKE BARRIERS IN ENTERTAINMENT

JOSEPHINE BAKER (1906-1975)

Of all the research we did for this book, here's one piece that really popped. How 'bout a woman whose robust résumé includes these ten tantalizing tidbits…

* First married at the age of 13
* Ten serious romantic relationships; six with men, four with women
* Achieved fame dancing nude except for string of fake bananas around her waist
* First Black woman to appear in a feature film
* Was an undercover spy during WW II
* Bought and lived in a castle
* Adopted twelve kids from different nationalities and religions
* Only female opening speaker at MLK's "I Have a Dream" Speech
* NAACP Woman of the Year
* Coretta Scott King asked her to lead civil rights movement after MLK's death

As we were assessing material for possible inclusion in this book, there was probably never a more OMG moment than when we read the life story of Josephine Baker. What a résumé this woman had! Seriously, how could one person parlay a nude dancing career into becoming the first Black female movie star, a WW II spy, and the adoptive mother of twelve children, all while carrying on bisexual relationships with a dozen different partners. Oh yeah, and then there was the time that Coretta Scott King asked her to become the leader of the civil rights movement after the assassination of her husband.

HUMBLE BEGINNINGS ~ Josephine Baker was born in St. Louis in 1906 and led an impoverished childhood. At the age of a mere 13 she found herself living on the street, married and eking out a survival by waitressing and dancing on street corners. She longed to be an entertainer and took the first step in that direction when at the age of 14 she joined the Jones Family Band, an organized street performance group in St. Louis.

Then, at 15, she joined the St. Louis Chorus vaudeville show which had been booked to play New York City. The Big Apple was like a steaming slice of hot juicy pie to Baker and she soon supped upon succulent success.

DANCING DIVA ~ She landed roles in the chorus lines of two extremely successful Broadway shows, *Shuffle Along* in 1921 and *The Chocolate Dandies* in 1924. The latter show billed Baker as "the highest-paid chorus girl in vaudeville," while employing an interesting motif with her dancing. She was strategically placed at the end of the chorus line where her shtick was to act confusedly discombobulated as if she were unable to keep up with the other dancers. The crowd-pleasing finale would feature a magical transition where Baker would suddenly become the most dynamic dancer on the stage, adeptly mastering her moves with even more sophistication and complexity than the other girls.

BON VOYAGE ~ Baker's New York City success earned her the opportunity to take her talent overseas and she chose Paris as her initial destination. It was a fateful decision as she would come to call this city home for the rest of her life, renouncing her United States citizenship. She was part of a wave of American pop media culture which stormed Paris in the 1920's. Other expatriates included authors Ernest Hemingway, F. Scott Fitzgerald, and Gertrude Stein, composers George Gershwin, Aaron Copland and Cole Porter, and dancer Isadora Duncan. Hail, hail, the gang's all here!

Baker loved France as it was an escape from all the racism and segregation in the U.S. and Paris could not get enough of what Josephine Baker had to offer. The French flocked to the Théâtre des Champs-Élysées to see her in a show called *La Revue Nègre*. What was furiously fanning the flames of the fans' fire? How about Baker's erotic topless dancing where she wore just a skirt of fake bananas and some beads around her neck?

> *I've a gift that exceeds even Santa's*
> *Showed it off at all kinds of cabanas*
> *See me dance like a banshee*
> *I sure hope that you can see*
> *Something tasty beneath my bananas*

The documentary *Josephine Baker: The Story of an Awakening* described the entertainer's success with the following words. "*Alternating between clown and seductress, the primitive and the American, Josephine hit Paris like a bombshell. She broke new ground embodying the audiences' fantasies, taking them to new heights.*"[1]

Baker's French success led to her touring throughout every major city in Europe, becoming easily the most high-profile Black entertainer on the continent, as well as the most high-profile female. About her, Ernest Hemingway gushed that, "Josephine Baker is the most sensational woman anyone ever saw." Pablo Picasso's paintings and drawings of her included "Black Pearl" and "Black Thunder." In 1927's *Siren of the Tropics* she became the first Black woman to star in a feature film. Simply put, she was the first Black international superstar.

During the 1930's Baker's career continued to flourish in Europe and she returned to the U.S. only one time during that decade, in 1936. The idea that she could perform in New York City, and then be denied a hotel room after the show, reminded her of why she had left the U.S. in the first place and she soon returned to the admiring crowds welcoming her back to Paris. The fact that her profile continued to rise in Europe was ironically laying the groundwork for the next twist that would be added to her résumé when she would become a French spy during WW II.

SPY GAMES - Because she had been an established fixture in the upper echelon of European culture and society, she was able to inconspicuously mingle with powerful people and high-ranking officials. As she performed in various countries and attended events at foreign ministries and embassies, she was able to charm and schmooze officials, as she always had, while gathering valuable intel regarding the war efforts of the Germans and Italians. Perhaps because she was a beautiful woman, the men whose security measures she breached were a little less on their guard.

It was all very cloak and dagger. There were examples of her smuggling information hidden inside her underwear because, as a celebrity and a woman, Baker was less susceptible to searches. On other occasions, she wrote messages in invisible ink on the pages of her sheet music. She was able to obtain information about troop concentrations of the Germans and Italians, as well as information about airfields and harbors.

When the Germans actually invaded France, Baker escaped first to the Château des Milandes castle which served as her rural retreat. She had rented the estate in 1940 and later bought it in 1947. As the Germans crept closer, she eventually fled to Northern Africa. Ironically, when American troops landed in Morocco in November of 1942, Baker was already there. During the rest of the war she organized a tour which entertained French, British and American troops. After the war French General, and future President, Charles de Gaulle ceremonially bestowed upon Josephine Baker multiple military awards and honors.

PLOTTING A RETURN ~ At this point Baker had not been back to the U.S. since 1936 and her attitude was that the only thing that could facilitate her return would be if she were able to make a significant contribution to the civil rights movement. Her fame had risen to the point where folks, both Black and White, were so enthralled with her that any tour was destined to be a resounding success.

Baker knew the power of the hand she was holding, and adeptly played her cards by taking the stance of…

I won't participate
'til you desegregate.

She would embark upon a full-fledged U.S. tour only if every venue she played was totally desegregated. The artist prevailed and she prepared to rock the states with a show like nothing they'd seen in years. The tour sold out to enthusiastic audiences while earning rave reviews. Baker's contributions to the civil rights movement prompted the organization to designate May 20, 1951 as "Josephine Baker Day" and the lovefest culminated with a New York City parade in her honor that drew over 100,000 people to Harlem.[2]

After exalting in this incredible comeback, we're going to pause at this point and sideways-saunter to cover a couple significant aspects of Baker's life. It seems like almost everything this woman did took on larger-than-life proportions. Well, that statement is also true of her libidinous love life and her passion for parenting.

LOVE IS IN THE AIR ~ As we are often wont to do, let's review the sex first. Josephine Baker was bisexual and had multiple romantic partners throughout her life. She was married four times, with several other significant relationships.

On both sides of this bisexual bonanza, we're just going to skip the names because if we start it's almost impossible to draw the line. Here's an example of that "other significant relationships" concept which ended the previous paragraph. At one point during the early 1920's in Paris, she was in love with a man she actually would have married, if only she had not still been married to a guy she had left back in the U.S.

As we segue from Baker's romantic life to her life as a mother, we'll mention that one of her sons, Jean-Claude Baker, researched and wrote a biography of his mother called *Josephine Baker: The Hungry Heart*. In this he documents the four significant relationships Josephine had with women.

STARTING HER OWN TRIBE ~ Baker never had any of her own children, but when she became seriously involved with the civil rights movement during her 1951 tour of the U.S. there arose one interesting manifestation. She decided to begin an adoptive family and it would be one with a purpose, as well as a catchy name, "The Rainbow Tribe." The purpose, as Baker put it, was "to prove that children of different ethnicities and religions could still be brothers."[3]

The Château des Milandes castle, in which she lived, turned out to be the ideal setting to host the tribe she was about to assemble. That tribe would grow to include 12 children, 10 boys and 2 girls. They came from a wide variety of countries including France, Finland, Israel, Morocco, Nigeria, Korea, Japan, Colombia, Venezuela, and the Ivory Coast.

Baker also factored in critical aspects of the children's background in order to facilitate how her entire program would further her model for world unity. We'll give you one example. At one point she adopted two children from Algeria and raised one Catholic and the other Muslim. You almost had to see this to believe it and guess what?... part of her whole plan was to actually have people see it!

How in the world did she accomplish that? Here's the scoop. She turned her Château des Milandes castle into a hotel, hired a huge staff, and as crazy as it seems, charged people admission to visit, engage in various activities, and watch the kids at play. Other attractions included a walk-through farm and amusement rides. At various scheduled showtimes the children would sing and dance for the assembled guests. She was a showgirl from the start.

CIVIL RIGHTS ICON ~ Somehow, amazingly, amidst this 12-ring circus in France, she managed to maintain a high profile in the civil rights movement in America. How high? Well, at the March on Washington, of all the opening speakers for Martin Luther King Jr.'s "I Have a Dream" speech, she was the only female. And when King was assassinated, his widow Coretta Scott King contacted Baker in Europe and asked if she would be willing to come back and take over the role of being the civil rights movement's leader. What could be bigger than that?

After a few days of careful consideration, Baker respectfully declined the offer saying she thought her kids, the Rainbow Tribe, "were too young to lose their mother."[4] Let's face it; replacing Martin Luther King Jr. was not a job that could be done in absentia.

How 'bout we share what we found to be the most moving moment of Baker's speech at the March on Washington event. Speaking about the time when she returned to the U.S. before WW II, she said, *"I have walked into the palaces of kings and queens and into the houses of presidents. And much more. But I could not walk into a hotel in America and get a cup of coffee, and that made me mad. And when I get mad, you know that I open my big mouth. And then look out, 'cause when Josephine opens her mouth, they hear it all over the world."*[5] You go, girl!

LAST HURRAH ~ After passing up her opportunity to become the symbol of the civil rights movement, she continued to oversee her castle while successfully touring to world acclaim. Her friends Jacqueline Kennedy Onassis, Prince Rainier of Monaco, and his wife Princess Grace Kelly had helped organize a retrospective show called *Joséphine à Bobino* celebrating her 50 years of entertaining in Paris. The sold-out opening night audience also included Mick Jagger, Diana Ross, Liza Minnelli and Sophia Loren.

As is the case with all great shows, the curtain must, at some point, fall for the last time. The finale for Josephine Baker appropriately occurred in Paris on April 8, 1975. After her 14th *Joséphine à Bobino* show, Baker was found dead from a cerebral hemorrhage, surrounded by newspapers with glowing reviews of her performances. It was probably an apropos visual to epitomize the image of a life well-lived.

ESTHER JONES (1918- ?) & BETTY BOOP

Are you ready
for Black Betty?

Our Storyline Sampler promised the revelations regarding the Blackness of Betty Boop and the Lone Ranger. Well, the Ranger will ride a few chapters down the road, but we're gonna bring on the Boop girl right now. Here's our storyline on how voluptuous cartoon character Betty Boop was Black.

There are three women who star in this story and we'll need to follow the thread that dot-connects Esther Jones to Helen Kane to Betty Boop. We'll start in the year 1918 when Esther Jones is born on the south side of Chicago which, as the song "Bad Boy LeRoy Brown" proclaims, is "the baddest part of town." Her parents try to steer her in a show biz direction early in the game.

ESTHER'S EMERGENCE ~ At the tender age of six she wins a Charleston dancing contest in Chicago. With her parents billing her as "Little Esther," Jones begins making regular appearances singing and dancing at Chicago's Cotton Club. Her trademark jazz vocal style of using "boops" and other childlike nonsense-word "scat" sounds catches on and by 1929, an article in the *Chicago Defender* describes her as "the highest-paid child artist in the world."[6]

During 1929 Esther Jones undertakes an extremely high-profile tour of Europe. She performs for the King and Queen of both Spain and Sweden, while also singing and dancing for nobility and high society in England, France and Germany. The *London Sunday People* newspaper travels to Paris to see Esther perform so they can publish a review prior to the youngster arriving in England for the final leg of her European tour.

Check out this exuberant report where the magazine writes, *"Thousands of people flock no longer to the Moulin Rouge to see Mistinguett herself or the clever American ballet girls, or the beautiful women of the chorus, but to applaud a little 10-year-old mite, who has won fame and wealth within the space of a few weeks. We are living in an age of speed but this amazing little child has broken every record of sudden theatrical success."*[7]

Esther's 1930 world tour takes her through South America. When she plays in Rio de Janeiro, American Ambassador Edwin Morgan comes backstage to congratulate her after the show. The next day the newspaper quotes the president of Brazil, Getúlio Vargas, as saying, "It was my great pleasure to see such a capable Black American artist perform in Brazil."[8]

The same article includes a quote from Esther who is asked how she has avoided the racists who lynch and burn Black people in Texas and Alabama. Esther replies by saying that she theretofore has "escaped their wrath by staying out of the South."

MYSTERIOUS DISAPPEARANCE ~ At this point, Esther's career takes a dramatic and inexplicable downward turn. As we researched her life, everything from this point forward is paradoxically plagued by a perplexing lack of detail and documentation. She has a few more performances in the U.S. that are briefly reviewed in media outlets, but the last published words about her career appear in 1934.

There is documentation that in July 1934 Esther Jones performed, along with numerous other African-American stars, in Philadelphia at a midnight benefit performance for the NAACP. The *Baltimore Afro-American* wrote about her performance that "Little Esther had charm and grace and her acrobatic dance number was very good."⁹

The final Esther Jones news article we could find appeared in a *Philadelphia Tribune* article from September of 1934. That paper mentioned Little Esther appearing at a benefit for the Douglass Hospital which was hosted by the famous black dancer William "Bojangles" Robinson. Yep, he was the man after whom the classic song "Mr. Bojangles" was written in 1968 by Jerry Jeff Walker.

So, the strangest aspect of the Esther Jones story is how the girl could be the highest-paid child star in the world at the age of ten in 1929 **and** manage to totally drop off the radar by five years later in 1934. There is no record whatsoever of her whereabouts after that year and the time and place of her death are totally undocumented.

Therein lies the tantalizing roller coaster story of Esther Jones, so at this point please allow us to connect the dots between her and Betty Boop. Betty was the first cartoon character to become a sex symbol. The animated sweetheart was known for her revealing dress, curvaceous figure and signature "boop-oop-a-doop" vocal. There is one person who serves as the go-between in the Esther-Betty connection and that person would be Helen Kane. Here is her story…

KANE CONNECTION ~ Helen Kane is a singer who specializes in the "scat" style of jazz vocal improvisation featuring wordless nonsense syllables, for example the "boop-oop-a-doop" that becomes the signature line for Betty Boop. In 1928 Helen Kane sees a performance of Little Esther and adapts her scat style to incorporate elements of Esther's act such as the high-pitched baby-style voice, frequent use of the "boop" syllable, and the childlike gesture of rolling her eyes while touching her index finger to her cheek.

In the late-1920's to the early-1930's Helen Kane becomes quite popular in the New York City theatre circuit and Fleischer Studios clearly bases their Betty Boop character upon Helen Kane. The facial resemblance, as well as the style, is undeniable, so it is not surprising when, in 1932, Helen Kane sues Fleischer Studios for appropriating her persona for their Betty Boop character. But sometimes it becomes hard to determine whether someone is the lighthouse or the storm.

During the trial, Fleischer Studios is able to introduce testimony that Kane had indeed seen Little Esther in 1928, and they are also able to produce film of an Esther performance to corroborate the connection. It's truly a shame that film was not carefully preserved because from an historical perspective, it would certainly be an enticing piece of video to be able to see today. There is no record of what might have happened to that film after the trial, and there's no existing video of Esther Jones.

THE VERDICT IS IN - The way the lawsuit plays out, Fleischer Studios essentially prevails by establishing that while their Betty Boop character was based upon the Helen Kane persona, that persona had in turn been based upon Little Esther. The judge's ruling includes the explanation that "the vocals 'boop-oop-a-doop' and similar sounds had been used by another performer prior to the plaintiff."[10]

That ruling would seem to lay the groundwork for Little Esther to launch a successful suit of her own against Fleischer Studios and it's interesting to ponder how history might have played out had such a lawsuit been filed. But by the time the final ruling in the Kane v. Fleischer case is rendered in 1934, Little Esther is just on the cusp of her mysterious disappearance where she just seems to have evaporated off the face of the earth. The only consolation we're left with is that part of Little Esther will always live on in the character of Betty Boop.

> *Glass house folks shouldn't really throw stones*
> *Don't claim fame for the Boop milestones*
> *Helen Kane tried to sue,*
> *but the judge really knew*
> *The real star was that sprite Esther Jones*

GLADYS BENTLEY (1907-1960)

From a century before anybody ever strung the letters LGBTQ together to form an acronym, we have a story which the aforementioned group would have absolutely adored. The star of our story is one Gladys Bentley and during her heyday, adoration was bestowed upon the musical performer not only by the LGBTQ community but also by the Hollywood mainstream as well. Among her ardent fans were included Cary Grant, Cesar Romero, Langston Hughes and Barbara Stanwyck.

How 'bout we lay out the lowdown on our gal Gladys. She was a heavyset, deep-voiced, openly-lesbian Black woman gender-bender who envelope-pushed New York City during the 1920's like the Big Apple had rarely been pushed. Her typical attire was a top hat and tux with tails, and her preferred clothing color was white.

Her genre was the blues, and her shtick consisted of playing the piano while belting out raunchy parodies and lewd cover versions of well-known songs, as well as her own original tunes. As her sultry success soared, she enhanced her presentation, augmenting the show with a chorus line of backup singing drag queens, and further engaged the crowd by openly flirting with the women in her audience.

During the 1920-1933 Prohibition Era, when everything going on at the New York City speakeasies was illegal anyway, Bentley's act was the perfect fit. No prominent performer of the era stretched the boundaries of the sexual norm more than she did, and Bentley was clearly able to tap into the tempestuous tastes of the times. By the mid-1920's Gladys Bentley had been anointed the "Drag King of Harlem."[11]

So how 'bout we score some new digs for our queen? In 1928 Harry Hansberry's Clam House opened up on Manhattan's 133rd Street and latched onto Bentley as its house performer. It was a killer combination and the Clam House rode Bentley's white coattails to the top of the club scene as the most popular LBGTQ speakeasy in the city.

Following the repeal of Prohibition, there was no longer a need for underground speakeasy districts which essentially led to the collapse of the nightclub scene in this part of Manhattan. Bentley took her career to

LA at that point, but she would never again enjoy the lofty heights of success that characterized her glory years in NYC.

In his book *Bulldaggers, Pansies, and Chocolate Babies: Performance, Race, and Sexuality in the Harlem Renaissance*, James Wilson summed up Bentley's style as follows… *"Differing from the traditional male impersonator, or drag king, in the popular theater, Gladys Bentley did not try to 'pass' as a man, nor did she playfully try to deceive her audience into believing she was biologically male. Instead, she exerted a Black female masculinity that troubled the distinctions between Black and White and masculine and feminine."*[12]

HATTIE McDANIEL (1893-1952)

Let's start out with this tantalizing teaser regarding Hattie McDaniel. We're thinking that most of the people reading this could not identify her by name, which oddly conflicts with the fact that the majority of our readers have probably seen her. Hattie McDaniel was the Black actress who played Mammy in the classic 1939 film *Gone with the Wind*.

How 'bout we all go back to the 1939 Academy Awards which was the setting for one of the most bizarre moments in Oscar history. In an oxymoronic sense, that year's ceremony was wonderfully terrible. The positive was that Hattie McDaniel became the first Black to take home the highly coveted award which she had deservedly captured for her aforementioned performance in *Gone with the Wind*.

So what was negative about this breakthrough event? The ceremony took place at the Coconut Grove Restaurant in the Ambassador Hotel in Los Angeles, an establishment which continued to maintain a policy of segregation at that point in time. While the Ambassador waived its policy and allowed McDaniel to attend, she and her guest were required to sit at a separate table in the back of the room.

This story is of course so paradoxically sad in that it juxtaposes the grandeur of the fact that a Black person would be awarded with an Emmy for the first time with the ignominy of a seating schematic that is certainly not one to be wished for. But of course, if wishes were dollars, paupers would be kings.

Hattie McDaniel was one of the most successful Black movie stars of the era having roles in about 70 films prior to her Oscar-winning performance. In addition to Clark Gable and Olivia de Havilland with whom she co-starred in *Gone with the Wind*, she acted alongside many major Hollywood heavyweights of the time who were also her friends. That list would include James Cagney, Henry Fonda, Bette Davis, Joan Crawford and Ronald Reagan. Despite their age difference, she was also close friends with Shirley Temple.

AWARD ACKNOWLEDGED – The day after the award the *LA Times* described her moment as follows, *"Hattie McDaniel earned that gold Oscar by her fine performance of 'Mammy' in* Gone with the Wind. *If you had seen her face when she walked up to the platform and took the gold trophy, you would have had the choke in your voice that all of us had when Hattie, hair trimmed with gardenias, face alight, and dressed up to the queen's taste, accepted the honor in one of the finest speeches ever given on the Academy floor."*[13]

Wondering what she said? Of course you are, and we're here for you. What follows is a transcript of Hattie McDaniel's 1939 acceptance speech. *"Academy of Motion Picture Arts and Sciences, fellow members of the motion picture industry and honored guests… This is one of the happiest moments of my life, and I want to thank each one of you who had a part in selecting me for one of their awards, for your kindness. It has made me feel very, very humble; and I shall always hold it as a beacon for anything that I may be able to do in the future. I sincerely hope I shall always be a credit to my race and to the motion picture industry. My heart is too full to tell you just how I feel, and may I say thank you and God bless you."*[14]

NICHELLE NICHOLS (1932 -)

Related to the theme of this book, Nichelle Nichols has a fascinating story which transcends the role that she is most known for, which was that of playing Lt. Uhura in the original *Star Trek* TV show, as well as the six subsequent theatrical movie sequels in the series. While exploring the universe for this book's topics, Nichols would rank amongst our Top 5 moments of arousingly righteous recognition.

Her first foray into showbiz came while touring as a singer in the early 1960's for both the Duke Ellington and Lionel Hampton bands. Next she hit the theatre stage appearing in *The Roar of the Greasepaint*, *For My People*, and *Blues for Mister Charlie*, a James Baldwin play which earned her rave reviews.

Nichols first shows up on *Star Trek* creator Gene Roddenberry's radar screen when she appears in an episode of his first TV series *The Lieutenant* in 1964. She makes a strong impression while playing her role in an episode dealing with racial prejudice called "To Set It Right."

Roddenberry is in the process of launching what would become his breakthrough *Star Trek* series, he is looking for ways to envelope-push, and he decides that Nichelle Nichols might provide a nicely-needed nudge. As Lt. Uhura, she becomes the first Black woman featured in a prominent supporting role on a network TV series. The acting accolades pour in and new offers follow. Nichols is offered a Broadway role and feeling this would be a natural progression to her career, she decides to accept. This leads into a great story.

Acknowledging a debt of gratitude to Roddenberry, Nichols writes a letter of resignation which she delivers to him in person on a Friday afternoon. He tells her to think about it over the weekend and if she doesn't change her mind, he will accept the letter and send her off with his blessings.

As fate would have it, Nichols attends an NAACP convention that weekend and in the midst of it, an organizer approaches her to say there is a fan here that wants to meet her. Assuming it is just another Trekkie, whom she will politely acknowledge as always, Nichols proceeds to meet the fan.

A FATEFUL MEETING ~ However, on her way, she is stopped dead in her tracks upon seeing Martin Luther King Jr. coming towards her and realizes the fan is going to have to be put on the back burner. Well, sometimes one surprise just follows another. Imagine how shocked she is to find out that the fan **is** Martin Luther King Jr.! At this point we would like to defer to the Nichelle Nichols' version of the encounter.

"I thought it was a Trekkie, and so I said, 'Sure.' I looked across the room and whoever the fan was had to wait because there was Dr. Martin Luther King walking towards me with this big grin on his face. He reached out to me and said, 'Yes, Ms. Nichols, I am your greatest fan.' He said that Star Trek *was the only show that he, and his wife Coretta, would allow their three little children to stay up and watch.* [Nichols then tells King about her plans to leave the series.]

I never got to tell him why, because he said, 'You cannot, you cannot – for the first time on television we will be seen as we should be seen every day, as intelligent, quality, beautiful, people who can sing dance, and can go to space, who are professors, lawyers. If you leave, that door can be closed because your role is not a Black role, and is not a female role, he can fill it with anybody, even an alien.'"[15]

At this point for Nichelle Nichols, leaving for Broadway is no more likely than her leaving with Lt. Spock to return to his Vulcan planet home. Her Monday meeting with Roddenberry is an absolute classic. When she shares the story of the weekend meeting with MLK and the impact *Star Trek* has made upon this icon of the civil rights movement, as well as his family, Roddenberry is brought to tears and pulls out the envelope with Nichols' letter of resignation which has already been torn into shreds.

That old sci-fi fix Martin did crave
Something he could not take to the grave
His true feelings professed
Who the Hell would've guessed
That Uhura would be Martin's fave?

You'd think this story couldn't get much better, but it does. Ramifications of the chance 1966 meeting between Nichols and King will resonate, believe it or not, for the next half-century. We promise to complete that fifty-year flight plan, but first let's skip ahead just one year.

KISS AND TELL ~ As she returns for the second season of *Star Trek* there is one script in particular that catches her eye. In the "Plato's Stepchildren" episode, which would air on November 22, 1968, Nichols becomes one-half of TV's first interracial kiss on a network TV drama, sharing the moment with William Shatner who plays Captain Kirk in the show.

According to the storyline of that episode, Uhura and Kirk are exploring a distant planet when their bodies become telekinetically controlled by aliens. The fact that the characters are "not themselves" enables the kiss to become a passionate one. Had the pair been "in character" the kiss never would have taken place at all.

In her 1994 autobiography, Nichelle Nichols shared a funny story about the kiss. She received a letter from one good ol' Southern White boy who was clearly conflicted over the episode. The guy wrote, "I am totally opposed to the mixing of the races. However, any time a red-blooded American boy like Captain Kirk gets a beautiful dame in his arms that looks like Uhura, he ain't gonna fight it."

TREKKING TO THE FUTURE ~ Whoopi Goldberg took her fandom of Nichols to a rather cool level. When the TV series *Star Trek: The Next Generation*, went on the air in 1987 she asked the producers if they would create a part for her. Subsequently Whoopi took on the recurring role of Guinan, who was a bartender in the Ten-Forward lounge on the starship.

How 'bout one more stellar example of Nichols' legacy? NASA astronaut Mae Jemison has made reference to the fact that seeing Lt. Uhura as a child inspired her decision to become an astronaut. 3-2-1 Lift off!

We mentioned earlier that ramifications from the 1966 Nichols meeting with MLK would resonate for 50 years. It would do so in the form of the volunteer work that Nichols would do for NASA. Between 1977 and 2015, she worked on a series of volunteer recruiting drives which sought to bring diversity to NASA by attracting more minority and women recruits.

Finally, let's end on a funny note which shows that not only could Nichols sing and act, she could also be quite the comedienne. On August

20, 2006, the Comedy Central network hosted a roast of William Shatner. At the podium Nichols paid her respects to Shatner and then closed by saying, "What do you say, let's make a little more TV history [and you get up here] and kiss my Black ass!" Hence…

Nichelle gave the all clear
for her final frontier.

How's that for a TV barrier deserving of some bare-ass breaking?

CHAPTER 5

FOUR FEMALES WHO BROKE BARRIERS IN MODERN COMEDY

TIFFANY HADDISH (1979 -)

Tiffany Haddish was born in South Central LA in 1979, beginning a childhood which was chaotically crazy by anyone's standards. Let's all get rowdy and ride the Terror Train to Haddish Hell on this frenzied foray with the absolute assurance that this nasty nightmare will eventually end and finally finish with our tempestuous Tiff in Haddish Heaven. All aboard…

Here's the family storyline. Her father, who was of Ethiopian/Jewish descent, left when Tiffany was just three. Her mother's volatile remarriage succeeds only on the level of achieving a family expansion adding four step-siblings to an equation already proving difficult to solve. So how 'bout now we toss a totally discombobulating factor into our equation? How 'bout the one where Mom suffers a serious automobile accident in 1988 leaving her with permanent brain damage.

How do all these contributing factors add up? Let's summarize. The accident leaves Tiffany's mother unable to overcome her impulsive anti-social outbursts which in turn leads to her being committed to a psychiatric hospital. Her step-father is an irresponsible reprehensible reprobate, at one point telling Tiffany he caused the accident by sabotaging the car in hopes of killing the entire family in order to collect an insurance payout.

It's always nice when the man of the house is gifted in both mechanics and finances! Throw all of those circumstances into a blender, press the pulverize-button, and you'll get the cataclysmic cacophony that effectively epitomizes the challenging childhood of Tiffany Haddish.

Subsequently, Tiffany does a two-year shuffle through a heartless and drug-ridden foster care system until her grandmother is able to gain custody, which serves as a temporary upgrade. This however comes to an abrupt end when Tiffany turns 18 and her grandmother shows her the door because there will no longer be any foster care money coming in to pay for her support.

We fully admit to having acquiesced to the long-story-short version of the rugged childhood because some of the details are downright difficult to digest. The devastating download is all there in Tiffany's 2017 bestseller *The Last Black Unicorn*. The best that can be said of the early struggles is that they serve to make the impending accomplishments even more exhilarating. And that's where we're headed next… high school here we come!

HIGH SCHOOL HIGHS ~ Tiffany Haddish went to El Camino Real High School in the San Fernando Valley region of LA. The student body was mostly rich, only 3% Black, and she had to get up at 5:00 am every day to catch a 6:15 bus traversing Los Angeles County from South Central to the Valley. On the surface it may not have seemed an obvious pathway to success, but for Tiffany the tide was high and the surf was up. Here's why…

She is quirkily charismatic and definitely different from the other students. Even the fact that she is at the opposite end of the socio-economic spectrum seems to work to her advantage because the other kids see her as "poor-as-fuck chic."[1]

FRESHMAN FROLICS ~ In her own words she enters 9th grade as basically illiterate, using her talents of humor and deception to navigate her way through classes. Her romantic pursuit of Audie, a boy on the football team, inadvertently leads to a few significant milestones in her high school career. She signs up for drama class because he is in it, and ironically the teacher of that class would be the one to detect her literacy deficiency and ultimately teach her to read and write.

The drama teacher arranges to have Tiffany pulled from nutrition class so she can provide one-on-one tutoring and in just one month's time, Tiffany skyrockets from a first grade to a ninth grade reading level. Once the basics have been achieved, Tiffany soon would be leaving the world wondering, "But soft, what light through yonder window breaks?" The drama teacher facilitates Tiffany's entrance in Shakespearian monologue contests, and that same year she ends up winning one with 375 participants! Let's chalk freshman year up in the win column.

SOPHOMORE SHENANIGANS – As a sophomore Tiffany is ready to move into a more high-profile on-campus role. So she considers trying out for the cheerleading team, but finds the rules too rigid and restrictive. Subsequently, she checks in with the advisor in charge of the school mascot and when informed that the mascot job does not come with any rules attached, her response is "That's what I want to be then – the mascot."[2]

So, at that point, Tiffany becomes the new official El Camino Real Conquistador. As you might have suspected, she turns out to be a mascot must-see. She runs up and down the field with her megaphone, leading cheers and shouting directions to the crowd. She studies ESPN taking note of the routines employed by the college and pro mascots and adapts their shticks for El Camino purposes. Between quarters, she pulls students down from the stands for dance-offs. The Tiffany show becomes an attraction in and of itself.

After establishing herself as a campus sensation, Tiffany uses her notoriety to renew her romantic pursuit of Audie, only to once again be rebuffed. "I can't date no mascot," Audie says. "They goin' to be callin' me the 'mascot assistant.' I don't think so."[3]

JUNIOR JUBILATION – By the time her junior year rolls around, Tiffany has opted for Boyfriend Plan B and is dating a different guy on the football team. The star continues to rise on her legendary status as the El Camino Conquistador and there is a sense evolving that as many people are coming to the football games to see her as are coming to see the game.

SENIOR SHOWSTOPPER – By the time senior year rolls around, she is arguably the most popular kid on campus and a plaque acknowledging Tiffany's role as the Conquistador has gone up on the wall in the school's lobby (where it is still on display today). But that fame comes with a cost. Her boyfriend (fulfilling Audie's earlier prediction) does become known on campus as the "mascot assistant." High school life in the shadow of the Conquistador is too stigmatizing and her boyfriend breaks up with her.

As a result, she tells the principal she's going to quit as mascot because she wants a boyfriend. Subsequently, she doesn't don the Conquistador costume for the first two games of her senior year. Previously stated suspicions about why people are actually coming to the football games prove to be true. When attendance drops by 50%, the principal calls her into the office and begins negotiations with, "What's it going to take to get you back on the field, Haddish?"

Her answer, "A boyfriend."[4]

The principal stays firm in his stance that while he can't get her a boyfriend, he may be able to get her a cut of the candy sales. After some intense student-principal negotiations they settle on a price of $50 a game. Tiffany the Mascot has gone pro!

PROFESSIONAL PARTY GIRL ~ And while that last statement was literally true, albeit on a relatively small scale, it actually leads to her big breakthrough in the world of entertainment. Here's what happens. Because of her notoriety at school, she becomes the center of attention at school dances. At one such event, when she is dancing up a storm, a circle of people forms around her, dancing along and chanting her name.

The DJ at the event is so impressed by the energy she generates that he offers her a job working executive parties and Bar Mitzvahs as an "energy producer" or "hype girl."[5] Her job description is basically that she is to work the crowd and get people excited, happy, and dancing. When her grandmother explains to her that the Bar Mitzvah piece actually connects to her Jewish ethnicity, she takes the job. Initially she makes $40 a party.

Tiffany's talent in this field is clearly in a league of her own. She ends up working 500 Bar Mitzvahs over the next eleven years. By the end of the run, she is knocking down $400 a party. Now that qualifies as some serious energy production!

LAUGH FACTORY COMEDY CAMP ~ Tiffany has two intriguing and basically unrelated story threads which overlap and run parallel through her high school years. In addition to the mascot→Bar Mitzvah storyline, here's the one that more directly leads to her career in comedy. And it actually develops from her getting in trouble at school.

Frequent disciplinary issues lead to Tiffany's principal and social worker making the following blunt offer regarding the summer between sophomore and junior years. Her social worker says, "Tiffany, you got two choices this summer coming up. You can go to the Laugh Factory Comedy Camp, or you can go to psychiatric therapy. Which one do you want to do, 'cause something is wrong with you."[6]

Not much of a choice there, and the comedy camp serves to dictate the direction in which her life would flow. People she meets at the camp, and cited as particular influences, are the Wayans brothers and Richard Pryor.

Soon after high school, she began picking up guest roles on a long list of TV shows before landing a permanent role for a two-year stint (2015-2017) with the NBC sitcom *The Carmichael Show*. Her role in the 2017 film *Girls Trip* served to launch her into the upper echelon of Black comediennes.

Since then, she's won an Emmy, starred in TV series on both TBS and Netflix, and released her first stand-up comedy special *She Ready* on Showtime in 2017. Finally, accomplishing something no other Black woman had done since Whoopi Goldberg in 1986, her comedy album *Black Mitzvah* won the 2021 Grammy for Best Comedy Album. Mazel tov, Tiff!

Please take a moment to reflect upon the title of that Grammy-winning album. Remember the ethnic background that has come up earlier in this component? Could any comedic title mirror Ethiopian/Jewish any better than *Black Mitzvah*?

Here's a further sampling of Haddish humor…

* (On the difficulty of driving to gigs when she was younger) Back then I was driving a little Geo Metro that sounded like a lawn mower. Ride in that shit for 2 hours, you feel like you done crossed America in a covered wagon.[7]

* No matter what the situation, I try to have fun. I get pulled over by the police, I'm like, "Oh, this is going to be the best arrest ever!"[8]

ISSA RAE (1985 -)

The work of Issa Rae first drew attention in 2011 when she initiated her internet series *Awkward Black Girl* on YouTube. When she released her autobiographical book in 2015 that title was altered to *The Misadventures of Awkward Black Girl*. From 2016 through 2021 she was the driving force and starred in the HBO series *Insecure*.

On October 17, 2020 she hosted *Saturday Night Live* and next we will share part of her opening monologue. After descending the stairs to the stage, she references several of the women who had preceded her down those steps including Tina Fey and Amy Poehler.

Issa proceeds to share how nervous she is before proclaiming, "I'm the first Black woman to host *SNL*." This brings the crowd to a thunderous applause before Issa brings them back to earth by acknowledging, "OK wait, that's actually not true. You all really clapped. What if I just kept lyin' to y'all all night? Half of y'all wouldn't even notice. But if this show goes bad tonight, just blame it on me, Mary J. Blige."[9]

The audience cracks up at Issa's deflection and please allow us to clarify a few fine points regarding her humor. For the record, while Mary J. Blige has appeared on *SNL*, it was never as the host. And in a second "for the record," the first Black female to host *SNL* was Cicely Tyson who did so on February 10, 1979.

Her *Awkward Black Girl* won the Shorty Award for Best Web Show and when she spins it into her memoir, she masterfully flashes her wry self-deprecating humor. Here's one story to illustrate. Her "Leading Lady" chapter begins with the opening line of "Several months ago, I was blocked on Twitter by a disabled, White stripper." How the hell can you **not** have to hear how this one turns out?

Well, it was Grammy night and, returning home with an admitted bit of a buzz, Issa initiates a Twitter thread by tweeting, "Sometimes I really wish I was a stripper. But a respectable one. I would always start off wearing pantsuits and dance to [Queen Latifah's] 'U.N.I.T.Y.'" She refers to this tweet as "earnest and, in my mind, harmless." Well, maybe not so much.

That tweet prompts a response of, "Wow. How BRAVE. Not like all us gross disrespectful sex workers." So at this point, it's game on. The verbal bitch-slap prompts Issa to explore the sender's timeline seeking a source for the vitriol. The long-story-short of it would be that the White "sex worker" is an insomniac, people-hating, wonted whiner who is particularly perturbed by the oppression of strippers in our society. Everybody needs a cause, right?

So Issa bandies back, "We should talk about this in the morning when you get some sleep, Grumpy McGrumperson."

Issa's "grumpster," now enraged and engaged, fires back with, "We should talk about this when you get some empathy, you whore-phobic asshole."[10] So, at this point the gloves are clearly off (always a great beginning to any striptease) and we'll refer you to *The Misadventures of Awkward Black Girl* to see how this one plays out. Also, if you're the type of person who looks for opportunities to drop seldom-used words into your everyday conversations, make sure you're locked and loaded with "whore-phobic" as a weapon in your arsenal.

We'll close with a few name-game notes. Issa Rae's birth certificate name is Jo-Issa Rae Diop and if you've never heard it pronounced the "I" in "Issa" sounds like a long "E" so the pronunciation is "E´-suh."

AMBER RUFFIN (1979 -)

Amber Ruffin broke into the big leagues of late night TV in 2014 beginning with her role as a writer for *Late Night with Seth Meyers*. Since then, she's parlayed the writer role into hilarious onscreen segments such as "Amber's Minute of Fury", "Amber Says What?", and our favorite "Jokes Seth Can't Tell." In the latter segment Ruffin costars with her lesbian co-writer Jenny Hagel, with Meyers sitting in between the two women.

The premise is that Meyers sets up jokes that, if he were to finish them, might come off as offensive to Blacks or lesbians. But if the jokes are finished by folks of the appropriate persuasion, the potential offense is mitigated. If you're intrigued by the premise, definitely YouTube it. But rather than having us divulge the nuances of lesbian credit card swiping, we are going to maintain our focus and go to a story about Black History Month 2017.

TRUMP TROUBLE ~ Beginning his first February in office, and facing his first Black History Month, you have to know that Donald Trump is looking at this dog as if white foam is oozing out of its mouth. He has to somehow acknowledge this Black event but needs to do so in a manner so as to disturb his racist White base as little as possible. So, he holds a press conference that is both pathetic and priceless.

While Trump's trappings are panned across the board by most intelligent media, *Late Night with Seth Meyers* uses Amber Ruffin to create our favorite response. Meyers sets up the bit by sharing that Trump has given his Black History Month speech and Amber is coming on to break down the speech and analyze it on a line-by-line basis.

The killer component comes when Trump attempts to go off script and expand upon the comments he has been provided about Black history. Seizing upon a name that Trump feels sure would resonate with the atypically Blacker audience he is addressing, the Commander in Chief spontaneously swivels to the topic of Frederick Douglass. What follows is the line from the president's speech followed by Amber's commentary.

Trump: Frederick Douglass is an example of somebody who has done an amazing job and is being recognized more and more, I noticed.

Amber: Now here we learn that he likes Frederick Douglass so much that he thinks he's still alive.[11]

Let's wrap this up with a few more Amber accolades…

* 2020 ~ Becomes the first Black woman to host her own late night talk show when *The Amber Ruffin Show* debuts on the streaming NBC/Peacock network.
* 2020 ~ Meyers also interviews Ruffin as a guest for his show's 1,000th episode.
* 2021 ~ The book *You'll Never Believe What Happened to Lacey: Crazy Stories about Racism*, which she co-wrote with her sister, is released and makes the *NY Times Best Seller List*.

Speaking of the book, we really enjoyed the unique style Amber and Lacey employ in their writing. In detailing Lacey's crazy stories, the entire work is written in the format of an ongoing dialogue between the two sisters. While they both grew up in Omaha, Amber has moved to New York City pursuant to her entertainment career while Lacey is still holding down the fort in Omaha.

As conveyed by the title, Lacey manages to find herself involved in more crazy-ass shenanigans than you would expect an Omaha girl to find possible. When shit happens, the phone rings in New York enabling Amber to process the details and provide her big-city spin on what's gone down in the badlands of Nebraska.

Here's one example… On one trip back home, Amber and Lacey get involved with an Omaha event called AfroCon which is "a Comic-Con for Black nerds." As fate would have it, the event takes place shortly after Disney had announced that it would be releasing a live action version of *The Little Mermaid* with a Black girl playing Ariel. Duly inspired, Lacey decides to make the Mermaid her AfroCon character costume.

At the event a young girl, ballpark 6-years-old, approaches Lacey and asks, "Who are you supposed to be?"

"The Little Mermaid," Lacey replies.

The girl looks at Lacey like she doesn't have both fins in the water and says, "You can't be the Little Mermaid, the Little Mermaid is White!" Lacey explains to the little girl that part of the magic of AfroCon is that you can be whoever you like.

"Fine," the little girl says, "but you're still not the Little Mermaid." At this point the girl's mother picks up on what's going down, scoops up her six-year-old, and delivers a firm scolding. Shortly thereafter, the girl contritely strolls back over to Lacey with the news that, "My mom says we can all be whatever we want to be… And that I need to hang out with you more."[12] The adults all share a laugh.

Mama said, "Fare thee well
as the Black Ariel."

PHOEBE ROBINSON (1984 -)

In researching this project one of the more exhilarating events we experienced was reading Phoebe Robinson's book *You Can't Touch My Hair*. Her writing manages to strike an engaging balance between innocent honesty and street-smart savvy. She unabashedly tackles tricky topics like race and sex in her free-flowing style which is peppered with pop culture references. And, oh my God, is the girl funny!

LET'S START THE STORIES - Here's one of our favorite stories to illustrate the concept of her honesty managing to wrap her overt sexuality in a cloak of innocence. We have to put this in Phoebe's own words to allow her to flash her style. She writes about, "*That time when I tastefully explained what the X-rated term 'hummer' meant during dinner with my ex-boyfriend's family, and somehow ended up charming everyone in the process. Seriously, I was breaking down a randy sex act to his family, and I was like Jennifer-Lawrence-falling-up-the-stairs-at-the-2013-Oscars charming.*"[13]

HONESTLY, OLIVIA - One motif of which she makes particularly effective use appears in a chapter called "Letters to Olivia." Who's Olivia? That would be her 2½-year-old biracial niece and "all-time favorite person." In setting up her shtick, Phoebe explains that while she's sure her brother and sister-in-law, PJ and Liz, are certain to flash incredible parenting skills in raising Olivia, she wants to take a proactive approach to make sure that none of her pearls of wisdom slip through the cracks.

At the point she writes the book, Phoebe has spent 31 years accumulating those pearls and she puts together a plan to pay them forward to Olivia. How will this be achieved? The mission will be accomplished through a series of "Dear Olivia" letters. Phoebe's directions call for Olivia's parents to decide at what point in life she has reached the level of maturity for the material to be appropriate.

This is an important component to the concept because, despite the fact that the letters are addressed to a 2-year-old girl, Phoebe does not dial down the edginess of her material one bit. With letter titles like "Use

Your Vagina Powers For Good," the book is clearly not going to make it onto Olivia's shelf for many years to come.

The next one we'd like to share is classic Phoebe throwing Olivia's parents under the bus, but with a decade in the rear-view mirror we need a little set up. A breakthrough hit of the 2012 TV season was the political thriller *Scandal* starring Kerry Washington as an administrative press aide whose acting gimmick was that she gave new meaning to the lip quiver. Her name in the show was Olivia Pope and she was such a beautiful compelling character that one result was a spate of Black parents naming their daughters Olivia.

Keep that fact in mind for this next dose of Phoebe-funny. One of her letters to Olivia is titled "Your Parents Might Say They Didn't Name You After *Scandal*'s Olivia Pope, But They Totally Did."[14] Well, we guess the cat's out of the bag on that one now.

THE PLAY'S THE THING ~ Another chapter we'll highlight is called "The Angry Black Woman Myth." This would support the stereotype of the Black woman as being some combination of the following characteristics which Phoebe traces back to the character of Sapphire Stevens on the 1930's-50's radio/TV show *Amos 'n' Andy*. How 'bout we go interactive with you guys right now? Listed below are 10 adjectives that came up as we researched the myth of the angry Black woman.

* shrewish
* ungrateful
* nagging
* demanding
* emasculating
* hellacious
* manipulative
* ill-tempered
* domineering
* overbearing

We always like to do things in groups of three so, after perusing the list above we'll ask you to pick any three and apply them to the character in our next story who will play the stereotypical angry Black woman. How would you respond given the situation that we're about to present? Returning to our regularly scheduled program, let's take a look at Phoebe's take on the topic at hand.

She applies the Angry Black Woman litmus test to herself and, in asking herself if she is an ABW, her initial reaction is to say no. Then she goes on to describe some of the situations that have befallen her in life where circumstances force the question, "How can I **not** be angry?" We'll share with you what we thought was her funniest example.

She's in college at Pratt Institute, it's her senior year, she's in her advanced writing class, and of the 15 students she is the only Black. As a final project, students are directed to write a culminating piece that would be representative of who they are as an artist. This written work could be anything from a collection of poems or short stories, to some creative fiction, non-fiction, or a play.

A stated component of this project's process was that the writing would be shared with the class and feedback from fellow students would be made available. When it became time to share, one of her classmates revealed that she had written a play. Not that it was mentioned during her classmate's project explanation, but as soon as the plot was leaked it became evident that the storyline brought with it an awkward connection to Phoebe. Brace yourself for this preposterous plot.

It starts out somewhat celebratory with a Southern female slave from that era discovering that she has been blessed with a ticket to freedom via the Underground Railroad. Glory hallelujah! But as the group of escaping slaves prepares for departure, one of them bestows shocking news upon her entourage. She is going to take a hard pass on the escape. Why, you ask? According to the storyline of this salacious Southern slavery soap opera, the Black girl declining to exit stage left is doing so because she has fallen in love with the slave owner's daughter!

As we re-rank our list of greatest lesbian lover losers ever, this chick shoots to #1 like a bullet. So, try if you can to put yourself in Phoebe's head at this point. She has to be thinking, how can this get any worse? Well, we have an answer for you. How 'bout if the professor assigns Phoebe to read the part of the lesbian slave as the class acts out the play?!

Phoebe's our thespian
slave who's a lesbian.

So, at this point in the story, Phoebe makes a devoted effort to not become the Angry Black Woman. But knowing our Pheebes, as you do by now, for how long is she really going to be able to sit on this? Admittedly, right now, we're going to leave you in a bit of a lurch. We will tell you that the way this play plays out is one of the funniest stories we've ever heard. If you're at all curious, we urge you to seek out Phoebe's book as soon as you finish this one.

YOU TOO, U2 – Then, after you finish Phoebe's first book, if you're anything like us, you'll soon be seeking out the follow up called *Everything's Trash, But It's Okay*, which published in 2018. The best "to-complete-the-story" moment of the second book is one we'll title "The U2 Follow Through." Pheebes is passionate about her music and her favorite band since the age of 13 has been U2.

One component of the first book that is the epitome of the unbridled unabashed honesty which makes her writing so captivating is that after she explains her fandom of the band, she proceeds to rank order the four members of U2 in terms of who she would most like to have sex with.

While that makes for some interesting reading first time around, when you flip through Book Two and realize there's a chapter on the two personal encounters she has shared with U2 in between books, you can't help but start sliding toward the edge of your seat. Here's how this plays out, beginning with the fact that some of U2's entourage were fans of Phoebe's podcast so the band had become aware of the Phoebe fandom phenomenon.

Phoebe and Jessica Williams, co-hosts of the podcast *2 Dope Queens*, receive flowers from U2 lead singer Bono which leads to the girls going to the Bonnaroo Festival where the band is playing. The day before the show there's a charity dinner which they attend thinking Bono might do a surprise fly-by. Turns out there's no Bono, but his rep blows their minds by letting them know that Bono wants to meet them before the show tomorrow.

So, we're sure we've got you wondering how this one is going to go down but, before we get to the meat of the story, allow us to throw in this titillating detail. Certain to make for the ultimate conversation starter is the fact that Bono was #2 on her list in Book One regarding which band members she'd most like to bone! For the record, here's the Top 4 list: 1) The Edge, 2) Bono, 3) Adam Clayton, 4) Larry Mullen Jr.[15]

At any rate, the meeting all works out with Pheebes and Bono bonding, as well as posing for some crazy pictures, for example Bono dropping to his knees and hugging Phoebe's legs as if to juxtapose the whole fan-worship theme. That pic is in Book Two and it makes for an endearing "humbled-fan-meets-her-idol" story. At this point we're going to "long-story-short" this and let you know that the Phoebe-Bono lovefest is continued with a second meeting before a concert in her hometown of Cleveland.

PHOEBE FINALE ~ Here's a concise version of her backstory and we'll finish up with some of her one-liners, or "Phoebe Funnies" as we've come to call them. Phoebe Robinson grew up in Cleveland, a midwestern girl as she often shares, before attending Pratt Institute in New York City and making the move to the Big Apple. Her résumé of TV appearances includes the *Today* show, *Late Night with Seth Meyers*, NBC's *Last Comic Standing, Last Call with Carson Daly*, and various appearances on Comedy Central.

Here's a sampling of Phoebe's humor…

* I mean… I was such a cute little kid that if I were up for adoption, Angelina Jolie would have surely snagged me.[16]

* (Expressing the joy she felt after cutting out a glowing *NY Times* review of her podcast show *2 Dope Queens*) I felt like I was being baptized in Oprah's titty sweat, which I believe is how you know for certain something should be framed.[17]

* Look, I love me some Val Kilmer. Anytime I watch *Batman Forever*, there's light precipitation going on in my vagina walls.[18]

* (Based upon the story we previously shared, this is her prediction on the conversation that would **not** take place between the slave owner father and his daughter upon discovery of the relationship between the daughter and the slave. The father is **not** going to say…) OK, wow. So you're a lesbian. You're in an interracial relationship. You're sleeping with the hired help. Cool, cool. Congrats on that![19]

* Nope. You can't touch my hair. Even if my hair catches on fire, do not come to my rescue; just let me do a Michael Jackson spin move to put the blaze out.[20]

We are worshipping her from afar
Phoebe rocks, she is our superstar
No, you can't touch her hair
So, don't even go there
Give it up for our girl, Phoebe R.

CHAPTER 6

FROM SITTING ON A BUS TO SITTING IN THE WHITE HOUSE (A GRAND SLAM OF POLITICAL PROGRESSION)

CLAUDETTE COLVIN (1939 -)

Rosa Parks was famous for the fact that it was her Supreme Court case that led to the desegregation of bus transportation in the United States. But the Rosa Parks bus seat story actually comes with an asterisk-outright. Before there was Rosa, there was Claudette Colvin. While the Rosa Parks incident occurred on December 1, 1955, it was on March 2nd of that year, nine months earlier, that the 15-year-old Colvin refused to move to the back of a Montgomery bus. For her efforts, she was arrested and thrown in jail.

There were a handful of other similar incidents throughout the course of that year, all of which contributed to the subsequent court case. So why did Rosa Parks emerge as the face of the Montgomery bus boycott?

Rosa Parks was an adult and also the secretary of the NAACP. With her maturity, experience and established level of respect, and knowing the gravity of what was at stake, the consensus feeling was that Parks would be a more appropriate icon for the movement than a teenage girl. It was a logical decision that had a solid outcome. That being said, the role of Claudette Colvin in the cause must always be acknowledged. While history never repeats itself, it sometimes rhymes.

Colvin had an absolutely wonderful quote about the incident. When *Newsweek* interviewed her, they asked what was going through her mind at the exact moment she denied the request to get out of her seat. She said, "I felt like Sojourner Truth was pushing down on one shoulder and Harriet Tubman was pushing down on the other. I was glued to my seat."[1] Yep, we can see how it would be pretty hard to get up under those circumstances!

My girl Sojourner Truth spoke to me
Harriet Tubman was loud as could be
Sit back down on your throne
And world, let it be known
That before Rosa Parks there was me

BAYARD RUSTIN (1912-1987)

How many of you would be surprised if we were to tell you that the following bullet points could all be found on the same man's résumé.

* Openly gay
* Worked on human rights movements in multiple countries
* Taught MLK the principle of non-violent resistance
* Primary influence in MLK giving up his guns
* Lead planner of event where MLK delivered his "Dream" speech
* Received Presidential Medal of Freedom from Obama in 2013

It's an impressive and somewhat startling list and the man who could boast those bullets would be Bayard Rustin. Rustin first becomes involved in the civil rights movement when he spearheads an effort to desegregate interstate bus travel in the South. We'll pick up the story in Louisville, Kentucky in 1942. There he boards a bus for Nashville, Tennessee and snags a prime seat right in the front of the bus. He subsequently ignores requests to move, well aware of the inevitable result. Before its arrival in Nashville the bus is stopped and Rustin's arrested, beaten, jailed, and then released. No charges are filed.

We found what we thought was a truly intriguing quote about this incident from Rustin which appeared in a Black Washington newspaper. Rustin said, *"As I was going by the second seat to go to the rear, a White child reached out for the ring necktie I was wearing and pulled it, whereupon his mother said, 'Don't touch a nigger.' If I go and sit quietly at the back of that bus now, that child, who was so innocent of race relations that he was going to play with me, will have seen so many Blacks go to the back and sit down quietly that he's going to end up saying, 'They like it back there, I've never seen anybody protest against it.' I owe it to that child, not only to my own dignity, I owe it to that child, that he should be educated to know that Blacks do not want to sit in the back, and therefore I should get arrested, letting all these White people in the bus know that I do not accept that."*[2]

During Rustin's work in aiding the Indian movement to gain independence from Britain, he had become a devout follower of the philosophy of Mahatma Gandhi who espoused non-violent tactics. In 1956 Rustin became an adviser to Martin Luther King Jr. and at this point it became impossible to ignore the impact that Rustin had on the civil rights movement.

MEETING MARTIN ~ It's perhaps surprising to hear that when the two men initially met, MLK was toting a gun. Yep, the King was packin' heat! That's how great Rustin's influence was. The imparting of the Gandhian philosophy upon King sparked a transformation, becoming the guiding force in King's teachings and practices for the rest of his life. How's that for being a major factor in the civil rights movement? Rustin continued his work with King, helping to found the Southern Christian Leadership Conference in 1957.

Fast forward five years to 1962 when plans begin to take shape for an epic march in Washington to commemorate the 100th anniversary of the Emancipation Proclamation. Bayard Rustin and A. Philip Randolph were designated to be the planners of the event. Rustin's responsibilities included the organization of security and traffic control, as well as coordinating the schedule of speakers.

Clearly, Rustin did the heavy lifting on planning the project but, because of his sexual orientation, he was relegated to behind-the-scenes advisor status. Amidst the inner-sanctum discussions of the Black hierarchy, MLK was not uncomfortable with Rustin's sexuality, but NAACP president Roy Wilkins expressed an opposing view saying, "This march is of such importance that we must not put a person of his liabilities at the head."[3] Subsequently, Randolph was listed as "director" and Rustin as his "deputy."

Despite efforts to squelch publicity about Rustin's involvement, the September 6, 1963 issue of *Life* magazine featured a two-man cover photo identifying Rustin and Randolph as the leaders of the movement. Good to see some acknowledgement given to a man who contributed so greatly to the cause while often being relegated to the shadows.

In our opening we mentioned Rustin's contributions to human rights movements around the globe. While we are not going to delve deeply into these, we do want to say the following. The importance of Rustin's efforts lies in the fact that they give a sense of the depth of this man's all-around compassion for humanity. We are going to opt for a bullet format in listing these accomplishments and share that Rustin...

* Worked to protect the U.S. property rights of the interned Japanese during WW II
* Contributed to the organization of independence movements in Nigeria and Ghana
* Opposed apartheid in South Africa
* Worked on refuge assistance projects in Vietnam and Cambodia
* Died while working on a humanitarian mission in Haiti

Bayard Rustin is by no means a household name so we felt a duty to do him justice in this component. Hopefully we can file this one in the "mission accomplished" column. The centennial of his birth was noted in 2012 and an appropriate acknowledgement of his work occurred when Barack Obama posthumously awarded the Presidential Medal of Freedom to Bayard Rustin on November 20, 2013.

SHIRLEY CHISHOLM (1934-2005)

"If they don't give you a seat at the table," she said, "bring a folding chair."[4] In this quote, who would our "she" be? Ladies and Gentlemen, please welcome Shirley Chisholm to our show. She was never one to passively submit to a back seat. When she made her historic run for president, her campaign motto was "Unbought and Unbossed."

Chisholm was born in Brooklyn, New York in 1924, the daughter of a father from British Guiana (in South America) and a mother from the Barbados (in the Caribbean). Her political career began in 1964 when she was elected to the New York State Assembly. In 1968, she became the very first Black woman to be elected to the United States Congress, where she would serve seven terms spanning from 1969 to 1983.

When she announced her candidacy for the Democratic presidential nomination in 1972, she became the first Black candidate to run for a major party nomination and the first woman to run for the Democratic nomination. (White U.S. Senator Margaret Chase Smith had previously run for the Republican presidential nomination in 1964.)

Chisholm mounted a gallant campaign during which she survived three assassination attempts. You know what they say... ya just can't keep a good girl down. Obviously, Chisholm's efforts were somewhat symbolic in the sense that she had a much greater chance of making a statement than she had of actually winning.

Her strongest showing was in North Carolina where she achieved a third-place finish. She had a respectable showing in several states and wound up taking 152 delegates to the Democratic National Convention. At the convention she galvanized the delegates when she proclaimed, "I am the candidate of the people and my presence before you symbolizes a new era in American political history."

A unique aspect of the 2008 Democratic presidential primary process served to bring Chisholm's legacy back to the forefront. As Barack Obama and Hillary Clinton battled for the nomination, it became clear that the Democrats were going to nominate either their first Black or their first woman. Ironically Shirley Chisholm had paved the way for both of them.

Please let us allow our girl Shirley to sum this thing up in her own words... *I ran for the presidency, despite hopeless odds, to demonstrate the sheer will and refusal to accept the status quo. The next time a woman runs, or a Black, a Jew, or anyone from a group that the country is "not ready" to elect to its highest office, I believe that he or she will be taken seriously from the start.*[4] Those words certainly rang true, didn't they?

How 'bout we close with three tributes and acknowledgements to Chisholm…

* 2001 ~ Her "For the Equal Rights Amendment" speech, given in 1970, is listed as #91 in *American Rhetoric*'s Top 100 Speeches of the 20th Century.
* 2015 ~ Barack Obama posthumously awards her the Presidential Medal of Freedom at a ceremony in the White House.
* 2021 ~ During Kamala Harris's Vice-Presidential inauguration she wears a purple dress, which she acknowledges as a tribute to Shirley Chisholm, who was noted for her purple attire.

Mountain-top, standing tall, I profess
That someday, my impact, would impress
Down from Heaven, I see
Kamala hailing me
Paying tribute, in that fine purple dress

We'll close by sharing a Shirley line we like from the 6/6/82 *Washington Post* which references the classic Sidney Poitier film *Guess Who's Coming to Dinner*. In response to an invitation to the male-only gridiron dinner in 1972, she fired off a classic response, "Guess who's **not** coming to dinner."[5]

BARACK OBAMA (1961 -)

Barack Obama boasts a very unique ethnicity package. His father was born in Kenya and grew up herding goats. From those humble beginnings Barack Obama Sr. studied hard enough to earn a scholarship and fulfill his dream of going to college at the University of Hawaii. It was there that he met his wife Ann Dunham, and the couple was married on February 2, 1961. And yes, for the record, Barack Obama was born in Hawaii. Conspiracy theories notwithstanding, this young University of Hawaii couple did not fly to Kenya for the birth of their child.

Obama entered politics in 1996 winning a seat in the Illinois State Senate. In 2004 he launched a campaign which would land him in the United States Senate. He began to attract national attention and was invited to deliver the keynote speech in support of John Kerry at the 2004 Democratic National Convention in Boston. After the convention, he returned to focus on his U.S. Senate bid in Illinois. When he won his senatorial race in 2004, he became only the fourth Black elected to the U.S. Senate.

It would be February of 2007, when Obama made headlines by announcing his candidacy for the 2008 Democratic presidential nomination. His primary contender was former first lady and then-U.S. senator from New York, Hillary Clinton, who he defeated to win the nomination. On November 4, 2008, Obama defeated Republican presidential nominee John McCain, to win the election and become the 44th president of the United States, and the first Black to hold this office.

As we stated in the opening to the book, when it comes to the historical thread, our objective is to stay off the beaten path and share with our readers some hidden gems. To that end, how 'bout we bullet-list Barack into the White House and then cue up his most humorous highlights…

* Born in Hawaii in 1961
* Elected to Illinois Senate in 1996
* Elected to U.S. Congress in 2004
* Elected President of the U.S. in 2008

Now that we've gotten him into office, let's have a little fun with Barack. In terms of comedic timing and delivery, Obama is certainly in the discussion as to who was the funniest president ever. We've scoured through his eight years of speeches and plucked out his very best lines for you.

On Trump Reversing His Birther Conspiracy Theory

There's an extra spring in my step tonight. I don't know about you guys, but I am so relieved that the whole birther thing is over. I mean, ISIS, North Korea, poverty, climate change, none of those things weighed on my mind like the validity of my birth certificate.[6]

Thoughts on Getting Older

These days, I look in the mirror and I have to admit, I'm not the strapping young Muslim socialist that I used to be.[7]

Analyzing the 2012 Election

I know Republicans are still sorting out what happened in 2012, but one thing they all agree on is they need to do a better job reaching out to minorities. And look, call me self-centered, but I can think of one minority they could start with. Hello? Think of me as a trial run, you know? See how it goes.[8]

At the 2013 White House Correspondents' Dinner Just After Hillary Clinton Had Been Caught on Video Drinking Beer and Dancing While on a Summit Meeting in Cartagena, Colombia

Despite many obstacles, much has changed during my time in office. Four years ago, I was locked in a brutal primary battle with Hillary Clinton. Four years later, she won't stop drunk-texting me from Cartagena.[9]

On love at the 2010 White House Correspondents' Dinner

There are few things in life harder to find and more important to keep than love. Well, love and a birth certificate.[10]

Ribbing Donald Trump at the 2011 White House Correspondents' Dinner

Now, I know that he's taken some flak lately but no one is prouder to put this birth certificate matter to rest than The Donald. And that's because he can finally get back to focusing on the issues that matter, like, did we fake the moon landing? What really happened in Roswell? And where are Biggie and Tupac?[11]

On his library at the 2013 White House Correspondents' Dinner

I'm also hard at work on plans for the Obama Library. And some have suggested that we put it in my birthplace, but I'd rather keep it in the United States. (to the laughing audience...) Did anybody not see that joke coming? Show of hands?[12]

Putting the Nerd Prom in perspective

The White House Correspondents' Dinner is known as the nerd prom of Washington D.C. – a term coined by political reporters who clearly never had the chance to go to an actual prom.[13]

On Dick Cheney at the 2009 White House Correspondents' Dinner (soon after former VP Cheney had accidentally shot a hunting partner)

Dick Cheney was supposed to be here, but he is very busy working on his memoirs, tentatively titled, "How to Shoot Friends and Interrogate People."[14]

Describing Often Crass Chief of Staff Rahm Emanuel on Mother's Day

This is a tough holiday for Rahm. He's not used to saying the word "day" after "mother."[15]

Disclosing his bucket list at the 2013 White House Correspondents' Dinner

My advisors asked me, "Mr. President do you have a bucket list?" I have something that rhymes with bucket list. Take executive action on immigration. "BUCKET!" New climate regulations "BUCKET!"[16]

Warning the Jonas Brothers at the 2009 White House Correspondents' Dinner

The Jonas Brothers are here, they're out there somewhere. Sasha and Malia are huge fans, but boys, don't get any ideas. Two words for you: predator drones. You will never see it coming. (in response to laughter…) You think I'm joking?[17]

On the new media landscape at the 2010 White House Correspondents' Dinner

The media landscape is changing so rapidly. You can't keep up with it. I mean, I remember when BuzzFeed was just something I did in college around 2:00 a.m.[18]

Ribbing Bill Clinton regarding smoking marijuana

Look, when I was a kid, I inhaled frequently. That was the point.[19]

Describing the closeness of his relationship with his vice president

I'm more relaxed than ever. Those Joe Biden shoulder massages… they're like magic.[20]

I was the first Black to reside in
The White House which I took great pride in
College BuzzFeed review
Every morning at two
And those magic massages from Biden

Chapter 7

THE MALE COMEDY ROLL CALL FROM THE MODERN ERA

JAMIE FOXX (1967 -)

What was the first sign that Jamie Foxx was destined to be a comedian? When he was in third grade his teacher would use his talent for the purpose of facilitating appropriate student behavior. She would tell the students that if all class rules were followed, she would let their comedic classmate tell them jokes.

We were a little careful with the wording of that previous sentence because that "comedic classmate" was known as Eric Bishop at the time. The Jamie Foxx name-game story is an interesting one, in and of itself. When he began to perform on the amateur comedy club circuit in 1989, he decided he needed a stage name.

Seeming to notice a let-the-ladies-go-first preference at the clubs, he latched onto Jamie, as it had a dual-gender sound to it. And the inspiration for the last name, as you may have perhaps guessed, is a tribute to comedian Redd Foxx. The newly renamed Jamie Foxx proved impressive on that club circuit and would soon advance to the next level.

FOXX ON FOX - *In Living Color,* on the Fox network, was the groundbreaking Black comedy show of the 1990's and Foxx was there from the start. He was named to the cast in the debut year of 1991 and stayed throughout the entire run which ended in 1994.

With his rising-star status at that point, Foxx weighed his options and found the pitch with the most potential coming from the WB network. They gave him the opportunity to be the creator, producer, and star of his own sitcom which would be called *The Jamie Foxx Show*. The premise of the show was that Foxx's character was a struggling musician who had moved to LA from Texas in hopes of hitting the big time. While pursuing that aspiration he worked with a comical cast of characters at his family's hotel. The show was an early feather in the cap for the WB network (which eventually merged into the current CW network) and it ran for five seasons from 1996-2001.

Foxx has also put together an impressive musical career including four Top 10 albums and a Grammy Award. His musical talent contributed to his critically acclaimed performance as Ray Charles in the 2004 biopic *Ray*. This role enabled him to become only the second person to be named Best Actor by all of the "Big 5" award groups (Academy Awards, Golden Globes, Critics Choice, Screen Actors Guild, British Academy Awards). At this point Foxx has starred in about 55 movies with other standouts including…

* Collateral (2004)
* Django Unchained (2012)
* Baby Driver (2017)

Beginning in 2017, the Foxx-on-Fox tandem has been rejuvenated with Foxx producing and hosting the game show *Beat Shazam* which is basically a newer hipper version of *Name That Tune*.

A couple lines from Foxx's *I Might Need Security* (2004) stand-up special…

* But you gotta hand it to George Bush, when they start talking about wars that motherfucker came out with a new walk. (Going into his Bush impersonation) We're gonna get those motherfuckers. We ain't gonna take it easy on those sons o' bitches. We're gonna get the fuckin' Taliban, we've gonna get KC and the Sunshine Band, don't give a fuck if it's the Gap Band, the Average White Band. We gonna get all the bands.[1]

* (Foxx does a hilarious shtick about going on a safari in Africa and what carries the bit is his vocal prowess in recreating a wide array of authentic-sounding jungle noises. Those, of course, can't be transcribed to the written page but here's his funny take on the quantity and size of the flies in Africa…) Flies… Millions and millions of flies. I think flies from other countries go vacation in Africa. The biggest out-of-shape flies you ever seen. They don't even fly; they are just walkin' on your table. When's the last time you saw a fly have to get a running start to have to get up in the air?[2]

KEVIN HART (1979 -)

Kevin Hart was born in Philadelphia in 1979 and grew up in basically a single-parent household with his heroin-addicted father in and out of the picture. After high school he left Philly for Boston which he used as a home base launching pad to play the amateur comedy club circuit throughout New England.

Success here culminated in Hart landing a role in the Fox sitcom *Undeclared*. While that series was short-lived, it did lead to follow-up movie roles including his debut in *Paper Soldiers* (2002), then *Scary Movie 3* (2003), and *Little Fockers* (2010). He has continued on a prolific movie career with a résumé that currently features 60 films.

Hart has also released five comedy specials beginning with *I'm a Grown Little Man* in 2009 and *Laugh at my Pain* which grossed $15 million in 2011. In 2017, he founded Laugh Out Loud, which he describes as "a global media and production company to provide opportunities for top comedic talent of all ethnicities worldwide."

Kevin Hart has also hosted a wide variety of award shows with typically successful results. That being said, he did have to give up the hosting gig at the 2019 Oscars amidst a firestorm regarding his history of homophobic tweets. The whole thing turned into a meandering brouhaha where he didn't apologize, and then he did, but it was too late and he wasn't going to host, and then Ellen got involved, and he was going to host again, and then there was a screw-Ellen backlash, and then he wasn't hosting.

At this point, if you can overcome the dizziness and continue to read, the eventual outcome was that the Oscars were held without a host that year.

RAFTING TRIP – Here's a great bit that Hart sometimes uses to close his live show…

"I'm gonna tell you a funny story before I let you go. I'm about to do a show where I'm doing everything they say Black people are afraid to do, like bungee jumping, skiing, skydiving, and eating dinner with my family with the TV off. Everything we as Black people don't do, I'm about to do."

The first Black fear to be overcome is whitewater rafting so, while in Chattanooga to do a show, Hart, his wife, and friends Nate and Nyene book a whitewater gig on the Tennessee River. Wanna know how scared Hart is of water? Here's our take on Hart's baptism as potentially told by baby Kevin… "So today at church a guy in a suit tried to drown me. And, no shit, my family just stood there takin' pictures."

That being said, what happens next is not surprising. Upon arrival Hart immediately gets cold feet and rattles off an array of crazy excuses to avoid the excursion as the tour guide recites the rules and regs of the outing.

Lines that particularly unnerve Hart are, *"If you fall out of your raft you must be a part of your own rescue,* and, *last but not least, we got a lifeline; lifeline is 7 feet long and if you fall outta the raft we can throw it to you. If you at 8 feet I suggest you get to 7; it's the only way we can get you back in the raft."*[4]

A petrified Hart is basically shamed into embarking upon the raft ride and sure enough, at one point, their raft flips and everyone is dumped into the drink. After Hart is able to scramble onto a rock, he proves of scant assistance in rescuing the others. The last person to be retrieved from the water is Nyene who is being kept afloat by his life jacket while frantically waving his paddle in the air. Here's what happens when one of the White crew members goes out to remove him from the course. As we turn this story back over to Hart, he leads with Nyene's background.

Nyene is a Muslim, he's been a Muslin his whole life. A serious Muslim, like not a half-ass Muslim, he's like one of those Muslims that reads the back of food packets. You know what I'm talking out.

"[Someone say,] Hey man, do you want a Starburst?"

He say, "Let me see the packet. Give it to me, let me see it. [After intensely scrutinizing the list of ingredients] Uh huh, you see that? That's pork right there! I told you man, that's pork!" He's one of those Muslims, right?

This is why I tell the story. He's in the middle of the river, waving his paddle back and forth, and this White guy is going right for him. White guy smacks his paddle out of the way, and say, "Move man, you messin' up the trail, man."

And Nyene without hesitation say, "Jesus please help!" He didn't even ask Allah for help; he went straight to Christianity. He wasn't like Allah, I'm about to die, where you at man? He's like Jesus come help. I told him he's a phony. He should eat a pork sandwich and kill himself immediately.[5]

DIABOLICAL DOLPHIN ~ Hart has another bit where he talks about different animals he's afraid of. The best one is the dolphin story and we'll share that one next.

I don't like dolphins; I'm scared of dolphins. Me and my wife, we was in Maui, right. She say, "Come on, baby, we should go swim with the dolphins."

I'm like "Nah, I told ya how I feel about the dolphins."

She goes, "Stop bein' a bitch and let's just do it."

[I say,] "Don't call me no bitch, Bitch. Man, whatever." We go and they got these dolphins in this tank; it's like eight dolphins in this tank, right? When I get there, I see this old lady on the back of a dolphin and see this little boy. [I say,] "You know what babe I might just be overreactin'; get the camera, take some pictures of me on the back of the dolphin."

I was hyped, right? I get in the water, I'm on the back of the dolphin, and the instructor, he's like, "As soon as you grab the dolphin's fin, dolphin gonna start takin' you around. So whenever you're ready, grab its fin."

Then I say, "Alright, cool." Soon as I grab my dolphin's fin, my dolphin went straight to the bottom of the tank. So because I was scared I didn't let go, I held on like, you know, when you're scared you start to mentally create shit in your own mind, I was like, "I've got a racist dolphin. He don't like Black people."

So I let go, I get to the top and I'm so scared I start snappin' on the instructor as soon as I see him. I'm like, "Nobody saw fuckin' dolphin #8 missing? You all didn't notice I was gone 30 seconds? He tried to kill me, he tried to kill me!" I was mad, I was so fuckin' scared. [I say,] "You all saw the old lady and the boy but nobody saw the Black fuckin' swirl missin'? Nobody noted that the Black guy wasn't goin' around? You all didn't notice that?"

He's like, "Calm down man, calm down. It's three feet deep. Just stand up."[6]

MARTIN LAWRENCE (1965 -)

Martin Lawrence's pathway to success involved him parlaying strong reviews at The Improv in New York City into an appearance on the CBS show *Star Search* and then into Colombia Pictures Television offering him a role on the syndicated sitcom *What's Happening Now!!* in 1987. His next big gig was being chosen to host *Def Comedy Jam* on HBO in 1992.

During his HBO run, Martin Lawrence landed his own sitcom, the self-titled *Martin* which ran from 1992-1997 on Fox. It was a major breakthrough for both the man and the network. Airing on Thursday nights, the show was a major hit which took the "Must" out of NBC's "Must See TV" advertising pitch. During an era when Fox was evolving from the "fourth" network to "one of the major four" networks, Lawrence was leading the charge.

Martin Lawrence has continued to star in various TV shows and movies. The IMDb movie website rates his top three movies as being:

* Bad Boys (1995)
* Do the Right Thing (1989)
* Boomerang (1992)

Lawrence's stand-up routine is not for the faint of heart. But if you like your comedy with heavy doses of profanity, drugs and sex, he could be your guy. We'll share with you here his take on a brother getting high and watching *The Wizard of Oz*...

"Brother sittin' there chillin' with the herb [he takes a drag on an imaginary joint]. I watched it last week on TV, The Wizard of Oz [another drag]. You know it had the Tin Man [drag]. The scarecrow [drag]. The lion [drag]. That motherfucker lookin' for a heart [drag]. Courage [drag]. And a motherfuckin' brain [drag]. None of these people are lookin' for no pussy [drag]. And they skippin' down the street with a bitch [drag]. Shit, had that been me I would have fucked Dorothy right there on the Yellow Brick Road [drag]. They ain't no place like home is they Dorothy? Ain't no place like home."[7]

TRACY MORGAN (1968 -)

Tracy Morgan was born in Brooklyn in 1968 and, perhaps not surprisingly, faced a difficult youth. His father was a Vietnam Vet and recovering heroin addict who died of AIDS at the age of 38. Tracy dropped out of high school and undertook the difficult dual street career of selling crack cocaine while performing street theater for money. How's that for a juggling act of absurdity?

When he realized that he was making more off the comedy than the coke, his future course was confirmed. Why get your ass thrown in jail when you can just joke your way to the jackpot? Go joke, no coke, right? Morgan parlayed a successful comedy club stint into a role on the *Martin* sitcom, which we mentioned in the previous component. On this show he played a street-savvy huckster salesman known as Hustle Man.

One good thing would lead to another. In a down-to-the-last-man decision, Lorne Michaels gave him the nod over Stephen Colbert for the last spot in the 1996 cast of *Saturday Night Live*. His *SNL* run as a regular would last from 1996 to 2003.

Tracy Morgan's next big gig would be to land a starring role in the NBC sitcom *30 Rock* along with co-stars Alec Baldwin and Tina Fey. That show would enjoy an awesomely award-winning run from 2006 to 2013. Most recently, he has been starring on the TBS comedy *The Last O.G.*

Morgan has also starred in multiple movies throughout his career with the Flickchart website listing his best three performances as…

* Top Five (2014)
* Jo Jo Dancer, Your Life is Calling (1986)
* Cop Out (2010)

There have also been some significant bumps in the road for Morgan, the most significant of which was on June 7, 2014. On that date, he was a passenger in a vehicle returning from an engagement in Delaware when they were rear-ended by a Walmart tractor trailer on the New Jersey Turnpike. The crash killed Morgan's collaborator and friend James McNair and seriously injured Morgan. After a helicopter-hospital transfer, he was diagnosed with a broken nose, several broken ribs, and a broken leg.

He has also encountered some bad-ass bumps of his own making with various comments that have crossed the lines of political correctness regarding women, gays, and handicapped people. Just to provide one of the relatively more lighthearted examples… here's what happened when Morgan appeared on an NBA pregame show in 2011. TNT hosts Kenny Smith and Charles Barkley asked Morgan who he thought was better looking, Tina Fey or Sarah Palin. What would prompt such a quirky question? Keep in mind that at the time Morgan was co-starring with Fey in *30 Rock* while Fey had previously made her Palin impersonations a mainstay on *Saturday Night Live*.

So it was a question rife with potentially funny answers, but even the never-nonplussed Charles Barkley was seen shifting in his seat a bit when he heard Morgan respond by saying, "Well, Palin is certainly good masturbation material."[8] Right now would anybody like to talk about free throw percentages?

And perhaps an even more interesting question. If you're Tina Fey at this point, are you relieved or offended?

When the talk turned to guys masturbatin'
Morgan had one chick he would be nailin'
His own horn he would toot
And then he would shoot
On a mag with a picture of Palin

TREVOR NOAH (1984 -)

Trevor Noah was born in Johannesburg, South Africa in 1984 and as he details in his 2016 memoir, he was literally *Born a Crime*. Why would that be? In those waning years of apartheid, it was still a crime for his parents to have done what they did. And what was that? His Black South African mother and White Swiss-German father had sex and created Baby Trevor.

Noah's book which is aptly subtitled "Stories from a South African Childhood" compellingly details his experiences growing up on the streets of Johannesburg. Prior to making his way to a career in entertainment, he used his considerable technology savvy to survive by bootlegging CDs and serving as a party DJ.

He developed some serious people skills along the way which served him well as he moved on to the world of entertainment, becoming one of the most successful comedians and talk show hosts in South Africa. He made the move to the U.S. in 2011, taking our country by storm as he had done his. Let's highlight some milestones…

* 2012 ~ First South African comedian on *The Tonight Show with Jay Leno*
* 2013 ~ First South African comedian on *The Late Show with David Letterman*
* 2014 ~ Becomes writer for *The Daily Show with Jon Stewart*
* 2015 ~ Comedy Central announces Noah will be taking over as host of *The Daily Show*; he's currently under contract through 2022.

How's that for rapidly ascending the ladder?

The man certainly has a way with words, both verbally as well as on the written page. Noah speaks seven languages and that first book which we mentioned, *Born a Crime* hit #1 on the *New York Times* Bestseller List. His follow up release, *The Donald J. Trump Presidential Twitter Library* (2018) also charted high on the *NYT* list. *Time* magazine included him on their "100 Most Influential People in the World" list in 2018 and further proving his diversity, Trevor Noah also hosted the 63rd annual Grammy Awards in 2021.

Here's a sampling of Noah's comedy…

* (from *Born a Crime*, a thought that occurred to him while sitting in church as a child) I learned about how Christianity works: if you're Native American and you pray to the wolves, you're a savage. If you're African and you pray to your ancestors, you're a primitive. But when White people pray to a guy who turns water into wine, well, that's just common sense.[9]

* (from *Born a Crime*, acknowledging the fact that his expertise with technology exceeded his success in the dating game) The only girls in my life were the naked ones on my computer. While I downloaded music

and messed around in chat rooms, I dabbled in porn sites here and there. No video, of course, only pictures. With online porn today you just drop straight into the madness, but with dial-up it took so long for the images to load it was almost gentlemanly compared to now. You'd spend a good five minutes looking at her face, getting to know her as a person. Then a few minutes later you'd get some boobs. By the time you got to her vagina, you'd spent a lot of quality time together.[10]

* (speaking about the Ku Klux Klan) The KKK as they're affectionately known… has nobody ever bothered to tell them that you do not spell clan with a "k"? Even in America, clan is spelled with a "c". The Ku Klux Klan, they are the KKC not the KKK. In fact the name is wrong, the whole thing, the Ku Klux part of it is just horrible. They got that, as you know, from Ancient Greece, the ku klux alpheon, meaning a circle of brothers and that's how they got their name. They call themselves a Greek circle of brothers. Which is wrong for two reasons. One, if your sole purpose as an organization is to hate Black people, don't you find it strange that you've now named yourselves the "circle of brothers." And secondly, did they realize that in Ancient Greece the circle of brothers were doing very different things with one another, very loving things.[11] (All of which has us casting allusions upon the time-honored question of, "How do you separate the men from the boys in a Greek Army?" the answer of course is… "with a crowbar.")

* A lot of Americans are learning Chinese. It's one of the hardest languages in the world. How do you even learn Chinese? They've got over 10,000 characters in the alphabet. 10,000 characters… we've got 26 in English, and there's still people going, "What comes after q?" With 10,000 characters they must have the worst *Sesame Street* in the world. It must suck being a Muppet in that country. You see them on a Monday morning singing to the kids [cheerfully starting the Chinese alphabet] … five years later [mournfully, they're just finishing the alphabet].[12]

* (On Bruce Jenner's gender reassignment) Looking at how successful all the Kardashian women are, I don't blame Bruce Jenner at all.[13]

* I find comedy is very similar to sex for me… it's exactly like sex if you think about it. Me, a comedian, playing the role of the man and you, the

audience, the role of the woman. Because it's my job to satisfy you. You just have to sit there. And then just like sex, my success or failure is somehow determined by how much noise you make during my performance.[14]

THE WAYANS CLAN

This is the only one of our components of comedian coverage that clamors for inclusion in a family-friendly format. We are going to throw all of the Wayans under one tent and actually, truth be told, it isn't even all of them. The breakthrough show for the family was the Fox sketch comedy series *In Living Color* which ran from 1990-1994. Of the ten Wayans siblings, six of them appeared on the show in some capacity.

The creator and host of the show was second-oldest sibling, Keenen Ivory Wayans. He also was involved in the writing, directing and producing of multiple movies including *Hollywood Shuffle* (1987) and *Scary Movie* (2000). The latter was the highest grossing film directed by a Black up to that point in time. More recently, in 2014, he appeared as a judge on the TV series *Last Comic Standing*.

Also playing a major role on the show *In Living Color* was Damon Wayans. Prior to the family show, Damon had played on the comedy circuit throughout the 1980's and gained notoriety during his stint as a regular on *Saturday Night Live*.

He was a writer as well as a performer on *In Living Color* before leaving the show halfway through its 4-year run. Damon has maintained an active and diverse career ever since, including various movies, TV shows and stand-up comedy.

As mentioned earlier, six of the ten Wayans siblings appeared on *In Living Color*. Here's a quick rundown of the rest of the clan. Brothers Shawn and Marlon Wayans went on to collaborate, writing and starring in *The Wayans Brothers* sitcom which ran on WB from 1995-1999. Kim Wayans starred on the NBC/UPN *In the House* sitcom from 1995-1998. Oldest brother Dwayne was a production assistant and played minor parts in both *In Living Color* and Damon Wayans' sitcom *My Wife and Kids* which ran on ABC from 2001-2005.

W. KAMAU BELL (1973 -)

Walter Kamau Bell was born in Palo Alto in 1973 and after some geographic gyrations around the country, he has landed back in the San Francisco area, now residing in Berkeley. He was living in Chicago (which he hated) when he finished high school and decided to go to college at Penn. After spending a year and a half at the Ivy League school, things just weren't clicking so he withdrew and headed home.

It was at that stage of his life that the notion of becoming a comedian kicked in. The drop-out decision, in retrospect, seems to have been a wise one, as he became a comedian and more. What do we mean by "more"? It's actually a bit hard to define because there's nobody else on the planet whose job description reads quite like Kamau's.

In addition to his stand-up comedy gig, which has resulted in multiple albums and TV appearances, he is a political activist who uses his forum for sociopolitical commentary. He also has a book out, hosts multiple podcasts and a live radio show, and is a multi-Emmy Award winner for his CNN series *Shades of America*. Oh, did we mention the wife and two kids? How 'bout we throw in a shout-out to Melissa, Sami and Juno for good measure!

Next, let's go to a timeline approach to capture the Kamau career crescendos.

* 2007 - First comedy album, *One Night Only* is released
* 2007 - Begins performing his one-man show, *The W. Kamau Bell Curve: Ending Racism in About an Hour*
* 2010 - Second album, *Face Full of Flour*, is named one of Top 10 Comedy Albums of the Year
* 2012 - FXX series *Totally Biased with W. Kamau Bell* debuts, produced by Chris Rock
* 2012 - Named San Francisco's Best Comedian in various publications
* 2016 - *Debut of Semi-Prominent Negro*, his third album and first stand-up comedy TV special
* 2016 - *United Shades of America* debuts, produced and hosted by Bell, multiple Emmy's ensue
* 2017 - First book published *The Awkward Thoughts of W. Kamau Bell*

LOOKING BACK ~ One of the funniest parts of the book was Kamau's self-reflective analysis of some of the TV shows he watched as a kid. Our favorite was his take on *The Dukes of Hazzard*...

In 1977 my favorite TV show was The Incredible Hulk, *and my second favorite was* The Dukes of Hazzard, *where every week the bright orange car named the General Lee, with the Confederate flag painted on top, would save the day as the two hillbillies, Bo and Luke, inevitably screamed, "Yee-haw!" My Mom was so proud.*

So this show, even though it was set in Hazzard County, Georgia, a place where there would have been boatfuls of Black people, only had like one Black dentist, according to my memory of watching it. I remember thinking to myself, "He must be a really good dentist." I would sometimes get excited and scream out, "YAY! The General Lee saved the day." Yup, that was the name of the car: the General Lee.[15]

Kamau wrote the following about his passion for Bruce Lee as a kid… "*My walls were covered in Bruce Lee posters, [still would be if my wife would let me]. This was the '80s, when finding Bruce Lee stuff meant going to Chinatown and doing a deep dive in the tourist traps. At that point he hadn't been taken fully into the bosom of mainstream pop culture. A few years ago, I saw a Bruce t-shirt at Target; I was horrified that his image was in such a crass store, and I bought it immediately. To this day I wish I had bought two.*"[16]

> *To Bruce Lee he still shouts out a "Wow!"*
> *But the choice that he must disavow*
> *Was when nothing else mattered*
> *When those Dukes of Hazzard*
> *Hit the Wonderful World of Kamau*

Here's some more of Kamau's humor…

* The reason that every modern Superman movie sucks is because we all sit in the audience thinking, "So wait… Lois is a Pulitzer Prize-winning journalist and she can't figure out that the key to Superman's secret identity is his glasses?"[17]

* (Describing his comedian friend Dwayne Kennedy at the No Exit Café in Chicago) He came in and did a joke about what it would have been

like to be Jesus Christ's bitter brother, Steve Christ. He leveled the place, absolutely killed it, and then immediately got offstage.[18]

* (watching Chappelle at the Punch Line in San Francisco, when he wasn't big yet, but everyone knew he would be) And I was there one night when a KKK member went on stage and hurled insults at the audience. It was hilarious, because we could see his black hand under his white sheets. Later we all realized that we were there during an early tryout of Clayton Bigsby, the blind Black KKK member that Dave played on the debut episode of his behemoth of a sketch show, *Chappelle's Show*.[19]

* (his suggested title for Obama's autobiography)
I Can't Believe Nobody Shot Me Either[20]

* Donald Trump, oh my god, Donald Trump is like the nagging cough that has turned into full blown AIDS, you know what I'm saying? If we'd only nipped him in the bud when we had the chance. It would just be HIV, but we let it go and now he's going to kill all of us.[21]

* So I find myself in this weird position now because I've got a little bit of a public profile. I'm in this thing that's called "Semi-Prominent Negro" status where I get asked the questions when Al Sharpton can't take the phone call. Sometimes I feel I get sandbagged: [for example] I was doing interviews to promote a tour I was going on and this guy called me to do an interview and he was a White reporter. And he goes, "Can I ask you a question?"
I go, "Sure."
[He says,] "When is it okay for a White person to use the word nigger?"
I went, "Well first of all, not right then. That's not a good time. Take that one back; you can't do that one. And second of all, why you askin' me? When did **I** get put in charge of **that**?"[22]

* Kamau has some humorous takes on the challenges of being in a biracial marriage, including how his wife's research on how to best take care of their daughter's hair led her to an actual website designed to help White women with that challenge. Name of the website… "Chocolate Hair, Vanilla Care." No kiddin', true story.[23]

* (Then there's the story of having his daughter process the fact that the skin color of everyone in the family is a little different.) And now she's come up with a whole system for what color everybody is and [She says,] I'm chocolate (crowd is quiet, wondering what's coming next), she calls herself peanut butter (crowd "oohs" and "aahs" at the cuteness), and mama is oatmeal (crowd laughs uproariously. Then, after a well-timed pause...) That may be the first documented case of reverse racism. Because nobody likes oatmeal.[24]

* (Regarding the fact that the situation has gotten so bad for Black people, things that would have been upsetting before, now have to be just dropped because they don't have time to deal with them.) Came out recently that Hulk Hogan had said nigger [conveys exasperation, then says...] Come on man! People are dying, Hulk, so we gotta let that one go. The best we can do for you is put you in the Black Rage Waiting Room over here.[25]

CHAPTER 8

SOME BELOW-THE-RADAR BLACK SPORTS HISTORY

JACK JOHNSON (1878-1946)

CHAMPIONSHIP ASPIRATIONS ~ Heavyweight boxer Jack Johnson, who was known as the "Galveston Giant," attained the title of Black Heavyweight Champion in 1903. He subsequently sought to fight for the world title but the White reigning champions of that era refused for years to fight him. It would be 1908 before he would get his chance and Johnson ascended to the overall heavyweight championship by knocking out Tommy Burns. He would hold that title until 1915.

During his reign, Johnson was a controversial and polarizing figure. While he was certainly a victim of racism, several aspects of his personal life definitely inflamed the situation. He had three White wives and frequented White prostitutes, often simultaneously, at a time when such behavior was prone to make a Black man the target for lynching. That screw-the-world approach was part of his appeal.

Add to this the fact that he lived a totally flamboyant lifestyle characterized by a deep down disrespect for White authority and it's not surprising why Johnson became a target of that authority. More on that in a minute, but first we'll share the fact that his way of life became the source of a number of Black rhymes and legendary stories. Here's one example of each.

First the rhyme which plays upon the fact that so many White people were despondent over the fact that the heavyweight champion of the world was Black.

Our World Champion's still a Nigger
The Yankees hold the play
The White man pull the trigger
But screw what the White man say
The World Champion's still a Nigger
And it's true all live-long day[1]

STORY HOUR ~ And we'll follow that up with our favorite Jack Johnson story.

It was on a hot August day in Georgia when Jack Johnson drove into town and man, he was really flyin'! Behind his fine car was a cloud of red Georgia dust as far as the eye could see. The sheriff flagged him down and said, "Where do you think you're goin', boy, speedin' like that? That'll cost you $50."

Johnson never looked up; he just reached into his pocket, handed the sheriff a $100 bill and started to gun the motor. Just before Johnson pulled out the sheriff shouted, "Don't you want your change?"

Johnson replied, "Keep it, 'cause I'm comin' back the same way I'm goin'."[2]

Now, back to the topic of Johnson's battle with White authority… In 1913 he was sentenced to a year in jail for violating the Mann Act which prohibited transporting women across state lines for immoral purposes. He subsequently fled the country for seven years before returning in 1920 and serving his term at the Leavenworth Federal Penitentiary.

Next, returning to his boxing career, after Johnson captured the heavyweight crown many racially motivated fans began clamoring for a "Great White Hope" to reclaim the title, but they would find themselves clamoring for years to come. Johnson would defeat all challengers for the next seven years before ultimately losing his title in Havana, Cuba in 1915. His career record finished at 70-11-11.

And somewhere in Georgia he should still have a $50 credit at the Sheriff's Department.

> *Sex with White girls I sure recommend*
> *Boxing crown I would surely ascend*
> *Many punches to land*
> *Yes indeed, it felt grand*
> *"Great White Hopes" to bring those to an end*

And a final fun fact… Jack is also said to be the inspiration for the concept that a Black man's genitalia is sometimes referred to as his "Johnson."

JOHN BAXTER TAYLOR (1882-1908)

Becoming the first Black athlete to win an Olympic gold medal was certainly an achievement destined to notch a niche in history for John Baxter Taylor. Perhaps equally notable is that upon the occasion of his premature death, the consensus opinion was that he was an even better man than he was an athlete. High praise indeed.

Born to former slaves in Washington D.C., his family moved to Philadelphia where he grew up and excelled as the only Black on his high school track team. An excellent student, Taylor was accepted into the University of Pennsylvania in 1903 and joined the Ivy League school's track team. Among his accomplishments was breaking the collegiate record in the quarter-mile run. Also, while at Penn, he was a member of Sigma Pi Phi, the first Black fraternity.

In June of 1908 Taylor graduated from Penn with a degree from the School of Veterinary Medicine. Just one month later he would board a ship, crossing the Atlantic to England where he was to compete at the 1908 Summer Olympic Games in London. He was the first Black to represent the U.S. at the Olympics.

Taylor ran in both the 400-meter relay final and the 1600-meter medley relay and he might have won two gold medals had not there been some controversial "home field shenanigans" in the 400-meter event. British officials claimed that one of their runners was fouled by an American competitor, subsequently awarding the gold to the British team.

But the 1600-meter medley relay would enable Taylor to establish his spot in history. He ran the third leg of the relay, being handed the baton with the U.S. in the lead and passing that lead on to his teammate who completed the final leg to secure the gold medal.

Unfortunately, Taylor would have precious little time to savor his Olympic medal or his veterinary degree. A scant five months later Taylor would be dead, succumbing to typhoid fever at the age of just 26.

Upon his death, the President of the U.S. Olympic team, Harry Porter, wrote a letter to Taylor's parents which contained the following passage. "It is far more as the man [than the athlete] that John Taylor made his mark. Quite unostentatious, genial, [and] kindly, the fleet-footed, far-famed athlete was beloved wherever known ... as a beacon of his race. His example of achievement in athletics, scholarship and manhood will never wane, if indeed it is not destined to form with that of Booker T. Washington."[3] Being placed on the same stage as Booker T. is certainly nothing to scoff at.

The New York Times obituary saluted him as "the world's greatest Negro runner."[4] So sad that the world's greatest had to exit that stage so soon.

All those obstacles he overcame
The gold medal that he would first claim
His legacy hewn
He left much too soon
Going out at the top of his game

MACK ROBINSON (1914-2000)

While we will tacitly acknowledge the discussion of other candidates, it seems consensus-clear that the most iconic Black athlete in history would have to be the man that broke the color barrier in the National Pastime of baseball, Jackie Robinson.

But how many of you know the story of his older brother Mack? As stated from the outset, a goal of this project has been to tell some untold stories rather than repeat the renowned.

So what are Mack's facts? At the 1936 Summer Olympics in Berlin, when Black American athletes were taking the theory of Aryan supremacy and shoving it down Adolph Hitler's throat, Mack Robinson broke the world record for the 200-meter dash. Especially for you sports fans out there this might beg the question, "Why have I never heard of this dude?"

Well, we have the answer for you. In that very same race, Jesse Owens also broke the world record while beating Robinson by 0.4 seconds. When Owens went on to win four gold medals in the 1936 games, that achievement became the definitive one of that Olympiad and Robinson's silver medal was overshadowed.

Mack Robinson earned accolades later in life for leading a campaign against street crime in Pasadena, California which was the hometown of both he and his brother Jackie. In 1997 the city erected the Pasadena Robinson Memorial paying tribute to both of the Robinson brothers.

NEW YORK RENAISSANCE (1923-1949)

The first Black induction into the Basketball Hall of Fame occurred in 1963 and that first inductee was actually a team, one called the New York Renaissance. It's an interesting story and one that we feel most people have not heard, so here's the scoop…

In the 1920's the only major team sport that had an efficient level of organization was baseball. When it came to basketball and football, teams could spring up anywhere and play anybody they wanted to. The goal was to draw enough spectators to pay the players a modest salary and it was all very spontaneous and unofficial. A general practice was that teams would "barnstorm," or travel around the country looking for opponents to play, with the financial arrangements worked out on a game-by-game basis.

It was amidst this backdrop that Bob Douglas became the organizer and head coach for an all-Black basketball team called the New York Renaissance. How did they get their name? Well, they needed a place to play, so in 1923 Douglas negotiated a deal with the Renaissance Casino and Ballroom which was located in Harlem at the intersection of 7th Avenue and 138th Street. The ballroom component featured in that establishment was large enough to install a basketball court and some seating, enabling it to serve as the team's home court. It was all quite festive as following each game the court transitioned to a dance floor and a Harlem hoedown ensued.

TEAM CHEMISTRY CLICKS ~ The team, which came to be known as the Rens, achieved amazing success during the 1920's and 1930's. The aforementioned helter skelter nature of the basketball world's organization during that era resulted in their being some all-Black teams, some all-White teams and some integrated teams.

Obviously, games pitting the best all-Black teams against the best all-White teams were racially charged. Black athletes were provided with the opportunity to prove their prowess, in a scenario of which they were deprived in pro baseball, a sport which operated under strictly segregated ground rules. We should note that there were occasions in baseball where Black teams would play White teams in exhibition games, but at the highest level of the sport, Major League Baseball was totally segregated until 1947.

Emerging as the dominant Black basketball team in the country, the Rens ultimate rival became the Original Celtics, a White team from New York City which, by the way, did not have any connection with the organization that would eventually become the Boston Celtics. The Rens lost their first four encounters with the Celtics before finally beating them on December 20, 1925. It was the Christmas gift they had been hoping for.

The Rens/Celtics rivalry became one of basketball's most bitter, intensified by the fact that the teams played each other quite evenly. And the Rens took on not only the best White teams but the best Black teams as well. Not surprisingly, one of their big rivals was their Manhattan neighbors, the Harlem Globetrotters.

KAREEM CLIMBS ON BOARD ~ Basketball legend Kareem Abdul-Jabbar took the Rens' story under his large wingspan by writing a book about them called *On the Shoulders of Giants* in 2007 and followed that up with a documentary in 2011. "I tried to spread the word [about the Rens and Douglas] with my book and documentary," said Abdul-Jabbar.

"I did both to make people aware of the Rens' contribution to basketball because it's important that we honor those pioneers who made this billion-dollar industry possible," Jabbar said. "It's also important that we recognize the people of color who did so much, but history deliberately ignored."

"Bob Douglas was the first Black man to own a basketball team," Abdul-Jabbar went on to say. "Not just any team, but the greatest team of the time. The early rivalries with the Original Celtics and Harlem Globetrotters gave basketball exciting teams to support."[4]

A LEGACY LEFT - The Rens compiled a record of 120 wins and 8 losses during the 1932-33 season. Obviously stellar by any standards. They actually put together a winning streak of 88 games that season, a record never matched in pro basketball history.

Moving to the end of the 1930's, a "World Professional Basketball Tournament" was organized for the first time and held in Chicago in 1939. Teams competed on an invitation-only basis. In the semifinals, the New York Rens defeated the Harlem Globetrotters, advancing to the finals. That championship game was contested between the Rens and the all-White Oshkosh All-Stars with the Rens prevailing 34-25 to claim what is considered to be the first world title in basketball.

In 1940, the Globetrotters turned the table and defeated the Rens on their way to the championship. In their final decade of existence, the Rens most impressive finish in the tournament came in 1948 when they finished second to the Minneapolis Lakers of the National Basketball League. Yes, those Lakers are the franchise that moved to Los Angeles in 1960 and yes, the NBL is the league that morphed into the NBA in 1950.

When Blacks began playing in the NBA in 1950, it signaled the end of an era for the New York Rens. Their reason for being had essentially ceased to exist and Bob Douglas folded up shop after the 1949 season. The Rens final line would be that in their years of competition from 1923-1949 they would compile an overall record of 2588-539. A Renaissance indeed!

SATCHEL PAIGE (1906-1982)

Leroy Robert "Satchel" Paige was one of the most entertaining professional baseball players of all time, both on and off the field. Almost unbelievably, his Hall of Fame career spanned five decades. He was arguably the best pitcher in the Negro Leagues, was able to achieve success at an advanced age in Major League Baseball, and his final appearance in MLB was one choreographed for the ages. Stay tuned for that.

Paige's Negro League career was characterized by his ability to perennially lead the league in wins, strike outs, and one-liners. It was a triple threat that made him legendary. In exhibition games he had a variety of shticks he would employ to entertain audiences. One was to have his infielders play sitting down as he would strike out the side and/or induce harmless fly balls.

On other occasions, if he had two outs and the other team's best hitter was four batters away from coming to the plate, he would intentionally walk three batters just so he could retire the other team's star with the bases loaded.

MAJOR LEAGUE STORY ~ When Jackie Robinson broke the MLB color barrier in 1947, Paige was already 41 years old. But that did not stop him from becoming the oldest rookie in MLB history when he took the field for the Cleveland Indians halfway through the 1948 season. At the age of 42 he compiled a record of 6 wins and only 1 loss with an earned run average of just 2.48 per game.

The Indians made the World Series that year and he subsequently became the first Black player to pitch in the World Series. There's an irony from that World Series which haunts professional sports to this day. The Indians won that World Series and they've never won one since. In all of the four major professional sports (baseball, football, basketball, hockey) no franchise has currently experienced a longer drought without winning a championship.

Paige was just the seventh Black MLB player and the first Black pitcher in the American League. He finished his original MLB career pitching for the St. Louis Browns (current Baltimore Orioles franchise) and made the American League All-Star team in 1952 and 1953.

RAMBUNCTIOUS RETIREMENT ~ After his original retirement from MLB, Paige's love of the game was such that he could never quite leave it. He continued to pitch in various minor, semi-pro, and international leagues until approaching the age of 60. At that point he was blessed with the cherry to place on top of his career.

In 1965, the Kansas City Athletics signed the 59-year-old Paige to pitch for one game against the Boston Red Sox, making him the oldest MLB player ever. In some avenues it was viewed as just a publicity stunt and the Athletics invited several Negro League veterans back for a pre-game ceremony that seemed more about show than substance.

The A's of that era were owned by Charlie Finley who was noted for his showmanship. Billing themselves as "the Swingin' A's," they were the first MLB team to wear colored jerseys and white spikes and Finley paid team members a bonus if they would grow a mustache. Some said they looked like a cross between a bunch of turn-of-the-century gangsters and modern urban pimps.

At any rate, the Satchel Paige stunt had showboating written all over it and many feared that it was sure to provide an ugly and embarrassing ending to what had been a storybook career. Turned out all those praying for all that Satchel-salvation needn't have been worried at all. He pitched three innings, giving up no runs and one hit while retiring the last six batters in a row.

True to form, Finley and the A's turned it into a show. Between innings Paige sat in the bull pen which was on the side of the field along the wall back then, so in full view of the crowd. Posing in his rocking chair he was served coffee each inning by his "nurse."

He went to the pitching mound in the top of the 4th and, as had been planned, the manager walked to the mound and took him out to a thunderous applause. As Paige walked to the dugout the lights dimmed as the PA announcer encouraged fans to light matches and cigarette lighters while he led the crowd in singing "The Old Gray Mare." It was Paige-perfection at its finest.

Here's one of our favorite Satch stories. On various Cleveland Indian questionnaires, the players were asked to indicate whether or not they were married. Sometimes Paige would answer yes and sometimes no. Every game day he would leave a ticket at the box office to be picked up by Mrs. Paige and when the organization noticed that a variety of different women were picking up the tickets each day, Paige was pressed for an explanation. "Well, it's like this," Satch said, "I'm not married, but I am in great demand."[5]

Here's a sampling of Paige's humor…

* (describing the speed of a Negro League opponent) One time Cool Papa Bell hit a line drive past my ear. I turned around and saw the ball hit him in the ass sliding into second base.[6]

* Work like you don't need the money. Love like you've never been hurt. Dance like nobody's watching.[7]

* Sometimes I sits and thinks and sometimes I just sits.[8]

* I never threw an illegal pitch. The trouble is, once in a while I would toss one that ain't never been seen by this generation.[9]

* (his signature line, with which he closed is Hall of Fame induction speech) Don't look back. Something might be gaining on you.[10]

> With romance I have more than nine lifes
> Love life's plagued with great perils and strifes
> I am in great demand
> Just how I have it planned
> Please don't tell any one of my wifes

MUHAMMAD ALI (1942-2016) (THE LOUISVILLE LIP'S TOP 7 QUOTES)

From the perspective of whit and whimsy, boxer Muhammad Ali was certainly the funniest and most entertaining athlete ever to emerge from that sport. And how famous was Muhammad Ali in his heyday? There was a time when if the Pope, in full regalia, was walking down the street with Muhammad Ali, people would look at the pair and say, "Who's that with Ali?" Here are our seven favorite Ali quotes ranging from hilarious to inspirational.

#7 ~ Service to others is the rent we pay for our room in the Hereafter.[11]

#6 ~ I'm so quick I could punch you before God got the news.[12]

#5 ~ If you even dream of beating me, you better wake up and apologize.[13]

#4 ~ If they can make penicillin out of moldy bread, they can sure make something out of you.[14]

#3 ~ It isn't the mountain ahead to climb that wears you out; it's the pebble in your shoe.[15]

#2 ~ I'm so fast that last night I turned off the light switch in my hotel room and was in bed before the room was dark.[16]

#1 ~ Live every day as if it were your last because someday you are going to be right.[17]

For Ali, that day came on June 3, 2016. Rest in peace champ, and may you always float like a butterfly and sting like a bee!

CHAPTER 9

THE GATEWAY FROM THE CHITLIN' CIRCUIT TO THE MAINSTREAM

PIGMEAT MARKHAM (1904-1981)

Who was the burly man who billed himself as "Sweet Poppa Pigmeat?" That would be Dewey "Pigmeat" Markham and that Dewey could do it all. With such an outlandishly porky name, a full explanation is probably appropriate. Sweet Poppa Pigmeat was a character in an old vaudeville routine who "stood with the river Jordan at my hips, and all the women is just run up to be baptized!"[1] We suppose there are worse positions in which a man could find himself.

Pigmeat was a talent-tempestuous tornado whose manic moves included singing, dancing, acting and comedy. His showbiz career began on the Chitlin' Circuit in the 1920's where he was once a member of *Bessie Smith's Traveling Revue.* He continued touring during the 30's and 40's, with the latter decade seeing him increasingly appearing in movies.

The Apollo Theatre in Harlem was a frequent Pigmeat haunt which he first visited in 1935, sometimes performing at the venue at least once a week for a year at a time. The book *Showtime at the Apollo* (1983) claimed, "He probably played the Apollo more often than any other performer."[2]

TIME FOR TV ~ During the 1950's Pigmeat Markham made the move to television, appearing frequently on *The Ed Sullivan Show*. His signature routine became his "Here Come Da Judge" take on a riotously out-of-control courtroom in which Pigmeat would play "Da Judge," who was "high as a Georgia pine," seated on an elevated bench bedecked with a wig and robe.

Da Judge would be confronted by an array of malcontents and miscreants upon whom he would bestow courtroom justice profusely punctuated by the verbal and physical abuse of the defendants. There was something about courtroom chaos where the geriatric judge was beating the defendants with a rubber chicken that just never seemed to grow old.

Toward the end of his life in the late 1960's, Pigmeat was able to add a few nice closing lines to his résumé. One of the most celebrated comedy shows of the era was *Rowan and Martin's Laugh-In* and of course one of the most famous Black entertainers of the time was Sammy Davis Jr. who helped contribute to a Pigmeat Markham comeback. They actually both performed the "Here Come Da Judge" sketch on *Laugh-In*. The expression became a catch phrase on the show specifically and around the country in general.

That sketch actually ended with a song which Chess Records had him record and release as a single. Under the grammatically corrected title of "Here Comes the Judge," the recording provided a pleasant surprise by rising to #19 on the *Billboard* charts in June of 1968. Pigmeat was definitely eating high on the hog. Because of the vocal stylizations, various music publications have referred to this recording as the first rap song. How's that for Pigmeat's persona permeating the present? Rap on, Bro!♫

Channeling that rap vibe, we'll toss out a little poetry of our own. Before we start, we'll begin by sharing one of our favorite Pigmeat quotes. Regarding the depth of his human virtue, Pigmeat once said, "Outside of booze, broads and bread, I have no vices."

> *Wine and women he found really sweet*
> *His court sketch was truly a treat*
> *Here does come da judge*
> *No way to begrudge*
> *That man known as Sweet Poppa Pigmeat*

FINAL WORDS – Let's close this with fellow comedian George Kirby's tribute from the liner notes for Markham's *Here Comes the Judge* album. Kirby wrote, "This comic was one of the few greats who walked in the back door so that we young comics of today could walk in the front, and thank God he has a chance to walk in the front with us… Pigmeat Markham is the greatest."[3]

SLAPPY WHITE (1921-1995)

Here's a unique hook for this next component. No comedian in our book could say that he was married to two more high-profile musical icons. Slappy White was married to both jazz legend Pearl Bailey and Rock and Roll Hall of Famer LaVern Baker. Not at the same time, of course. That would have cranked this "unique" hook to erotically epic proportions.

Melvin Edward "Slappy" White experienced his modestly humble entertainment beginnings at the age of just 10, dancing for coins outside the Royal Theatre in Baltimore. At 13 he ran away from home to join the circus where he told jokes and tap danced. By the 1940's he was touring the Chitlin' Circuit performing with the likes of Louis Armstrong, Duke Ellington and Count Basie.

White's profile on the circuit was elevated during the 50's and 60's when he teamed with Redd Foxx. At that point he was poised to cross over into the mainstream, making guest appearances on TV shows such as *Sanford and Son*, *That's My Mama*, *Cybill*, and *Blossom*. He was also a frequent guest on talk shows as well as a panelist on game shows. In his later years he was a regular participant in the series of Dean Martin's Friar's Club roasts of various celebrities.

Here's a sampling of White's humor...

* The trouble with unemployment is the minute you wake up in the morning you're on the job.[4]

* I asked my date what she wanted to drink. She said, "I guess I'll have champagne."
I said, "Guess again."[5]

* (when asked how he felt about sex in motion pictures) I think sex should be confined to the privacy of the home. And I don't mind goin' from house to house.[6]

* (when told that Los Angeles has a number of honest policemen) Yeah, the number is 6.[7]

* (when asked about sex education films in the classroom) They should be shown in the drive-in theaters, so you can see what you're doin' wrong while you're doin' it.[8]

* (when asked about the war between the Arabs and the Jews) I was rootin' for the Jews myself, 'cause you know I'm not going to be rootin' for a bunch of guys runnin' around in white sheets.[9]

> One thing does make me feel quite happy
> My sex life was really quite snappy
> Pearl did have her turn
> And then came LaVern
> How'd you feel if they both called you Slappy?

NIPSEY RUSSELL (1918-2005)

Julius "Nipsey" Russell was a man of many talents which were featured on American screens from the 1960's through the end of the century. His arsenal of talents included comedy, poetry, dancing and the area where he was probably most prevalent, that of the ubiquitous TV game show panelist. In 1964 he became the first Black to appear on network TV in this capacity.

His game show résumé included all the standards of the era such as *Hollywood Squares, Password, To Tell the Truth, $10,000 Pyramid* and *The Match Game.* One of his unique shticks was interjecting his own poetry into his performances which caused the nickname "poet laureate of television" to be bequeathed upon him.

Here is a sampling of Russell's self-penned poetry…

If you ever go out with a schoolteacher
You're in for a sensational night,
She'll make you do it over and over again
Until you do it just right.

The young people are very different today
And there's one sure way to know,
Kids used to ask where they came from
Now they'll tell you where you can go!

Spanking a child to get him to learn
Is something I cannot defend.
How can you knock any sense in his head
When you're whacking him on the wrong end?[10]

Here are a couple of our favorite Nipsey Russell stories...

"Train to New York"

Got on the train in Tampa, Florida, on the way to New York. Conductor came around, said, "Give me your ticket, Boy." Gave him my ticket; he punched it and gave it back. Came around again in Richmond, Virginia, said, "Give me your ticket, Boy." Gave him my ticket; he punched it and gave it back. In the Lincoln Tunnel on the way into New York City, the conductor came around and said, "Give me your ticket, Boy." Turned around to him and said, "Who the hell you callin' Boy?"[11]

"Ain't Ghana Eat"

An African delegate was driving along Highway One between Baltimore and Washington D.C., and stopped at a restaurant to dine. When he entered, they told him they didn't serve Blacks. The delegate, flustered with embarrassment, pulled up all of his dignity and said in a loud voice, "I'm the African delegate from Ghana." The waitress looked him straight in the eye and said, "Well, you ain't Ghana eat here!"

We'll use our limerick to provide a quick history of Russell's dancing career.[12]

Dancin's part of the heart of show biz
Yep, for me that is just how it is
When I danced that hand jive
People just came alive
As the Tin Man I danced in The Wiz

FLIP WILSON (1933-1998)

Upon coming under frequent criticism from her husband for too many impulse purchases, the reverend's wife deflects the blame by declaring, "The Devil made me buy this dress!" In this particular Flip Wilson sketch, the reverend's wife was a variation of the Geraldine character who was the centerpiece of Wilson's comedy shtick. He often dressed like a woman to enhance the comedic effect. In 1970 he won the Grammy for Best Comedy Album for *The Devil Made Me Buy This Dress*. In the late-60's and early-70's no Black loomed larger on the comedy landscape.

Fashion sense, I succumbed, nonetheless
Purchase choices, I might reassess
God's advice I ignored
I proclaim to the Lord
That damn devil made me buy this dress

Now, let's lead with the story on the wacky name. After entering the Air Force in his late teens, Wilson's comedic talent rose to the surface and his superior storytelling often put him in the role of entertaining the troops. In describing his act, a phrase that became repeatedly used was that he performed as if he was "flipped out." Flipped turned into Flip and the name stuck.

His showbiz career began in the mid-1950's when he was working as a bellhop at the Manor Plaza Hotel in San Francisco. He convinced the hotel's nightclub manager to allow him to perform in between regularly scheduled acts doing a bit where he played a drunk. He was so well received that he managed to parlay these fill-in gigs into becoming a regular on the Chitlin' Circuit.

It was Redd Foxx who actually facilitated the breakthrough moment in Flip Wilson's career. During a 1965 appearance on *The Tonight Show*, Johnny Carson asked Foxx who his favorite comedian was. Expecting to hear a famous name, Carson was surprised to hear the Foxx fave being identified as one Flip Wilson, a man of whom Carson had never heard.

Following up on that surprise lead, Carson booked Wilson for an appearance on *The Tonight Show* and the comedic cat was out of the bag.

That led to follow-up appearances on *Ed Sullivan, Dean Martin,* and *Laugh-In.* By the end of the decade Wilson was one of the hottest comedians on the planet. And we're not talking just African American comedians; we're talking red and yellow, black and white, (referencing the classic "Jesus Loves the Little Children" song from days of Sunday school yore).

He landed his own variety show, *The Flip Wilson Show,* which ran on NBC from 1970 through 1974. It became a #1 show in the country earning him two Emmys and a Golden Globe. Two lines of his, delivered by his Geraldine persona, became national catch phrases during this era. Those would be "What you see is what you get!" and "The Devil made me do it!" If we had to pick one moment to anoint as the zenith of his career, we'd probably go to January of 1972 when *Time* magazine featured him in a cover story boasting the headline "TV's First Black Superstar."[13]

Here's a story we remember from our childhood when Flip describes a scene where he's visiting relatives. A pair of five-year-olds have gotten into a mess, are taken to the bathroom to cleanup, and the supervising adults leave to gather the materials necessary to accomplish that task. The five-year-old boy and girl find themselves standing naked face-to-face in the bathtub with questions on their mind about "private parts" that they clearly have not seen before.

Flip says, "I'm watchin' through the crack in the door, and the girl says to the boy, 'What's that?'"

And he says, "Where?"

She says, "Right there."

He says, "I don't know."

She says, "Well what's it for?"

He says, "I told you I don't know."

She says, "Can I touch it?"

He says, "Hell no. You broke yours off already."[14]

Here's a sampling of more Flip Wilson comedy…

* (This first one features Flip in his female Geraldine persona at the airport baggage counter)

Airport Clerk: We're sorry ma'am, but your bags didn't arrive on the plane. We don't know what happened.
Geraldine: If y'all can fly this airplane 600 miles an hour, in a thunderstorm, in the middle of the night, and find New York City, then y'all can find my luggage![15]

* Get well cards have gotten so funny that if you don't get sick, you're missing half the fun.[16]

* The secret of my success with Geraldine is that she's not a put-down of women. She's smart, she's trustful, she's loyal, she's sassy.[17]

* Don't order one for the road, because the road is already laid out.[18]

DICK GREGORY (1932-2017)

It would be difficult to pick any man who better straddled the line between stand-up comedian and civil rights activist than Dick Gregory. He was a prolific author, released multiple comedy record albums, and made frequent television appearances.

He first rose to fame on the Chitlin' Circuit in the 1950's with his cutting-edge act which focused on bigotry and racism as it existed in the United States. It was 1961 that became Gregory's breakthrough year with the flashpoint being when Hugh Hefner happened to catch one of his performances at a small club called the Roberts Show Bar in Chicago.

Hef booked Gregory to do a night at his Playboy Club right there in Chi-Town. That one night turned into six weeks and Dick Gregory was propelled down the pathway to fame. By the end of the year, he had been featured in *Time* magazine and appeared on *The Tonight Show Featuring Jack Parr*, as well as other shows.

As the decade wore on, Gregory's focus reflected the volatility of the changing times and he began to channel more and more of his efforts into activist causes, the primary two being racial injustice and opposition to the Vietnam War. To this end he went on multiple hunger strikes and was arrested numerous times.

During this era the line of "successful author" was added to his résumé. In 2017 when *Rolling Stone* published its poll of the "50 Best

Stand-Up Comics of All Time," Dick Gregory was rated as the 8th greatest Black comedian.[19]

Here is a sampling of Gregory's humor…

* They asked me to buy a lifetime membership in the NAACP, but I told them I'd pay a week at a time. Hell of a thing to buy a lifetime membership, wake up one morning and find the country's been integrated.[20]

* I waited at the counter for 11years. When they finally integrated, they didn't have what I wanted.[21]

* I never believed in Santa Claus because I knew no White dude would come into my neighborhood after dark.[22]

* We used to root for the Indians against the cavalry, because we didn't think it was fair in the history books that when the cavalry won it was a great victory, and when the Indians won it was a massacre.[23]

* I am really enjoying the new Martin Luther King Jr. stamp – just think about all those White bigots licking the backside of a Black man.[24]

* Last time I went down South I walked into this restaurant, and this White waitress came up to me and said, "We don't serve colored people here."

I said, "That's alright, I don't eat colored people. Bring me a whole fried chicken."

About this time three cousins come in, you know the ones I mean, Klu, Kluck, and Klan and they say, "Boy, we're givin' you fair warnin'. Anything you do to that chicken, we're going to do to you."

About then the waitress brought me my chicken. They say, "Remember, Boy, anything you do to that chicken, we're gonna do to you."

So I put down my knife and fork, and I picked up that chicken, and I kissed it.[25]

KKK did walk in, I be sickened
Thought for sure, my ass in for a kickin'
Back-up plan, did conceive
How to get them to leave?
Never thought I would kiss a damn chicken!

CHAPTER 10
NOTEWORTHY CONCEPTS & EVENTS

In the process of writing and organizing this book we took all the people we covered and clustered them into thematic groupings. At that point we realized we had half a dozen components that weren't actually about specific people, but rather about certain events and concepts. So those components get their own chapter and welcome to it.

We'll lead off by delving into the concept of interracial marriage and then we'll look into some interesting relationships between Blacks and two religious groups, namely the Quakers and the Jews. Juneteenth has achieved new prominence and was duly awarded with its own component. Finally, we'll close the chapter with the musical trio of *The Wiz*, *Motown 25*, and "We Are the World."

INTERRACIAL MARRIAGE

The timeline on the history of interracial marriage in the United States has some surprising numbers and dates. It was actually illegal for 303 years and we thought the storyline was interesting enough to deserve inclusion in this book.

The 16th century and the first half of the 17th century saw an increasing number of interracial marriages which were referred to as "miscegenation." The colony of Maryland passed the first law banning miscegenation in 1664 with several other colonies rapidly following suit. Penalties for White people violating this law included imprisonment, exile, and even enslavement.

It would be over three centuries before these laws would be unilaterally overturned. What were the circumstances that led to the lifting of the laws? Here's the scoop… We'd like you to meet Richard Loving and Mildred Jeter. The year is 1967 when Loving, a White man, and Jeter, a Black woman, are forbidden from marrying in their native state of Virginia because of the anti-miscegenation law that is still on the books there. As of 1967 Virginia is one of 31 states that still has such laws, so what is this couple to do? How 'bout...

for their marital decree
go to Washington D.C.

So, they go to the nation's capital to tie the knot. Upon their return, the state of Virginia has a whimsically wistful "congratulations and welcome home" present for them. They are arrested and convicted for the offense of dragging one of those nasty interracial marriages back onto their home turf. Their penalty for this heinous offense? How 'bout one year each in jail. We're thinking the option of conjugal visits is not even on the table. And if all this wasn't enough, the fact that someone feels compelled to rip their "Virginia is for Lovers" bumper sticker right off their car is probably one toke over the line.

These circumstances lead to the case of *Loving v. the State of Virginia* which goes all the way to the Supreme Court. The high court rules in favor of the Lovings, thus finally ending the 300-year ban on interracial marriages which had been in place in some parts of the country. The state of Alabama kept its miscegenation law on the books until the year 2000 even though it was unenforceable.

THE QUAKERS AND THE JEWS

In our research on this project, we found three examples of rather unlikely allegiances between primarily White religions and totally Black causes. What two religions are we talking about? How 'bout the Quakers and the Jews? Strange bedfellows, indeed!

PEACEMAKER QUAKERS - We'll tackle this timely topic chronologically and lead with the Quakers. America's earliest recorded protest against slavery came from the quills of the Quakers in 1688. It was a group of four Quakers from Germantown, Pennsylvania who penned the original protest. Using the Golden Rule as a premise for their thesis, they decried the grave injustice of slavery, writing...

"*We should do unto others as we would have done unto ourselves. Pray, what thing in the world can be done worse towards us, than if men should robb (sic) or steal us away, & sell us for slaves to strange Countries, separating housband (sic) from their wife and children..."*[1]

This document was presented to the Quakers' Monthly Dublin Meeting which was held in Philadelphia during that year of 1688. Kudos to the Quakers for taking this initial stand against slavery and human trafficking.

JEWISH CONFLUENCE ~ It would be almost exactly 250 years later when the Jewish and Black communities were brought together under somewhat surprising circumstances. To whom should we give credit? How 'bout that Hitler? We're sure at this point you're wondering how in the world we are going to dot-connect this one. Well, just watch.

As Hitler ascended to power during the 1930's, Jewish professors from both Germany and Austria were dismissed from their positions and many crossed the Atlantic to the U.S. in search of employment. Upon arrival in America, while they did not find a maniacal xenophobic dictator, they did find other circumstances working against them.

The Great Depression, combined with rising anti-Semitism, made the job search difficult for these academic Jewish immigrants. So how does the Black American community connect to this conundrum? At this point allow us to introduce an acronym which didn't even exist at the time this piece of history played out. Let's see how many of you know it before we tell you. The acronym is HBCU. What does it stand for? That would be the Historically Black Colleges and Universities.

These institutions originally arose to teach freed slaves to read and write. The first one (Cheyney University in Pennsylvania) was founded in 1837 and in the century that transpired between then and the 1930's story that we're in the midst of, about 100 HBCU's had come into existence. They were always looking for quality professors and with the commonality that they were both victims of discrimination in White America, the Black institutions along with the Jewish educators enjoyed a mutually symbiotic level of comfort in joining forces.

Subsequently, many Jewish professors took jobs at HBCU's. As history progressed, the two groups' interests did diverge, but it did make for one nice little nugget in time when the Blacks and the Jews all held hands and sang "Kumbaya." Now if only we could have gotten the

Quakers on board with this lovefest we might have achieved a level of never-before-experienced universal bliss.

We actually have one more interesting example of the coalescence of the Black and Jewish causes. The star of this story from the Black perspective is Bayard Rustin (who we saw back in Chapter 6). Rustin's choice to extend himself into the Jewish panorama was basically twofold.

* Rustin saw a parallel between the oppression of the Jews in the Soviet Union and the treatment of Blacks in the U.S. with shared problems including housing, education and employment.

* Rustin felt that a positive relationship between Blacks and Jews in America would produce positive consequences for both groups.

So how did he get involved? We'll lead with one high-profile example. In June of 1970, Rustin wrote an article for the *New York Times* in which he called for Israel to execute air raids on the Arab states. A companion piece to the article was a letter written to Israeli Prime Minister Golda Meir. In the letter Rustin wrote, "I hope that the article will also have an effect on a serious domestic question; namely, the relations between the Jewish and the Negro communities in America."[2] Rustin furthermore lauded Israel's democracy vs. the mostly autocratic governments of the Arab nations.

He also worked for the cause of enabling Jewish emigration from Russia. The status achieved by a Black American in this movement is striking, and a testimony to the global respect afforded Bayard Rustin. In 1966 he was appointed chairman of the Ad hoc Commission on Rights of Soviet Jews. We have some statistics conveying how successful this group was in facilitating Jewish emigration from Russia. In the 1960's, 4,000 Jews were allowed to leave the Soviet Union and in the 1970's that number increased to 225,000.[3] Nice work, Bayard.

These three groups could be barrier breakers
All their members were movers and shakers
How could it be, oh
This unlikely trio
The Blacks, and the Jews and the Quakers

JUNETEENTH

Whether you call it Jubilee Day, Black Independence Day, Emancipation Day or Juneteenth National Independence Day, it became official on June 17, 2021. That was the day that President Joe Biden signed the Juneteenth National Independence Day Act into law officially making June 19th the federal holiday of Juneteenth. It had been a long time coming, so let's rewind this story.

It wasn't until June 19, 1865 when Union troops arrived in Texas that the slaves in that state were freed. The reason for that delayed freedom is worthy of explanation, so here we go. The Emancipation Proclamation, which had been officially approved by Abraham Lincoln on September 22, 1862, actually took effect on January 1, 1863. So, at that point all the slaves in the eleven Confederate states were proclaimed to be free, with enforcement of course being a totally different matter.

The date upon which most slaves were effectively freed was April 9, 1865 when General Robert E. Lee surrendered at Appomattox Court House in Virginia. Meanwhile in Texas, the most remote corner of the Confederacy, there was an off-shoot Southern military force called the Western Army of the Trans-Mississippi. Who knew?

At any rate, these ragtag renegades refused to participate in the rest of the South's surrender. With bigger fish to fry in terms of patching the nation back together, rushing a regiment back to Texas, where only three Civil War battles had been fought, was not a huge government priority. Furthermore, enforcement of the Proclamation generally relied on the advancement of Union troops, so freedom in Texas lagged.

And so it goes in the circus of life…

Just when you think that you've been gypped
the bearded lady comes and does a double back flip.

It was June 19th, or Juneteenth, when the U.S. Army finally arrived in Galveston and broke the news to the state of Texas. Officially, Lone Star State slavery ceased to be. On June 19, 1866, the first Jubilee Day was celebrated in Texas and while the event has borne multiple monikers over the years, the consensus has landed on Juneteenth.

IT AIN'T OVER TILL IT'S OVER ~ As we continue on our mission to inform as well as entertain, at this point we're going to throw down a few related facts that surprised us as we did our research on this topic. We went into this Juneteenth thing thinking it was **truly** the **very** end of slavery in the United States. How many of you are riding on that same train? Well, if you are, get ready to deboard; not just once, but twice.

Truth be told, there were two dates **after** June 19, 1865 that still-held slaves were freed in the United States. Here's the scoop... The exact wording of the Emancipation Proclamation played into this storyline. That document proclaimed the freedom of all slaves in the eleven states that had seceded from the Union. However there were two "border" states, Kentucky and Delaware, that had slaves who were not freed by the Emancipation Proclamation because those states never seceded. Kentucky and Delaware slaves weren't freed until December 6, 1865 when the Thirteenth Amendment to the Constitution was ratified abolishing slavery in all of the United States.

So who's still holding out at this point? Some slaves were still held in the "Indian Territory" (outside the U.S.) which was a huge chunk of land starting in Oklahoma and spreading northwest all the way to Washington State. Slavery did not end there until April 28, 1866 when the United States signed a treaty with the Indians finally bringing a complete end to slavery in what is now the United States.

OPAL LEE ~ After watching her do her "Holy Dance" we knew we couldn't depart from this Juneteenth story without a shout-out to Opal Lee who has been described as the "Grandmother of Juneteenth." When President Joe Biden honored her at the signing of the Juneteenth National Independence Day Act, her goal of a lifetime had finally come true at the age of 94.

Upon retiring from teaching in 1976, Lee began a second career as an activist. Her causes included establishing the holiday for Martin Luther King Jr.'s birthday, Black History Month, and making Juneteenth a national holiday. For decades she advocated for Juneteenth by leading an annual 2½ mile walk every June 19th, the 2½ figure being reflective of how many years had passed between the Emancipation Proclamation and the freeing of the slaves in Texas.

How serious was she about this mission? On September 1, 2016, at the age of 89, she embarked upon the 1,362 mile walk from Fort Worth, Texas to Washington, D.C. If you're wondering how long it takes for an 89-year-old woman to walk 1,362 miles, we've got the answer for you. Opal arrived in Washington on January 10, 2017.[4]

When Congress finally passed the Juneteenth bill in June of 2021, she was invited to the White House bill-signing to be an honored guest at the ceremony. When President Biden gave her the pen he used to sign the bill, she received a standing ovation from the crowd in attendance.

When asked how she perceived her role in the Juneteenth initiative, she summarized the process by saying, "I'm just a little ol' lady in tennis shoes gettin' in everybody's business and I'm havin' a good time doin' it. I just know that the time has come for us to work together."[5]

THE WIZ

The Wiz, released in 1975, was a Broadway musical based upon *The Wizard of Oz*. It was basically a Black reimagining of the original *Oz*, with the same primary characters and basic storyline transposed to an urban setting with urban-inspired music and adventures. The rural poppy fields for example are replaced by flamboyant prostitutes known as the "Poppy Girls." Oh, those sordid city streets.

The musical which debuted on May 25, 1975, won seven Tony Awards including Best Musical. *The Wiz* ran for four years, closing on January 28, 1979 after 1,672 performances.[6]

The Wiz was also made into a movie which hit the big screen in 1978 and check out the killer cast that was assembled for this production.

* Diana Ross as Dorothy
* Michael Jackson as the Scarecrow
* Nipsey Russell as the Tin Man
* Ted Ross as the Cowardly Lion
* Richard Pryor as The Wiz
* Lena Horne as Glinda the Good Witch

The Wiz has stepped out from behind the curtain on a few occasions since its original 1970's run. The musical returned to Broadway during 1984 with Stephanie Mills reprising her role as Dorothy and it also played at the Lyric Hammersmith in London during 1984-85.

There was a U.S. concert version tour during 1996-97 which starred Tasha Scott as Dorothy. Other notable cast members included Peabo Bryson as The Wiz and Grace Jones as Evillene, the Wicked Witch of the West.

George Faison presented *The Wiz: A Celebration in Dance and Music,* at Summerstage in New York City during August of 2015. This production featured original song and dance numbers saluting the 40th anniversary of the original Broadway run. Several members of the original cast returned and the show was co-hosted by Phylicia Rashad who had played a munchkin in the original show.

Later that year, NBC blessed the nation with a holiday gift of *The Wiz Live!* which aired on December 3, and was rebroadcast on December 19. This new adaptation featured aspects of both the 1978 film and the original Broadway play.

Cast members included Shanice Williams as Dorothy, Queen Latifah as the Wiz, Mary J. Blige as Evillene, the Wicked Witch of the West, and Stephanie Mills (who had played Dorothy in the original on Broadway) as Auntie Em.

MOTOWN 25

As they say, it's all in the timing. That was the aspect of *Motown 25* which was the major factor contributing to its majestical musical perfection. What do we mean by that? Most all of the major Motown hits had been recorded by that point and were available for a performance. Most all of the major Motown performers were still alive and available to perform.

The full title of the special was *Motown 25: Yesterday, Today, Forever* and it aired on NBC on May 16, 1983, soaring to the top of the TV ratings for the week. Just writing about it makes us want to go back and watch the whole thing again but, for the sake of concision, we'll boil the highlights down to a manageable mound where reunions abound.

TOGETHER AGAIN - Smokey Robinson reunited with the Miracles for the first time since 1972. They reprised their greatest hits including "Shop Around" and "Tears of a Clown." Diana Ross had last sung with the Supremes in 1969. They reunited to perform their last #1 hit "Someday We'll Be Together," the irony of that title being impossible to miss. The 1983 performance fulfilled the prophesy of the 1969 song.

TEMPS & TOPS - The Temptations and the Four Tops performed an epic battle of the bands in which the groups stole each other's songs for parts of the shtick with the end result being one of the greatest Motown medleys of all time. But the hands-down highlight of the evening was what happened with Michael Jackson and the Jackson 5.

JACKSON JUBILATION - Michael's solo career had taken off at this point, so he was somewhat reluctant to revert back to the group scenario, but agreed to sign on when Barry Gordy promised him that a solo spot could follow the J5 gig. Brother Jermaine had left the Jacksons in 1978 so he was back in the fold for the first time in five years.

The entire reunited family performed a medley of their hits including "I Want You Back," "The Love You Save," "Never Can Say Goodbye," and "I'll Be There." Then as the family was leaving the stage Michael said, "*I have to say those were the good old days. I love those songs. Those were magic moments with all my brothers, including Jermaine. I like those songs a lot, but especially, I like the new songs.*"[7]

At that point the audio track of "Billie Jean" kicked in and Michael launched into the tune which, at that point, was in the midst of a 7-week run at the #1 spot on the *Billboard* charts. The single most mind-blowing moment of *Motown 25* was two-thirds of the way through "Billie Jean" when Michael Jackson debuted the moonwalk which would of course become his signature move.

In some ways the world would never be the same again. If you're thinking that statement might be a little too dramatic, please allow us to put it in perspective for you. It wasn't just that we had a new dance. Up until that point, MTV had not played videos by traditionally Black artists. After "Billie Jean," MTV caved and, as we said, the world would never be the same again. That's our story, and we're stickin' to it.

WE ARE THE WORLD

This really cool piece of Black music history came together in 1985. It was inspired by the previous year's video of "Do They Know It's Christmas" by Band-Aid. The concept behind "We Are the World" was to take the megastar charity-fund-raising music video concept and spin it Black.

Let's talk people first and then we'll talk statistics. It was originally conceived by 1950's-60's singing legend Harry Belafonte. If you want one song to put this very cool dude in perspective, YouTube his reggae classic "Day-O (The Banana Boat Song)."

Belafonte sold the idea to Michael Jackson and Lionel Richie who wrote the song. At this point we're not sure if we'd rather be dancing to "Thriller" or "Dancing on the Ceiling" but the whole thing seems like a temptingly tantalizing idea, doesn't it?

Okay if you're still skeptical, how 'bout we bring on 28-time Grammy Award winner Quincy Jones to be the producer? Next, let's line up some artists. For the sake of brevity, we'll highlight the list of performers we've got as follows: Diana Ross, Stevie Wonder, Tina Turner, Smokey Robinson, Dionne Warwick, The Pointer Sisters and the Jackson brothers.

The song permeated the planet, sold 20 million copies, and raised about 65 million dollars in relief aid for Africa and the world. In addition to the dollars, the recording also won a People's Choice Award, an American Music Award, and three Grammys. As Harry Belafonte sang back in the old days, "Work all night on a drink of rum, Daylight come and me wanna go home," but in our 1980's "We Are the World" corollary we'll add a bit about taking all that money to the bank on the way home.

Chapter 11

THE ORIGINAL LADIES OF BLACK COMEDY

BERTICE BERRY (1960 -)

Bertice Berry is a professor and author who has written passionately about her experiences as a Black woman. She had her own syndicated talk show for a few years in the mid-90's and when her show debuted in September of 1993 it was delayed because of a news bulletin regarding an Israeli-Palestine peace treaty. When she finally got on the air she began by saying, "We've got peace, now here's Bertice."

Here's a quick story we'll share from her memoir *The World According to Me.*

Hi, my name is Bertice Berry. I know, you're thinking I look like that other Black woman with dreadlocks. She's beautiful, but I'm not her. All Black women do not look alike. The other day I got on the bus and this woman said, "You look just like Whoopi Goldberg."

I told her, "You're fat and White, but you don't look like Mama Cass."[1] Well, Bertice, thanks for just tellin' it like it is! (For those of you too young for this reference to click, YouTube the Mamas and Papas "California Dreamin'". You'll recognize the song and get the gag.)

DARYL CUMBER DANCE (1938 -)

If you're a fan of colleges in Virginia, you're never going to get more bang for your buck than in this next short component on Daryl Cumber Dance. Born in Richmond in 1938, Dance went on to become an English professor and writer.

She graduated from (HBCU) Virginia State College in 1957. She subsequently taught college English at Virginia State before going to earn her doctorate at the University of Virginia. At that point she continued her college professorial career at the following institutions, in the following order: Virginia State College, Virginia Commonwealth University, the University of Richmond, and (HBCU) Howard University (which is in Washington D.C.).

Her writing résumé boasts eight published books and we really enjoyed the two following stories beginning with this parenting story she shared…

"You Rinate?"

I always used the proper names when I potty trained my daughter, so I would set her on the potty, and say, "Alright, sweetheart, urinate for mommy; come now, urinate in the potty."

At first I was somewhat nonplussed when upon succeeding, she gleefully yelled, "I rinated, Mommy, I rinated in the potty." It was some time before I realized that she had understood me to say to her, "you rinate," and thus she was responding, "I rinated."[2]

"The Missing Hat"

This Minister could not find his hat, and he finally decided that one of the members of his church must have stolen it. He was very disturbed, and he decided to talk to his Deacon about what he should do. The Deacon suggested, "Why don't you preach on the Ten Commandments next Sunday, and then when you come to 'Thou shalt not steal' really lay it on, so that the guilty person will repent and return your hat." The Minister said, "That's a good idea. I'll try it."

So the next Sunday he got up in the pulpit and he was really laying it on strong on those Ten Commandments. He preached on "Honor thy father and thy mother"; then he preached on "Thy shall not commit adultery." Then – he cut his sermon short.

After the service the Deacon said to him, "Reverend, you were doing so well, but you never did get to the main part of your sermon. What happened?"

He said, "Deacon Jones, I didn't need to use that part 'cause when I got to 'Thou shall not commit adultery,' I remembered where I left my hat."[3]

When it comes to Daryl Cumber Dance, we were honored that she was honored. Upon completion of our initial draft of this book, we sent her a copy and received the following response...

I am honored to be included in this inspirational, informative, entertaining, and often hilarious study – can't wait to give autographed copies to the favorite people on my Christmas list! Best wishes for the success of this project.

In addition to the college credits mentioned above, Dance is also the former advisory editor of the *Black American Literary Forum*.

LAWANDA PAGE (1920-2002)

LaWanda Page was a comedienne upon whom the nickname "Black Queen of Comedy" was bestowed. She was also an actress and dancer whose career spanned six decades. Her greatest fame was achieved during her 1972-77 stint playing Aunt Esther Anderson on the sitcom *Sanford and Son*.

Born in St. Louis in 1920, Page became a stalwart performer on the Chitlin' Circuit. For female performers of that ilk, she would probably be considered the second most famous behind only Moms Mabley. She had a reputation for the X-rated. While Chitlin' Circuit censorship was notoriously negligible, Page pushed even that envelope.

On *Sanford and Son*, Esther was a volatile, confrontational, bible-totin' firebrand. She parlayed her catch phrase on the show into a 1977 gold album called *Watch It, Sucker!*, which was one of five comedy albums that she released. Page became known as an advocate of equal opportunities for Blacks in the entertainment business.

Here is a sampling of Page's comedy...

* Little Red Riding Hood is walking through the forest you know, and all at once here comes this big wolf, and he says, "Little Red Riding Hood, I'm gonna eat you right up."
And Little Red Riding Hood was so disgusted she threw her basket down and said, "Oh, shit, hell. Ain't they fuckin' in these woods anymore?"[4]

* (At a George Burns roast) George, you're too old to get married again. Not only can't you cut the mustard, honey, you're too old to open the jar.[5]

* There's a guy who's in the service and got his arm cut off. So he goes to the doctor and say, "You know my arm has been cut off and I need a new arm."
 Doctor say, "We don't have no male arms," say, "all we've got is female arms."
[Guy say] "OK, put a female arm on." So they put a female arm on him. The doctor say, "You come back in about three weeks, and I'll see how you doin'." He comes back in about three weeks and the doctor say, "How's your arm doin'?"
He say, "It fits, it's fine, it don't give me no trouble, and it don't hurt, but I got one problem. I'll tell you what it is... Every time I go to take a piss, this bitch don't wanna let go."[6]

* There's a preacher in church who's up there just preachin', "We gonna take all the whiskey and we gonna throw it in the river. We gonna take all these cards and we gonna throw 'em in the river. We gonna take all the weed and throw it in the river. And we're gonna throw all these bad things in the river, and we gonna wash our hands of all these bad things. We ain't gonna stand this bad stuff no more. Now Sister Smith lead us in a song."
She got up and began singin' the hymn, "Shall we gather at the river?"[7]

* You know they've got a new douche product out now. This is made out of elm, LSD, and Kentucky Colonel Sanders chicken fat. It makes your pussy up tight, out of sight, and finger lickin' good.[8]

MOMS MABLEY (1894-1975)

How's this for the most unfunny bullet list beginning of any comedienne ever and we probably don't even need to include the qualifier Black comedienne 'cause this list seems to transcend all racial boundaries.

* Age 12 – baby #1, raped by elderly Black man
* Age 14 – baby #2, raped by White sheriff
* Age 15 – volunteer firefighter father killed in fire engine explosion
* Age 16 – mother dies, run over by truck, coming home from church on Christmas Day

On that note ♪, Let's cue up, I'll have a Blue Christmas without you.

MOVIN' ON ~ With that kind of start, there's pretty much only one way to go, right? And up she went. Loretta Mary Aiken, aka Moms Mabley was a trailblazer whom Whoopi Goldberg called "the first Black female stand-up comedienne."[9] She was the first Black female to perform at both the Apollo Theater and Carnegie Hall and she was a hit all over the country on the Chitlin' Circuit.

Her "Chitlin'" performances began in the 1920's and she was a storyteller from the get-go. In explaining to her audiences how she came by her name, she offered the following. One of her early romances that had gone sour was to a man named Jack Mabley and, as Moms put it, "He took so much from me, the least I could do was take his name from him."[10]

GOLDEN YEARS ~ Channeling a Grandma Moses type of vibe, Moms Mabley's greatest successes would be achieved at the backend of her life. Part of what fueled her success was how she managed to juxtapose her appearance and her material, which was always very cutting edge, tackling the subjects of race and sex.

How did her appearance manage to mitigate her material? She performed literally toothless, wearing a floppy hat, draped in gaudily-colored robes and dresses which always clashed. So no matter how controversial her material was, it was being delivered by your freakin' grandmother. How threatening could it be?

The 1960's turned out to be Moms Mabley's greatest decade, believe it or not. Between 1961 and 1972 she released 20 comedy albums, the last of which was called *I Like 'Em Young*, which was a frequent theme to her comic material. She appeared on numerous TV shows including *The Ed Sullivan Show, The Smothers Brothers Comedy Hour, The Bill Cosby Show* and *The Merv Griffin Show*.

And here's the craziest one of all… In 1969, at the age of 75, she became the oldest person to ever score a Top 40 hit when her cover version of "Abraham, Martin and John" went to #35. That song, which is a whimsical reflection upon the assassinations of Abraham Lincoln, John F. Kennedy, Martin Luther King Jr. and Bobby Kennedy, was originally a #4 hit for Dion in 1968.

Here is a sampling of Moms' humor…

* (Her advice to children crossing the street) Don't watch the lights. Damn the lights. Watch the cars. The lights ain't never killed nobody.[11]

* (exemplifying her go-to shtick of preferring younger men to old geezers her own age) Moms don't like old men. Anytime you see my arms around an old man, just know, I'm holding him for the po-lice.[12]

* After a funeral, for a lady who had died at 89, the preacher tapped her brother on the shoulder and said, "How old are you, Pops?"
He replied, "91."
The preacher said, "There ain't no need in you even goin' home." [13]

* (conversation with TV host Merv Griffin)
Merv: Do they like your act down South?
Moms: They do like me down South, but they keep thinkin' I'm Roy Rogers' horse.
Merv: Why do you say that?
Moms: They's keep callin' me Trigger, Trigger! Or at least I think that's what they's callin' me.[14]

When I ponder those Rebels, I snigger
Love they's horses, I know, but go figger
How 'bout dem way down South
What I hear from they's mouth
Is dem folks, they keep callin' me Trigger

Chapter 12

WAR IS HELL

CATHAY WILLIAMS (1844-c. 1893)

If we told you we had a good story about a Black woman recruited to help the Union Army efforts during the Civil War you might say, "Sounds interesting, you've got my attention, tell me more." How 'bout if we were to add the caveat that this same woman would later disguise herself as a man and succeed in completing the entire enlistment process, including the physical, to become the first woman to ever enlist in the U.S. Army.

Hopefully you'd be saying, "No freakin' way, can't wait to read this, bring it on." If that's your reaction, we've got good news; we're here for you." The lady who stars in this story is one Cathay Williams or, as she becomes known in the second half of the story when she flip-flops her name as part of her enlistment ruse, William Cathay.

One ironic thing about this story is that it almost slipped away with the sands of time. It had been almost a decade since Williams had left the Army when rumors of her story were shared with the *St. Louis Daily Times* in late 1875. The newspaper tracked her down in Colorado where she was living at the time and ran an extensive article about Cathay Williams on January 2, 1876.[1]

BACK TO THE BEGINNING ~ So the good news is that much of Williams' story you will be able to hear in her own words and we will defer to that option as often as possible. Resetting to the beginning of this saga when she was born in 1844, Williams said, "*My father was a freeman, but my mother was a slave, belonging to William Johnson, a wealthy farmer who lived at the time I was born near Independence, Missouri.*"[2] The laws of the time dictated that Williams was also a slave.

When Williams was a child, Johnson moved to Jefferson City, Missouri where he died in 1861 and his slaves were subsequently set free. Williams was destined to become a part of the Union Army effort in the Civil War in a process she describes as follows. "*United States soldiers* came to Jefferson City and they took me and other colored folks with them to Little Rock. Colonel Benton of the 13th army corps was the officer that carried us off. I did not want to go. He wanted me to cook for the officers, but I had always been a house girl and did not know how to cook."[3]

Well, at 17 years of age, Williams was apparently a quick learner as she assumed this cook's role and accompanied the Union brigade from Missouri, through Arkansas, Louisiana and Georgia, before eventually ending up in Washington D.C. There she became a cook and cleaning lady for General Phillip Sheridan and his staff.

ENLIGHTENING ENLISTMENT ~ However, during her Civil War years she had come to enjoy the Army life and wanted to return, but this time as an official soldier. Using the aforementioned name William Cathay, Cathay Williams managed to enlist in the Army on November 15, 1866, identifying herself as a 22-year-old cook. In his report, her recruiting officer entered a description saying "Recruit is 5' 9", with black eyes, black hair and black complexion."

Not casting the most positive light on the Army's medical process at the time, Williams was given a physical and described as "fit for duty." At that point her niche in history had been carved out with the designation that Williams would forever be the first woman to enlist in the Army. You go, girl!

You may be wondering at this point if anyone else was in on the ruse. About this, Williams said, "*The regiment I joined wore the Zouave uniform and only two persons, a cousin and a particular friend, members of the regiment, knew that I was a woman. They never "blowed" on me. They were partly the cause of my joining the army. Another reason was I wanted to make my own living and not be dependent on relations or friends.*"[4] Note: Her use of the word "blowed" as a verb seems to be derivative of the modern-day cliché "to blow somebody in," meaning to turn someone in.

At Fort Riley, Kansas, Williams was taken ill in April of 1867. This is the beginning of a 15-month period where she is in and out of the hospital with an illness which is eventually diagnosed as neuralgia, a nerve disease. Again, the Army's medical procedures are cast in a somewhat questionable light in that she could have spent that much time under medical care without her true gender being discovered.

PARTY'S OVER ~ When did the "jig-is-up" moment occur? An attending doctor made the discovery that Williams was a woman in October of 1868 and she was officially discharged on October 14th of that year. Thus, the run of service for the first woman to enlist in the Army was brought to an end, just shy of two years.

Here is Cathay Williams' summary of what happened after her service: "*After leaving the army I went to Pueblo, Colorado, where I made money by cooking and washing. I got married while there, but my husband was no-account. He stole my watch and chain, a hundred dollars in money, and my team of horses and wagon. I had him arrested and put in jail, and then I came here to Trinidad, (Colorado). I like this town.*"⁵

And it appears that it would be this town in which Williams would finish her life. There is a record of her being denied a military pension by the U.S. Pension Bureau in 1892, which seems patently unfair. That's the last we hear of Cathay Williams. She does not appear in the 1900 census and there is no recorded burial site, so the logical conclusion is that she died sometime between 1892 and 1900. Conjecture has landed on 1893.

When this whole sex change put-on began
Getting sick wasn't part of my plan
'Cause I had to concede
That as soon as I peed
The doctor would know I'm no man

6888ᵀᴴ CENTRAL BATTALION

During WW II there was only one Black women's military unit to serve overseas and their success story is worth sharing. After completing a rigorous training regimen, the battalion was sent to Birmingham, England and then, after the Allies' successful invasion of Normandy, they were assigned to stations in Paris and Rouen, France. Who were these gals? They were the 6888th Central Postal Directory Battalion which was formed in 1944 and commonly referred to as the "Six Triple Eight."

Next question… Who got this party started? Well, that would be civil rights activist Mary McLeod Bethune. She contacted First Lady

Eleanor Roosevelt and, citing the shortage of personnel to manage the overseas postal service during the war, she pitched the possibility of organizing a crew of Black women to tackle the task.

Various Black newspapers had also issued the challenge for the U.S. to find meaningful ways to use Black women in the war effort. Thus the impetus was provided for the Six Triple Eight. Most of the girls worked as postal clerks, but others were cooks, housekeepers, and mechanics assuring that the battalion would be a self-sufficient operation.

MISSION DESCRIPTION ~ The issue these women had to address was that undelivered mail intended for servicemen had become backlogged and was literally filling up overseas warehouses. This scenario subsequently had a negative impact on the spirits of the fighting men who were not receiving mail that they felt certain was being sent. The motto of the Six Triple Eight became "No mail, low morale."[6]

Because they were being stationed in a war zone where they could potentially be exposed to enemy bombing and troops, the battalion members had to be trained to deal with those possibilities. The women of the Six Triple Eight were sent to Oglethorpe, Georgia where they prepared by jumping over trenches, crawling under logs, and identifying enemy aircraft.

Once that training was completed the women set sail for England. It was estimated that the disarray of the postal system there would take six months to clean up. The plan was to work around the clock with three 8-hour shifts per day, seven days a week.

POOR WORKING CONDITIONS ~ Complicating the task was the fact that working conditions were less than ideal. The windows were blackened to prevent escaping light from making the warehouses targets during nighttime air raids. Thus the buildings were dimly lit, as well as unheated, necessitating that the women wear multiple layers of clothing.

Also, if you leave packages containing baked goods sent from home out in the warehouses for months, guess what happens? Yep, rats! Just what the girls needed. Despite these overwhelming obstacles, the job that was projected to be a six-month ordeal was wrapped up by the Six Triple Eight Battalion in half that time.

As the American troops advanced through France, logically the mail from home followed the Six Triple Eight as its operations moved across the English Channel to the French locations of first Rouen, and then Paris. The women seemed to particularly like their time in France.

A specific memory sited in multiple interviews was the time when they were invited to participate in a victory parade past the spot on the Seine River where Joan of Arc had been burned at the stake. The women were cheered and celebrated by the newly liberated French.

Team morale we would rejuvenate
By assuring the mail's not late
What's that crawling, oh "Drats!"
Could those really be rats?
We're the gals of the Six Triple Eight

HARLEM HELLFIGHTERS

This is the story of one of the most effective U.S. military brigades of WW I. When the war began and the U.S. realized it would be needing troops, the 15th New York National Guard Regiment, located in Harlem, was transformed into the 369th Infantry Regiment. In preparation for sending them to France to fight, they were assigned to Spartanburg, South Carolina for military training. On December 27, 1917 the 369th Regiment embarked to engage in the Great War (which is what WW I was called prior to WW II).

Upon their arrival in France, their combat efficiency was so great that they became known as the Harlem Hellfighters. Unfortunately, however, many White American soldiers refused to fight alongside the Hellfighters, leaving the U.S. military with a dilemma. Rather than waste their talent and the time and money that had been put into their training, on April 8, 1918 they were deeded to the French Army for the duration of the war.

What a blessing that turned out to be for the Hellfighters! With the French they were welcomed and integrated into the war effort, literally and figuratively. They fought hard, spending almost 200 days in frontline trenches, which was more than any other American regiment.

Reflective of this, their 1,500 casualties were also the most of any American unit. The French bestowed upon them the additional nickname of the Black Rattlers.

After the war, the French government awarded their army's Cross of War medal upon 172 distinguished members of the Harlem Hellfighters. Unfortunately, similar appreciation was a little slower coming from the United States. In 2019, a century after the fact, the 369th Infantry Regiment was recognized with the Congressional Gold Medal. To apply the cliché "better late than never" at this point actually rings a bit hollow.

There have been some subsequent recognitions of the Harlem Hellfighters. In 2003 Harlem River Drive was renamed as Harlem Hellfighters Drive, a gesture which was initiated by the New York State Department of Transportation. A monument was also erected there to honor the Hellfighters. It's a 12-foot-high black granite statue which contains the crest of the 369th Infantry Regiment along with its rattlesnake logo.

TUSKEGEE AIRMEN

Among their victims could be included 387 planes and 1,000 railroad cars and vehicles. But they weren't bad guys; they were heroes. Why? Because these victims were all taken during WW II and they were all from either Nazi Germany or Fascist Italy. Who were these guys that were driving Hitler and Mussolini crazy? They would be the Tuskegee Airmen and here is their story.

They were the first Black aviators in the U.S. Army Air Corps. The U.S.A.A.C. would officially evolve into the U.S. Air Force in September of 1947. The Airmen's name was derived from the fact that their training took place at the Tuskegee Army Air Field. This was also the site of the prestigious Tuskegee Institute in Alabama which had been founded by Booker T. Washington on the 4th of July in 1881.

Just to reset the racial table in America as the world was teetering on the brink of WW II, the military was still completely segregated. It would be another decade before Harry Truman signed Executive Order 9981 integrating the U.S. armed forces.

TAKING OFF – The training of Black airmen and support staff began in Tuskegee in January of 1941 and the competition to become involved in the program was stiff. This was by design. The government had put in place a system to help ensure the success of the Tuskegee Airmen. Of the many Blacks that applied, two key criteria were considered for acceptance. Candidates needed a high level of aviation experience and/or a high level of academic achievement.

One of the Tuskegee Airmen was Coleman Young who would go on to become the first Black mayor of Detroit. About just how competitive the Tuskegee program was, he said the following: *"They made the standards so high, we actually became an elite group. We were screened and super-screened. We were unquestionably the brightest and most physically fit young Blacks in the country. We were super-better because of the irrational laws of Jim Crow. You can't bring that many intelligent young people together and train 'em as fighting men and expect them to supinely roll over when you try to fuck 'em over, right?"*[7]

About 15,000 participants were accepted and trained with about 1,000 of those being pilots. The other positions needed to facilitate the overall operation included navigators, mechanics, bombardiers, and control tower operators.

FIRST LADY LIFTOFF – On March 29, 1941 the Tuskegee Program was given a significant boost by the visit of First Lady Eleanor Roosevelt. She went on a flight and was given an aerial tour by one of the Black pilots. Upon landing she ebulliently proclaimed, "Well, you can fly all right!"[8]

The whole thing turned into a wonderful public relations coup. Photos of the event showed up in newspapers and magazines across the country and a filmed account was published as a Pathe newsreel. This "newsreel" concept needs a note of explanation for modern-day readers. In that pre-TV era, Americans were generally provided with their visual entertainment at movie theaters. The newsreels were shown as lead-ins for the feature films, so they constituted the highest profile news outlet of the time.

DEPLOYED & DANGEROUS – Well, now that we have the team trained, how 'bout we send them out and see if this thing is going to fly, so to speak. It would be on April 2, 1942 when the Tuskegee Airmen would deploy to North Africa, which was occupied by the Allies at the time. Known and identified by the tails of their planes which were painted completely red, the Tuskegee Airmen took on the nickname of the Red Tails.

The Tuskegee Airmen made immediate contributions to the war effort. We'll share a few quick examples. Their first combat mission undertaken was an attack on the Italian island of Sicily. Here's a visual that may help you. If you conjure up that image with the map of Italy looking like a boot kicking a ball, Sicily would be the ball. It's that big island at the tip of the toe of the boot. The airmen spearheaded an attack which led to the surrender of over 11,000 Italians.

On one two-day occasion in January of 1944, Tuskegee Airmen pilots shot down 12 German fighter planes. Another service often provided by the Airmen was to "escort" heavy bomber planes deep into enemy territory to execute raids. The task of the Airmen on these missions was to fly alongside the bomber, fending off any enemy attacks to shoot the bomber down.

IN SUMMARY - By the time the Germans surrendered in May of 1945, the Tuskegee Airmen had flown over 15,000 missions during their three years in the European theater. As stated in our lead for this piece, they took out about a thousand enemy train cars and military vehicles, and 387 enemy planes, 112 in the air and 275 on the ground. Oh, by the way, they also managed to sink one German torpedo boat.

Also added to the accomplishments of the Tuskegee Airmen must be the acknowledgement that their achievements paved the way for Harry Truman to integrate the military. In latter-day accolades, more than 300 of the original Tuskegee Airmen were on hand to receive the Congressional Gold Medal from President George W. Bush in 2007. Then just two years later, many of them were back in Washington, having been invited to the inauguration of Barack Obama. Seems quite appropriate.

THE ROBERTS REPORT - One of the Tuskegee Airmen whose story takes on an added element of interest would be Lawrence Edward Roberts, Sr., who is the father of newscaster Robin Roberts. The senior

Roberts did his undergraduate work at Howard University and Morningside College before earning his master's degree at Tuskegee Institute.

He joined the U.S. Army Air Corps (precursor to U.S. Air Force) in 1943, then joined the Tuskegee Airmen program a year later. In addition to his service during WW II he also flew missions during the Vietnam War, winning 18 awards and service medals. After passing away in 2004, he was buried with full military honors, acknowledging his 32 years of service. Listed below are some posthumous honors Roberts received.

* 2004 ~ Mississippi Legislature resolution of honor
* 2007 ~ Congressional Gold Medal
* 2009 ~ Sculpture dedicated in Pass Christian, Mississippi
* 2009 ~ Keesler Air Force Base aircraft facility dedicated

Regarding his daughter Robin Roberts, we first loved her during her ESPN stint and we've continued to love her at ABC where her intelligent, compassionate style resonates in all her work. The piece her Dad would probably most prize would be her 2021 documentary *Tuskegee Airmen: Legacy of Courage.*

> *We never backed down from a dare when*
> *We rode on a wing and a prayer then*
> *Rejoiced in the splendor*
> *Italian surrender!*
> *All praise to the Tuskegee Airmen*

CHAPTER 13

THE ORIGINAL WAVE OF BLACK COMEDIANS

BERT WILLIAMS (1874-1922)

In our historical explorations for this book, truly one of the greatest treasures we unsurfaced was the story of the Black man who could lay claim to three amazing accolades in the first quarter of the 20th century. During that era he was the consensus choice as to being the funniest Black comedian, he sold more records than anyone else, and he also made the most money. Let's have a laugh, cue up a tune, and take it to the bank with Bert Williams.

In the early 1900's, when racial stereotyping was common place, Williams managed to envelope-push in multiple areas. In 1902 he became the first Black to assume the lead role in a Broadway play, *In Dahomey*, and in 1914 he became the first to land the lead in a film, *Darktown*. He was referred to as "one of the great comedians of the world"[1] by the *New York Dramatic Mirror* in 1918.

START UP STORY - Let's rewind to the beginning at this point. Bert Williams' entertainment career began in earnest when he joined Martin and Selig's Mastodon Minstrel Show in the 1890's and was partnered with George W. Walker. The Williams & Walker partnership soon evolved into one of the most successful comedy acts of the era.

They left the minstrel show to tour the vaudeville circuit, a trip they took all the way to Broadway. The pair produced the first Black musical comedy to open on Broadway. The full-scale production called *In Dahomey* debuted in 1902 with Williams and Walker as the writers and stars.

The duo was a popular and critical success throughout the first decade of the century. Tragedy however hit in 1909 when George W. Walker lost his life to syphilis. The death of his partner ended up presenting Williams with one of the greatest silver linings in the history of clouds. This was the era of vaudeville and the biggest show on the road was Ziegfeld's Follies. The entertainment world was shocked when in 1910 Flo Ziegfeld offered Bert Williams an opportunity to join the cast. (It turned out to be the greatest Black/Jewish collaboration until the 1930's HBCU partnership, which we covered in Chapter 10.)

FOLLIES PHENOMENON ~ Perhaps not surprisingly, the White cast members collaborated on an ultimatum that Williams not be allowed to join the show. You gotta love Ziegfeld's response in which he informed the participants in his Follies that, "I can replace every one of you, except the one you want me to fire."[2] Had the Jewish Ziegfeld not stood firm to the White resistance, American culture would have likely been deprived of a significant portion of the career of one of the greatest Black stars in media history.

How might Bert Williams have put this all into perspective? We're thinking he might have deferred to the wisdom of the ancient Chinese philosopher Confucius who said, "If they spit at you behind your back, it means you're ahead of them."[3]

The idea of a Black-featured performer amid an otherwise all-White show was certainly revolutionary in 1910. This is one revolution we're going to categorize as an unqualified success. The show opened to rousing reviews with the highlight sketch being a parody of the recent "Great White Hope" heavyweight boxing bout in which the Black Jack Johnson had defeated the White James J. Jeffries. As TV historian Tim Brooks wrote: "Williams had become a star who transcended race to the greatest extent that was possible in 1910."[4]

One unique aspect that characterized Williams' success was the degree to which the Ziegfeld Follies writers scripted him in equal roles with White performers. The two-man team of Williams and the White Leon Errol became the centerpiece of the Ziegfeld shows of that era, with Williams delivering as many, or more, of the punch lines as Errol. Williams also had numerous sketches in which he acted with White women which was not at all the norm.

Having established himself as the Follies featured star, Williams signed a three-year contract paying him $62,500 a year. In modern-day dollars this would equate to 1.5 million dollars annually. Here are a couple ocean-spanning accolades acknowledging just how renowned Williams became during the 1910's. He was summoned to Buckingham Palace in England to play a command performance before King Edward VII and back at home, New York's *Theatre Magazine* wrote that, "Bert Williams is a vastly funnier man than any White comedian now on the American stage."[5]

RACISM REARS ITS UGLY HEAD ~ Here's a story which exemplifies how Williams dealt with racism when exposed to it. Check out what happened at the ritzy Hotel Astor in New York City. He went to buy a drink and in a thinly veiled attempt to get rid of him, the bartender told Williams that the drink would cost him $50. Williams responded by slapping a stack of $100 bills on the bar and ordering a round for the house. Cheers!

While he was enjoying massive success in multiple facets of the entertainment world, life was not total bliss for Bert Williams. He was never able to fully reconcile the adulation he received from his audiences with the racist treatment he experienced while **not** on stage. In the latter stages of his career, he began to drink heavily and also battled chronic depression. In 1922, despite suffering from pneumonia, he tried to maintain his vigorous performance regimen until collapsing on stage during a show in Chicago on Saturday, February 25, 1922. A week later he would be dead at the young age of 47.

W.C. Fields, a friend and vaudeville co-star of Williams said, "He was the funniest man I ever saw – and the saddest man I ever knew."[6]

We'll close with a trio of quotes from Bert Williams…

* I named all my children after flowers. There's my daughters Lillie and Rose and my son, Artificial.[7]

* It's no disgrace to be colored, but it is very inconvenient.[8]

* Prejudice is not to be found in people who are sure enough of their position to defy it.[9]

THE TUTT BROTHERS

The Tutt Brothers make for a great story but before we get started, we need to straighten out the name game because it can be confusing. While they billed themselves as brothers, the two men featured in this component were, at most, half-brothers, and may have been totally unrelated. It's one of those mysteries that, at this point, seems destined to remain unresolved.

Another mystery is how the name "Tutt" comes up as one guy's middle name and the other guy's last name. And for the record, they also sometimes bill themselves as the Whitney Brothers, so the sibling situation is certainly sketchy. All that being said, here's the lowdown on the stars of this show. We have Salem Tutt Whitney born on November 11, 1875 and Jacob Homer Tutt born on January 31, 1882, both in Logansport, Indiana.

The Tutt Brothers were major players on the Black vaudeville Chitlin' Circuit from the late 1880's through the 1930's. They were performers, writers and producers throughout their careers which were summed up as follows by David Soren. In an article he wrote for the American Vaudeville Museum he said, "The fact that they were able to do this successfully for whole decades despite facing incredible discrimination and frustration which blocked them from performing in non-Black venues is a testament to the quality of the talent they put forward in their shows."[10]

Their musical comedy shows were known for their elaborately elegant costumes and sets, and their practice of reinvesting any profits back into the shows was certainly a secret to their success. Salem Tutt Whitney was noted for his extraordinary voice, both speaking and singing and by virtue of this he was able to provide a powerful presence while hosting their productions.

THE SHOW HITS THE ROAD ~ The Tutt Brothers first hit the road in 1888 performing with a show called *Silas Green from New Orleans*. This was a traveling tent show which toured all over the country. They did this from 1888-1905 when the show was sold. It ran under different ownership through the 1940's.

Their next entertainment undertaking they billed as the "Smart Set Company," which was in operation from 1910-1925. During that period the Tutt Brothers produced over 40 musical and comedy revues. These shows all consisted of Black performers, including themselves, presenting their talents to Black audiences.

Some of the Smart Set performers went on to achieve significant success on their own. Probably the most outstanding example was Mamie Smith, a jazz and blues singer who came to be known as the "Queen of the Blues." She would go down in history as the first Black artist to make vocal blues recordings.

Later career successes for the Tutt Brothers included getting one of their shows, *Oh Joy!* onto Broadway and appearing in multiple movies. David Soren said, "The Tutt Brothers were remarkable for their great talent in writing, producing and also [performing]. Ever hopeful and ambitious, they forged ahead where few Black Americans dared to go. They were among the great forgotten pioneers of African-American show business."[11]

BUTTERBEANS (1893-1967) & SUSIE (1894-1963)

The marriage of Butterbeans and Susie could be described as long, happy and productive. In life-for-real they were Jodie Edwards and Susie Hawthorne who met on the Black nightclub circuit in 1916. A year later, they were married in a ceremony which took place on stage in Greenville, South Carolina. Subsequently they pooled their talents to create a Black comedy revue in which they billed themselves as Butterbeans and Susie.

Butterbeans/Jodie portrayed a pussy-whipped husband dominated by an overbearing wife whose sexual schtick often called him to task for his inadequacies in the bedroom, but then paradoxically begged him for more. Here's a little ditty called "New Jelly Roll Blues" where Butterbeans seems ready to deliver the goods, so to speak, or at least he's talkin' a good game.

Jelly roll, jelly roll, ain't so hard to find
There's a baker shop in town bakes it brown like mine
I got sweet jelly, a lovin' sweet jelly roll
If you taste my jelly, it'll satisfy your soul[12]

SAUCY SHOW – The show featured racy songs and comedic dances all punctuated by the couple's marital quarrels. Their respective parts featured husband Butterbeans playing the clownish, and sometimes angry buffoon to Susie's sensuous seductress. When aggravated, Butterbeans would come out with hurtful lines such as, "I'd whip your head every time you breathe; rough treatment is exactly what you need."[13] His animosity however would always be quelled by Susie's charms.

As seen in the "New Jelly Roll Blues" above, censorship was not a concept deeply entrenched in the Black nightclub circuit of the era and Susie and Butterbeans often crossed the line of conservative acceptability. How 'bout we serve up another example, this one for the hot dog lovers in our audience? Ever hear the tune "I Want a Hot Dog for My Roll"? Its condiments included a healthy dose of Susie's secret sauce; they didn't call her the "Queen of the Double Entendres" for nothin'.

Playing upon the classic analogy of bread = pussy, check out these lyrics.

> *Well I want a dog without bread you see.*
> *Because I carries my bread with me.*
>
> *Give me a big one, that's what I say.*
> *I want it so it will fit my bread*[14]

In the midst of Susie's sultry lines, Butterbeans would employ the "call-and-response" technique of classic Black gospel music and punctuate Susie's singing by shouting out phrases such as "I got a hot dog for that roll!", "My dog's never cold!" and, always the crowd favorite, "Here's a dog that's long and lean!"[15] Susie would be a-dancin' up a sexy storm all song long.

The raucous sexuality of this segment would be juxtaposed with a romantic duet, just to show how happily married the couple actually was. And the grand finale was always Butterbeans doing his signature song and dance version of "The Heebie Jeebies."

The couple released many single records over the years culminating with the release of an album in 1960. They continued to perform through the early 1960's and always looked to extend a helping hand to the Black comic community. After meeting Moms Mabley early in her career they used their connections to help her secure gigs in more prominent venues. Also, when Stepin Fetchit (see next component) encountered financial difficulties he sometimes stayed with them during the 1950's and 1960's.

When someone's in the kitchen with Dinah
Those sex games could never be finer
Who knew those hot dogs
Could serve as sex logs
When the bread symbolizes vagina

STEPIN FETCHIT (1902-1985)

This dude, who was born with five fairly fancy regular names, ended up going with just two somewhat silly ones. Lincoln Theodore Monroe Andrew Perry was born in 1902 and is best known by his stage name Stepin Fetchit. He is generally considered to be the first Black to carve out a significantly successful career in the movies. How successful? We're talkin' millions.

Fetchit grew up in Florida and moved to Montgomery, Alabama when he was 11 years old. That stay didn't last long as he ran away to join a carnival where he made money by singing and tap dancing. On the carnival circuit during his teens he continued to hone his comedic skills, as well as his business savvy, and by the age of 20 he was managing and performing in a touring carnival show. Here's the story on the funky name.

There was a race horse called "Step and Fetch It" which he and a partner won some money on. In celebration of that victory, they put together a skit where one of them adopted the name of "Step" and the other became "Fetch It," hence the name of the overall act mirrored the name of the horse. Collectively, they were "Step and Fetch It." By the time the partnership ended, he had become attached to the name and subsequently contracted it to Stepin Fetchit, so it would work solo. The name was there to stay.

A career that would span over 50 films began in 1925 with his role in *The Mysterious Stranger*, but it was the follow up film *In Old Kentucky* (1927) which would provide his breakthrough and secure him a five-year contract with the (20th Century) Fox Film Studio. Billing his persona as the "Laziest Man in the World,"[16] Fetchit had come up with a shtick and he stuck with it. We would note that, in contrast to the character he played, Fetchit was actually a very intelligent man who coupled his movie career with a regular writing gig for the Black newspaper, *The Chicago Defender*.

Fetchit developed a close connection with fellow comedian Will Rogers which led to a series of successful collaborations during the 1930's. During 1934 and 1935 the pair made four movies together and it was during this time that Fetchit became the first Black to make a million dollars as an actor. That million in 1935 would be worth almost 20 million today!

While acknowledging the professional success he achieved, we must also acknowledge the criticism under which he came for the stereotypical roles he played in his movies. That "laziest man in the world" persona was not exactly the image Blacks were looking to portray as the movement for equality progressed and by the 1960's, Fetchit found himself criticized by some civil rights advocates for his past career.

The 1960's also took on an unusual storyline combining Stepin Fetchit and Muhammad Ali. On some levels the two men may seem to rest at opposite ends of the spectrum of Blackness, so what was it that brought them together? In 1965, with his first title defense coming up against Sonny Liston, Ali summoned Fetchit to his training camp essentially to become a channel.

What was Ali looking to channel? Well, Fetchit had been a friend of Jack Johnson, the legendary first Black heavyweight boxing champion of the world and Johnson (see Chapter 8) had spoken of possessing a mysterious "anchor punch"[17] which could drop opponents immediately when properly executed. Ali was hoping to channel that punch in order to prevail in the Liston bout.

So, in a sense it was kind of a novelty gimmick, but it was certainly in line with the unconventional approach that Ali often brought to his sport, as well as his life. Ali, of course, won the fight and then attributed the victory to the anchor punch. And if you're familiar with the storyline of that fight, the whole thing takes on an added element of bizarrerie.

The fight only lasted two minutes and Liston went down so quickly and easily that some in the crowd, as well as at home, were yelling "fix" and "fake." Some reporters referred to the blow that dropped Liston as a "mystery punch" and Ali himself referred to it as a "phantom punch."[18]

Actor, rapper and writer Will Power seized upon the storyline to write a book, which was also turned into an off-Broadway play. He titled it *Fetch Clay, Make Man*. Stepin Fetchit died in 1985 at the age of 83.

MANTAN MORELAND (1902-1973)

Mantan Moreland was born in Louisiana in 1902 and at the age of 14 he ran away from home to join a minstrel show where he sang and tap danced. His traceable professional career has him starting in 1927 with *Connie's Inn Frolics* in Harlem, then moving on to the musical revue *Blackbirds* in 1928. By the end of the decade Moreland had completed multiple vaudeville tours, performed on Broadway, and was touring Europe.

Moreland's bulging eyes and cackling laugh enabled him to quickly become a Hollywood favorite and led to his scoring bigger and better roles. He even escaped the confines of comedy when he starred as the sergeant in charge of an army brigade from Senegal fighting in colonial French Algeria in the 1940 film *Drums of the Desert*.

Moreland next played the role of the chauffeur Birmingham Brown in Monogram Pictures' Charlie Chan series. He appeared in this capacity for a run of 13 films lasting from 1944-1949.

In the 1950's, Mantan teamed with Ben Carter, both on and off screen, in a shtick which was referred to as their "indefinite talk" routine. With impeccable timing, they would rattle off conversations where each would interrupt the other mid-sentence with conversations continuing as if all the unspoken words had been heard and comprehended. After Carter's passing, Moreland recreated the bit on stage, and in films, with both Redd Foxx and Nipsey Russell.

Here's a fun "What if" for you which features the Three Stooges. After Shemp Howard died in 1955, lead Stooge Moe Howard, who had always been a huge Moreland fan, wanted him to replace Shemp as the third stooge. Columbia Pictures however deferred to budget constraints and demanded that the replacement come from someone they already had under contract, which turned out to be Joe Besser. But wouldn't a biracial Three Stooges have been a potentially hilarious undertaking?

A nice cherry on top of the Mantan Moreland sundae story is that he did live long enough to land some salutary roles in classic TV series just prior to his death in 1973. He was given nice guest spots on *Love, American Style* (1969), *Julia* (1969), *Adam-12* (1970) and *The Bill Cosby Show* (1970). In some significant Black TV history notes, please allow us to share that *Julia* was the first network TV series to feature a Black woman in a non-domestic lead role (Diahann Carole). And *The Bill Cosby Show* was the sitcom where he starred as a phys ed teacher as opposed to *The Cosby Show* which ran from 1984-1992.

The most current Mantan Moreland acknowledgement would have to be credited to Spike Lee. In his 2000 film *Bamboozled*, he features a fictional TV show called *Mantan: The New Millennium Minstrel Show* with a tap-dancing character called Mantan. This happens to set up the perfect segue to our next component. *Bamboozled* also featured a segment which paid tribute to Willie Best.

WILLIE BEST (1913-1962)

Willie Best was born in Sunflower, Mississippi in 1913 and in terms of all the Black "sunflower seeds" born in Mississippi during that era, his life proved more interesting than most. Before he died in 1962, he had starred in 124 films and 38 years after his passing he was acknowledged by Spike Lee in the 2000 film *Bamboozled* which we referenced at the end of the preceding component.

So here's our take on the best of Best. How does one get from Sunflower, Mississippi to Hollywood, California? As opposed to the Beverly Hillbillies who drove their jalopy to California, Best chauffeured a honeymoon limousine to the Golden State and just decided to stay.

After gaining attention on the vaudeville circuit, West began to get hired for movies in which he was sometimes billed by his stage name "Sleep n' Eat."

As implied by that stage name, Best's character persona was basically the same as Stepin Fetchit's, and hence carries with it all of the same racial stereotypical baggage. While limited in range, Best was good at what he did. Hal Roach, producer of the Laurel & Hardy film franchise and *The Little Rascals/Our Gang* series, claimed, "Best was one of the greatest talents I ever met."[19] While working together on the 1940 film *The Ghost Breakers*, Bob Hope said, "Willie Best is the finest actor I know."[20] So there are a couple of nice accolades from a pair of show biz legends.

Best worked in television in the 1950's, predominantly on two sitcoms. On ABC's *The Stu Erwin Show*, he played the handyman and housekeeper for the title character during the series' entire run from 1950-1955. Then he also played the elevator operator on CBS's *My Little Margie*, from 1953-1955.

CHAPTER 14

SETTING THE WAYBACK MACHINE FOR SOME VINTAGE STORIES

ONESIMUS (1680's-1730's)

Would it surprise you to be told that the first vaccination against disease in America was performed by an African slave in Boston? Well, it's true and it definitely makes for an interesting story which we will delve into next.

The man's name was Onesimus (pronounced: won-Zye´-mus) and he was born in sub-Saharan West Africa. There is no documentation whatsoever about what happened between his birth and his arrival in Boston but the first thing we do know is that in 1706 the congregation of the Puritan church in that city gave the enslaved Onesimus to its minister, Cotton Mather.

When a small pox epidemic hit Boston in 1721 few would have thought Onesimus would turn out to be an absolute life saver, literally. He initially went to Mather with information about a centuries-old process of vaccination practiced in his native land. Mather took Onesimus to meet with Dr. Zabdiel Boylston to share what he knew. It would certainly be logical for the Bostonians to be skeptical about Onesimus' process of extracting small pox fluid from an infected person and scrapping the fluid into a healthy person's skin.

But based upon Onesimus' assurances, the vaccine was offered to all those willing to try it. The percentage of people who chose to be vaccinated was expectedly low but the results were extremely telling. Of the 5,889 people who were not vaccinated, 844 died while of the 280 people who received the vaccine only 6 died.[1] Converting these numbers to percentages, 14.3% of the unvaccinated died while only 2.2% of the vaccinated died. It was perhaps the greatest leap of life since the amphibians hit the beach in the Paleozoic Era.

A result of these statistics was that, the Onesimus method of vaccination had become common practice in America and Britain by the mid-1720's. On the "100 Best Bostonians of All-Time" published by *Boston* magazine in 2016, Onesimus was ranked a very respectable #52.[2] We're sure it was a lifelong dream of his to end up on a list which also included Bill Russell. Chalk up another Black breakthrough in America.

PHILLIS WHEATLEY (c. 1753-1784)

You will absolutely love the story of the first Black, male or female, to have a book published on planet Earth. Hitting the presses in 1773, it features some fascinating nuances. Undoubtedly, the most fascinating of these would be the fact that it was written by a 12-year-old slave, Boston's Phillis Wheatley. Obviously we're looking at an off-the-beaten-path story here. How 'bout we head for some uncharted territory?

Around 1760, at the age of six or seven, Wheatley was taken from her home in West Africa, probably modern-day Senegal or Gambia. The slave trade brought her to America where she was sold to the wealthy Wheatley family. John and Susanna Wheatley were progressive people who, after they sensed a literary ability in Phillis, determined that her education and the development of her talent would become a family project.

By the time Phillis was 12, she was a prolific reader of the Greek and Roman classics and had begun to write poetry. She had an affinity and aptitude for the poems which were a particular passion of hers and the quality and quantity of the work she generated led the Wheatleys to establish the goal of publishing her collected poetry in a book.

Feeling that there was a better chance of getting the book published in England than the colonies, the Wheatley's son Nathaniel took Phillis to England in 1773. Phillis so impressed the Lord Mayor of London upon their meeting that he set out to arrange aristocratic sponsorship for the book. As of September 1, 1773, copies of *Poems on Various Subjects, Religious and Moral* were flying off the presses and selling like hotcakes!

Phillis Wheatley achieved fame on both sides of the Atlantic, enabling her to have contact with British royalty and American aristocracy. If we had to pick one example to illustrate, we'd probably go with George Washington as he and Phillis had a bit of a two-way admiration society. She wrote a poem for him called "To His Excellency, George Washington."

Take a minute to date-process this one, as it clearly picture-paints Wheatley as a poet ahead of her time. Not only was Washington not yet president, the Revolutionary War hadn't even begun. How did "His Excellency" respond to the prophetic poem? Washington liked it so much, he arranged to meet her.

Before Valley Forge
it was Phillis and George.

Phillis was invited to Washington's headquarters in Cambridge, Massachusetts, in March of 1776. With the Declaration of Independence less than three months away, George still found time to pay his respects to the 12-year-old girl who had penned a poem for him. We'll include an excerpt from this poem below, but first we want to share a bit about her writing style.

When you read her material, you are immediately blown away by the depth and sophistication of her vocabulary. Most of Phillis' poetry was written in iambic pentameter which was the style Shakespeare usually used. She has 10 syllables per line and a pattern of rhythm, where the accents fall on every other syllable. Here are the last four lines of her George Washington poem.

Proceed, great chief, with virtue on thy side,
Thy ev'ry action let the Goddess guide.
A crown, a mansion, and a throne that shine,
With gold unfading, WASHINGTON! Be thine.[3]

After the publication of her book, Phillis Wheatley was emancipated which would seem to lay the groundwork for a storybook ending. But alas, 'twas not to be. She married a man whose debt exceeded her income, and both John and Susanna Wheatley passed away soon after the marriage, eliminating the support system that had facilitated her success. Her later years she spent in poverty and died in 1784 at the age of 31.

BASS REEVES (1838-1910)

When he was born a slave on an Arkansas farm in 1838, the future that lay ahead of Bass Reeves turned out to be much different than anyone might have anticipated. The general expectation would have been a boring cotton-pickin' life, right?

Well, how about a storyline that has young Bass gaining his freedom before becoming a heroic Wild West lawman who apprehends thousands of villains and, with his Indian accomplices, manages to become the inspiration for the fictional Lone Ranger character!? "Hi ho, Silver," you didn't see that one comin' did you? Who knew that behind that mask the Lone Ranger was Black!

Let's rewind and dot-connect how Bass Reeves makes the transition from slave to ranger. He lives his youth as a slave with the only significant development being that William Reeves, his owner, moves from Arkansas to Texas in 1846.

When the Civil War starts, William Reeves makes Bass accompany his son to fight for the Confederacy. As his life plays out, this proves fortuitous for the reason that it is during his time with the Confederate Army that Bass first learns how to handle a gun. Marksmanship mastered, it slowly begins to occur to Bass that risking his life fighting for an army that is trying to preserve slavery is perhaps not the best use of his Black-Bass-ass time.

So one night, under the cover of darkness, Bass slips out of camp and heads toward the Indian territory of Oklahoma. There is a bit of geographic terminology which we should clarify at this point. In the mid-1800's there was a huge parcel of land relegated to the Indians which started in modern-day Oklahoma and extended in a northwesterly direction all the way through Washington State. For the purpose of this piece we will heretofore refer to the parcel as "Indian Territory."

That destination is desirous to those looking to elude the law, as the judicial system in place is Native American and its jurisdiction only extends to tribe members. So, with no local law enforcement, the influx of common criminals and runaway slaves is only subject to federal law and, oh yeah, there's that pesky Civil War going on. The Feds have little or no interest in what's goin' down in Indian Territory.

As the Bass Reeves story evolves, this experience becomes significant because he learns the lay of the land, as well as the customs of the Indians. He even learns to speak the Creek and Seminole languages, so we're clearly dealing with a man of superior intellect and initiative.

When the Civil War concludes, ending slavery, Reeves is able to return to his original home in Arkansas where he marries and begins a family that grows to include 10 children. During this time he earns a living as a farmer and rancher, while also serving as a guide into the Indian Territory for various U.S. government agencies.

In 1875, U.S. Marshal James Fagan is appointed by the U.S. government to head an initiative to quell the chaos in the Indian Territory which, as we've stated, has become a haven for thieves, murderers and criminals, thus creating a need for some kind of government law enforcement to be brought to the region.

When Marshal Fagan is charged with assembling this force to venture into the badlands, Bass Reeves is the perfect candidate to join the U.S. Marshal Team as a deputy. He stands 6' 2" tall, has superior shooting skills, knowledge of the physical terrain, and speaks the languages of the Indians whose aid will be of immense value in rounding up the bad guys. He's the total package; it doesn't get much better than Bass!

He signs on for the job becoming the first Black deputy U.S. Marshal west of the Mississippi, a capacity in which he serves for more than 30 years. Reeves is ambidextrous and he wears his two .45 caliber six-shooters with their handles facing forward. We're sure you're wondering why at this point and the answer is super cool.

Reeves employs a cross-handed draw whereby he simultaneously reaches across the front of his body with both arms. Subsequently his right hand grasps the handle of the gun on his left hip and vice versa. Since the backs of the handles are pointing forward, they are actually in the correct position to be grasped by each hand. Then Reeves swings each arm around and starts shooting the bad guys two at a time. He's like the Lone Ranger on steroids.

Solidifying the Lone Ranger/Bass Reeves connection, the fact that he frequently works closely with Native Americans serves to establish the connection with the "Tonto" character of the Lone Ranger legend. Furthermore, he is known to prefer silver or white-colored horses, so all the Lone Ranger stars seem to align. As the Lone Ranger religiously reprised upon mounting his gallant white steed, "High ho, Silver!"

A primary source for this component is the 2006 Art T. Burton book *Black Gun, Silver Star: The Life and Legend of Frontier Marshal Bass Reeves,* which was the first to undertake a significant effort to establish the linkage between Bass Reeves and the Lone Ranger. In his book, Burton shares dozens of stories depicting how Reeves used deception and disguises to prevail over his adversaries. Here's our favorite.

One time, while based at a camp in central Oklahoma, Reeves receives information telling him a pair of brothers, escaped murderers, are laying low at their mother's house 28 miles away from his location. He decides to undertake the mission to apprehend the two men.

What's his first step? An element of deception deemed necessary to maximize the chances of success in this particular mission is that Reeves has to walk from his camp to the criminals' Mom's house. So he laces up his boots to start the sojourn.

Upon arrival at Mom's place, Reeves takes on the persona of a dusty beggar on the run from the law. Illegally sheltering two fugitives of her own, Mom extends her compassion to the stranger and invites him to stay for the night. Won't Mom be surprised in the morning! What does she find?

By the time Mom wakes up, Reeves has rounded up every weapon in the house and both boys are handcuffed to their bedposts. After sunrise, Reeves unshackles his captives and begins the 28-mile walk back to camp holding his prisoners at gun-point. This is a classic example of the circumstances which bring Bass to the heroic status we want to afford him.

Wanna hear the biggest headache of Reeves' arrest story? The mother of the arrested brothers, stripped of her weapons, has no recourse other than to follow the departing trio on foot, cursing Reeves for three miles before accepting the reality that she has no choice but return home.

According to Burton's book, Reeves apprehended more than 3,000 criminals, many of which were perhaps ironically sent to the Detroit House of Corrections. Why is this ironic you ask? Detroit would be the city where radio station WXYZ would first introduce the Lone Ranger to the world on January 30, 1933.

We'll close with the line from the Burton book that best summarizes his case making the connection between Bass Reeves and the Lone Ranger. "Although there is no concrete evidence that the real legend inspired the creation of one of fiction's most well-known Western Heroes," Burton wrote, "Bass Reeves is the closest real person to resemble the fictional Lone Ranger on the American western frontier of the nineteenth century."[4]

> *Oklahoma was just wrought with danger*
> *The game changer came from a stranger*
> *By U.S. request*
> *He braved the Wild West*
> *High Ho Silver, here comes the Lone Ranger!*

BILL PICKETT (1870-1932)

Next, let's saddle up and kick off our salute to Bill Pickett, the legendary Black cowboy, rodeo star and Wild West show performer. He will be the only person in our book whose ability to bite live animals proves to be an integral part of his success. Stick around for that story.

Pickett was born in Taylor, Texas in 1870, descending from an eclectic collection of American Indians and Black former slaves. After 5th grade, he abandoned the path of formal education and became a ranch hand where he began to master his skills at riding and roping. Here's his story…

His talents are such that he begins to emerge as a popular showman whose skill eventually leads to his professional route as a rodeo performer. Steer wrestling is an early and integral part of the rodeo routine, and Pickett innovates a stunt so unbelievable you'll be biting your lip when you read this next paragraph.

Pickett perfects a steer wrestling technique which comes to be known as bulldogging. The event starts with the bulldogger and his hazer (a second rider who keeps the steer running straight) on either side of the steer's chute.

Pickett rides his horse alongside the steer waiting for the opportunity to leap from his horse onto the back of the steer, which he grabs by the horns, then hangs on for dear life. Next, he maneuvers into a position where he can wrap his arms around the steer's neck and spin his body around so as to be under the neck of the animal as it is running.

If this doesn't seem dangerous enough, coming next is the one part you really won't believe. Pulling himself up to face the steer, Pickett then proceeds to sink his teeth into the animal's lip. Yep, Pickett bites the steer on the mouth, which they apparently hate. Thusly compromised, Pickett is then able to wrestle the beast to the ground for the requisite hog-tying. Thunderous applause inevitably ensues.

Here's our limerick on this one written from the perspective of the steer, and we've changed it up a bit from the one in the Storyline Sampler that opened this book.

> *While it's hardly my style to complain*
> *And quite rarely do I wax profane*
> *God damn legs on my hip*
> *Then that bite on my lip*
> *Which I must say I truly disdain*

Pickett soon became known for his tricks and stunts on the local country fair circuit. In 1900, he recruited his four brothers to form "The Pickett Brothers Bronco Buster and Rough Riders Association." Local success spawned taking his act on the road to neighboring states including Oklahoma, Colorado and Wyoming.

The 101 Ranch Wild West Show recruited Bill Pickett to join their roster in 1905. This high-profile operation included several big names of the era such as Buffalo Bill Cody, Tom Mix and Will Rogers. For this show, Pickett took on the stage name of "The Dusky Demon." This Wild West show toured much of the United States serving to cement Pickett as a pantheon in the genre.

The resulting fame led to the budding of a second mini-career as Pickett became a silent film star of sorts. In 1921 he starred in *The Bull-Dogger* in which he was able to showcase his steer-wrestling skills. That was followed up with a Western crime drama called *The Crimson Skull*. Spoiler alert on this one... Don't be scared; it's only a mask.

We're going to start to wind down by going to a Bill Pickett quote we came across that really resonates. "I'm promised to this world just so long," Pickett said, "and when I go that will be the end of it.... Sometime, I suppose, I'll make a mistake, a fatal mistake, and it will be all over."[5] That "sometime" turned out to be April 2, 1932 when he was kicked in the head by a bronco and killed.

MATTHEW HENSON (1866-1955)

Google "Who first reached the North Pole?" and the big-black-block-letter flash-up you'll get is "Robert Peary." Well, we're here to tell ya that you can't believe everything you read. The dude who actually flagpole-rammed the Stars & Stripes into the Arctic ice was a Black man named Matthew Henson and here's his story...

Henson was born near Washington D.C. just after the Civil War in 1866. Before we get him connected with Robert Peary, we'll share with you what Henson considered to be the most memorable event of his childhood. One day in 1876 he saw Frederick Douglass give a speech at a ceremony honoring Abraham Lincoln. At the speech Douglass charged the Blacks in the audience with two tasks.

* always fight racial prejudice
* passionately pursue your education

Henson accepted these challenges with a vengeance.

Fast forward a decade to 1877 when Henson was working at a clothing store in D.C. and guess who happens to stroll in looking for some new threads? Could that be U.S. Navy Commander Robert E. Peary over there? Well, sink my battleship if it isn't him. The two men strike up a conversation and before you know it, a mutually symbiotic relationship is brewing. That "brewing" reference is apropos because these two guys are going to be doing some serious coffee drinking together over the next four decades.

The mutually symbiotic thread that initially links the men is that Henson has significant seafaring skills and Peary is about to embark upon a voyage and surveying expedition to Nicaragua. Peary asks Henson to join him on the mission and, not that a career hawking clothes at B.H. Stinemetz and Sons isn't something every Black guy dreams of, Henson decides he's outta there.

Peary sails with a crew of 45 men on the Nicaraguan expedition and Henson's seafaring talents so impress Peary that he is soon named the "first man" on the mission. If you haven't sailed to Nicaragua recently, that "first man" term may not be familiar to you, but it means exactly what you're probably thinking it means; Henson becomes Peary's primary assistant on the mission.

Hopefully Henson enjoys this trip 'cause that warm toasty feeling of the Central American sunshine will not be something he'll be enjoying again soon. The Peary pair next turns its attention northward to begin a decades-long quest to reach the North Pole.

It is 1891-92 when Peary and Henson embark upon their first Arctic expedition and it certainly marks the beginning of an era. The two men will spend 18 of the next 23 years together on a series of seven expeditions. Conquering the North Pole proves to be no easy feat; on one failed attempt their party has six men perish from starvation.

While success would be elusive, it will not prove impossible. On April 9, 1909 instruments reveal that the six-man team of Peary, Henson and four native Inuit Eskimos are within striking distance of the North Pole.

As the party approaches their goal, Peary is relegated to riding on a dog sled due to a combination of frostbite, illness and/or exhaustion. Henson is sent ahead with a scout team which originally overshoots the pole before returning to verify its location. At that point Henson plants the U.S. flag.

When the men return home, because the "Peary Expedition" under the leadership of Robert Peary had reached the Pole, Peary ended up getting most all of the credit while Henson languished in virtual anonymity.

In 1912 he published a book called *A Negro Explorer at the North Pole* which, not surprisingly, didn't change much of history's perspective. The Explorers Club, which is an honorary worldwide society for explorers and scientists, did make Henson their first Black member in 1937.

Next, here's one we really had to chuckle at – in 1944 he received the Peary Polar Expedition Medal. Could we please call a timeout here to point out the irony of this one? Wouldn't a more appropriate gesture than giving him the medal have been to rename it the "Henson Polar Expedition Medal?" What the hell, we'll even give one to Peary.

During his later years he was a White House guest of both Harry Truman and Dwight Eisenhower and he did have one symbolically important posthumous honor bestowed. In 1988 the bodies of both he and his wife were exhumed and honored with a permanent resting place at Arlington National Cemetery. What a long strange trip it had been since Peary had found Henson hawking clothes at B.H. Stinemetz and Sons!

> *History books never paid me my dues*
> *Sometimes you regret what you choose*
> *Could've stayed nice and warm*
> *Screw that damn Arctic storm*
> *Should've kept selling clothes for the Jews*

C. J. WALKER (1867-1919)

How 'bout we do the first Black female millionaire ever! Born Sarah Breedlove, Madam C.J. Walker founded a company which featured Black women's hair care products in 1906. The Madam C.J. Walker Manufacturing Company achieved vast success and, in addition to her philanthropical endeavors, as well as political and social activism, that millionaire milestone was a gaudy one to add to the résumé.

Let's lead off with the name game. It came from her husband at the time the company was founded when she was Mrs. Charles Joseph

Walker. At that time many Black women, including herself, were subject to multiple hair-related problems such as dandruff, baldness and skin disorders. Why were Black women such frequent victims of these conditions?

It was a combination of the facts that during this era many Blacks were not blessed with quality health care and lived in homes without electricity, indoor plumbing, or consistent heating. The secret to her success was that she developed products specifically suited to target the issues that were relevant to Black women at the time.

In an address at the National Negro Business League she summarized her pathway to success by saying, "I am a woman who came from the cotton fields of the South. From there, I was promoted to the washtub. From there, I was promoted to the cook kitchen. And from there, I promoted myself into the business of manufacturing hair goods and preparations. I have built my own factory on my own ground."[6]

Among her posthumous accolades here are our two favorites…

* In 1993 she was inducted into the National Women's Hall of Fame which is located in Seneca Falls, New York.
* In 1998 the United States Postal Service honored her with a commemorative stamp in its Black Heritage series.

BESSIE COLEMAN (1892-1926)

She may have lost her life in an airplane crash on April 30, 1926, but Bessie Coleman's star will always shine aloft. Let's take off with her story next. She was born of African American and Cherokee Nation parents in Atlanta, Texas in 1892.

After a Texas childhood characterized by poverty, segregation and discrimination she decided to take her chances up north, moving to Chicago in 1915. Her financial status did not immediately change, but she developed a passion which would become the driving force in her life. Or perhaps we should say the "flying force."

As pilots began returning home after WW I she became captivated by the wild tales of their flying exploits which she heard while working at the White Sox Barber Shop in Chicago. Bessie was convinced that she wanted to become a pilot. Okay, noble dream and all, but how much is the deck stacked against her? Sure, people have overcome obstacles to achieve success, but how much of a deck-stacked dilemma is hovering over our hair-to-air heroine?

Think about the stupid-tough stigma-triple facing Bessie… She's part Black, part Indian, and all woman. Clearly she is not a baseball player because, despite already having three strikes against her, Bessie is definitely not out.

In assessing her strategy moving forward, she feels France forebodes favorably. There, the combination of being an African American as well as a Native American, is more of a novelty than an impediment. She really doesn't have much of a choice. At that time, there are no aviation training opportunities for Blacks or women in the U.S.

Bessie studies and masters French to pursue her initiative. Her drive and determination impress Robert Abbott, the wealthy Black owner of the *Chicago Defender* newspaper. Abbott helps publicize her story which facilitates sponsorships and financial support for the French foray.

On November 20, 1920, Bessie sets sail for Paris. Over the next half year, she learns how to fly and on June 15, 1921, she is awarded her pilot's license by France's Fédération Aéronautique Internationale. It is a success story that manages to supersede racial boundaries and she returns home to virtual celebrity status, among Blacks and Whites.

I can no longer sit on my pants
Fulfill dreams, roll the dice, take a chance
In my country denied
Request not dignified
For to fly, I must travel to France

While the notoriety is nice, it doesn't pay any bills and Bessie's "What's next?" options are limited at that point in history. Widespread commercial air traffic is still a decade down the road and the only viable outlet to sustain her passion is to enter the dangerous world of stunt flying. So of course Bessie tackles that titanic task with the tenacity that characterized every aspect of her life and personality.

It is her goal to encourage other Black people to pursue flying and she becomes a role model for not only Blacks, but also Native Americans and women. She quickly gains a reputation as a skilled and daring pilot who fears no attempt to complete a dangerous stunt.

Over the next five years Bessie performs at air shows around the country, always refusing to perform at any show where Blacks are not admitted. She becomes such a draw that her fame empowers her to effect societal changes.

Her typical performances include stunning demonstrations of daredevil maneuvers including figure eights, loop-de-loops, and dive-toward-the-earth dips. On a dollar-for-dollar basis, things don't get much better in the early 1920's. True, you could go see the Yankees play, but Babe Ruth only comes up to bat about five times a game and you have to wait during the interim. Bessie offers a non-stop 20-minute show that blows the socks off every attendee, Black or White, Yankee or Confederate.

It would be "off she goes into the wild blue yonder" for Coleman for the next five years. She tours extensively throughout North America and Europe. She is triply unique in terms of the dangers she faces and also the amazing skills she exudes. She achieves groundbreaking aviation accomplishments for women, Blacks and Native Americans.

The end comes on April 30, 1926 when a plane she is flying in suffers mechanical difficulties, spirals out of control, and crashes. She actually is not piloting the plane at the time of the crash. The purpose of the flight is to plan a parachute jump, and Coleman is not at the wheel because she wants to examine the terrain below to pick the best spot for her jump. At the time the plane spins out of control, Coleman has her seat belt off, so she can lean over the cockpit sill to look down.

Subsequently, she is thrown from the plane and falls to her death from 2,000 feet as the plane crashes to the earth killing the pilot. Coleman's eventual fate had been determined the very second that control of the plane was lost. All of which gives us pause to reflect upon the old adage that you only live once, which of course is inherently false. You live every day… but you only die once.

An obituary in the Black newspaper, the *Dallas Express,* stated, "There is reason to believe that the general public did not completely sense the size of her contribution to the achievements of our race as such."[7]

The air is the only place free from prejudices. I knew we had no aviators, neither men nor women, and I knew the Race needed to be represented along this most important line, so I thought it my duty to risk my life to learn aviation... Bessie Coleman[8]

THE SCOTTSBORO BOYS

The sounds of the old freight train clickety clacking along the Tennessee tracks echo mournfully through the tunnels of time, ruefully resonating the resignation regarding one of the most manic miscarriages of justice in the history of the U.S. legal system. But as we all know, history can be a very tricky thing. You absolutely cannot get it mixed up with the past. The past actually happened, while history is just what somebody wrote down.

This story spans a spectrum that begins with the accusations and ramifications of race and gang rape within the Alabama legal system. Then it spirals outward to ensnare the Communist Party of the United States and a Jewish New York City lawyer, before finally winding up in the U.S. Supreme Court. Buckle your seat belts.

Our story begins March 25, 1931, as we're onboard a Tennessee freight train heading west from Chattanooga to Memphis on the Southern Railway Line, with a remarkable story about to unfold. In addition to its freight, the train is also hauling a few dozen hobos some Black and some White. After a don't-step-on-my-foot incident escalates, the Whites try to force the Blacks off their "White train" near the Lookout Mountain tunnel. A fight ensues in which the Blacks prevail and drive the Whites off the train.

The whipped Whites report to the local authorities that a gang of belligerent Blacks has assaulted them on the train. Word is wired ahead to the train's next stop and here kicks in the first of so many intriguing nuances in this story. On its westward Tennessee trek from Chattanooga to Memphis, the train line dips south into Alabama for just a few miles and one stop. That fateful stop would be in Scottsboro, Alabama. Had this whole thing played out in Tennessee, you can't help but wonder how differently the chips may have fallen.

COMIN' IN TO THE STATION - As the train is stopped and searched in Scottsboro, nine Black male hobos are rounded up along with two White females, Victoria Price and Ruby Bates. The two women come forward with a graphic tale of how they have both been gang raped by the nine Blacks who range in age from 13 to 19. The teenagers are taken into custody and it is only an intervention by the National Guard that keeps them from being lynched by the angry White mob that almost immediately descends upon the jail house. The mob is out for blood and like mosquitoes at a nudist colony, they just don't know where to start.

Why do Price and Bates concoct an outright lie? Is it nothing more than vindictive racism? Turns out there is a little more to it than that. The women both have a history of prostitution and the Mann Act creates even more severe penalties for anyone crossing state lines to engage in immoral sexual behavior. This one all boils down to that old cliché that sometimes the best defense is a good offense. Why not say, "We're not prostitutes; they're rapists."

Prior to a hastily arranged trial, a doctor who examines Price and Bates for signs of rape, finds none. Hired with the $60 their parents are able to scrape together, the boys are represented by a real estate lawyer and a 69-year-old attorney who has not worked a case in decades. The Scottsboro Boys are convicted by an all-White jury, despite the total lack of any evidence a crime has actually taken place. Eight of the nine are given the death penalty, with a 13-year-old sentenced to life in prison.

COMMUNIST COLLABORATION - While the case is being appealed, it ironically becomes a subject of international headlines. Why, you ask? It's all because the Communist Party of the United States takes the Scottsboro Boys under its wing and manages to gain control of the boys' legal defense. How's that for a WTF moment? If you're thinking there must be some kind of ulterior motive here, right you'd be.

At this point in time, the Communist Party is well-funded, efficiently organized and opportunistic. They have used the Great

Depression to raise doubts about the viability of capitalism, and they have specifically targeted southern Blacks as a source for increased party membership and support. It is certainly a logical strategy in a society where Blacks are clearly disenfranchised.

The Communists feel that their platform espousing a proletariat of the people where societal assets would be equally distributed should be enticing to the Blacks because the status quo is clearly not currently providing them with much equality.

The clever Communist strategy is essentially that if they can take the forefront in organizing the defense of the Scottsboro Boys, that action could serve to ingratiate Southern Blacks who might then subsequently join the Communist party. So, that's why the Commies are comin' down to Dixie!

Because of the international network it has in place, the Communists are able to orchestrate huge demonstrations around the globe decrying the fate of the Scottsboro Boys. With all the injustices that have been perpetrated on Blacks in Alabama with virtually no response anywhere, ulterior motives notwithstanding, it is certainly strange to see thousands of people rallying in Madrid, Berlin and Moscow singing songs and carrying signs in support of the Scottsboro Boys!

HERE WE GO AGAIN ~ Meanwhile, as we continue to sustain the suspense, in a landmark decision, the Supreme Court grants new trials for all the boys based upon the woefully inadequate defense they had received. There are a couple key developments in between the first and second trial.

1) Ruby Bates recants her testimony and acknowledges that the rape allegations are fictitious.
2) The Communist Party hires Samuel Leibowitz, a legendary New York City defense attorney who has never lost a murder case. Of the 78 murders he has tried up to that point, he has won 77 and had one hung jury. He struts into Alabama with a swaggering over-confident arrogance, fully intending to keep his undefeated streak alive.

Adding to the drama as the second trial approaches, Ruby Bates, who is to be the star witness for the defense with her revised story, goes missing a few weeks before the trial. She vanishes from her Huntsville, Alabama home and despite the best efforts of authorities, she is nowhere to be found as the trial begins.

Leibowitz initiates the proceedings by exposing the flaws in the Alabama legal system which creates the circumstances whereby there are no Blacks in the jury pool. He then goes on to present an overwhelmingly convincing argument that the White girls were not raped by the Black boys, nor anybody else for that matter.

With no evidence to support the charges, the prosecution's primary weapon is the testimony of Victoria Price who takes the stand, repeating the allegations of rape she had issued in the first trial. Upon cross-examination Price proves to be a difficult witness, even for Leibowitz. The crude and depraved Southern prostitute adopts a hardened façade of sarcasm and evasion that isn't quite like anything Leibowitz has ever encountered in the Big Apple. Leibowitz is left as frustrated as a pyromaniac in the Petrified Forest.

THE STINK OF THE NORTH ~ And while Leibowitz doesn't like Price, likewise neither she, nor any of the White members present in the jury box or courtroom, are enamored of the Jewish New York City lawyer who has been hired by the Communists to invade their Southern home turf. Leibowitz's efforts to compromise the firmly entrenched White stranglehold on the power within the Alabamian judicial system are fiercely resented. National Guard troops are, for good reason, stationed outside his door every night as a safety precaution.

Summing up the trial, it would be fair to say that Leibowitz does an excellent job of debunking the testimony of every prosecution witness, but it would be to little or no avail because the Southern animosity toward this "Yankee Jew"[9] is destined to overshadow all the legal prowess Leibowitz is able to exhibit. His harshly caustic cross-examination of Price essentially turns the trial into a referendum on the respect of Southern womanhood, in general, more than a trial of the Scottsboro Boys' guilt in particular.

As the trial chugs toward a conclusion, he needs a miracle. So what happens next? Leibowitz has an ace up his sleeve, and he's ready to play it. Just as it seems he's about to close his defense, having worked all the way through his submitted witness list, Leibowitz approaches the bench and asks if he can call just one more witness. Ready for some New York drama? OMG-gasps are heard throughout the gallery when the rear doors open and Ruby Bates is escorted into the courtroom by two Alabama National Guardsmen. Ruby Bates? Ruby's back!

At this point, the whole thing begins to take on the feel of a made-for-TV movie. Turns out Bates' disappearance was a result of her having been whisked away to New York City by the Communists for safe keeping. What could be more dramatic than the sudden appearance of the one witness who can totally disavow the testimony of the only significant witness the prosecution has? Can you feel the pendulum begin to swing toward the defense?

TRUTH BE TOLD - Dressed in a newfound air of classy sophistication, Bates draws stares from everyone in the courtroom and a glare so intensely hateful from her former partner in prostitution that Bates is preemptively told to hold her temper. We'll bullet-list the highlights of Bates' testimony.

* On March 25, neither she nor Victoria Price were raped, touched, or even spoken to by any of the Scottsboro Boys.
* The reason she'd lied was because Price had told her they might go to jail for prostitution if they didn't "frame up a story."
* Price had added that, "She didn't care if all the Negroes in Alabama were put in jail."[10]

We can only assume that Price's glare intensifies during this testimony. Everything points toward that swinging pendulum having dealt a deadly blow to the prosecution's case.

Upon cross-examination, Bates is asked where she has gotten her flashy new clothes and she acknowledges that the Communists had bought them for her when she was in New York City, which sends a wave of derisive gasps throughout the courtroom. One witness at the trial described the scene by saying, "The jury smelled the North on Ruby."[11] Can you feel the pendulum swinging back in the other direction now?

By the time closing arguments are over, prosecuting attorney Wade Wright refers to Bates' boyfriend (who had testified) as "the prettiest Jew

I ever saw," and makes disparaging anti-Semitic remarks about Leibowitz. His closing line is, "Don't you know these defense witnesses are bought and paid for? May the Lord have mercy on the soul of Ruby Bates. Now the question in this case is this – Is justice in the case going to be bought and sold in Alabama with Jew money from New York?"[12] Leibowitz's objections are subsequently overruled. It is the perfect playing of the Jew card by Wright and it serves to bring home a second guilty verdict for the Scottsboro Boys.

Further legal maneuvers and wranglings lead to the granting of a third trial and we will let you know that the drama that has characterized the story up to this point is mostly missing from the last chapter in this sad saga. It ends with a whimper rather than a bang and, that being said, we'll give you the long-story-short version.

As things gear up for the third trial, basically Alabamians are beginning to grow weary of the whole affair, as well as its cost. Most, in their hearts, know that the boys are not guilty and the national embarrassment, as well as the international shaming, is making the whole ordeal no longer worth the price of propping up the false façade.

SAVING FACE – Grover Hall, Editor of the *Montgomery Advertiser*, once one of the most ardent of the Scottsboro prosecution advocates begins to wonder if something has not gone terribly wrong. To this effect he writes, "*The* Advertiser *knows, and all of its readers know, the whole of this sordid sickening story. Scottsboro has stigmatized Alabama throughout the civilized world. We herewith suggest and urge that the state now move for a decent dignified compromise. Nothing can be gained by demanding a final pound of flesh. Throw this body of death away from Alabama.*"[13]

At this point, let's put this whole case in perspective. Of the nine Scottsboro Boys, one had such a severe case of syphilis he was incapable of even having sex, one of the boys was legally blind and two had only been 13-years old at the time of the incident. Those were the first four to be pardoned and released in 1937. Other pardons and escapes followed and by 1946 all of the Scottsboro Boys were free through one means or another.

We do have some additional reading on this in the addendum beginning on page 177 which includes an individual synopsis on each of the nine Scottsboro Boys and how their lives played out.

If one were wont to extract any kind of a silver lining from this grave injustice it might be that the series of trials did serve to unite Blacks and Whites in the United States on a level not seen since the abolitionist movement some seventy years earlier. In much of the country massive demonstrations in support of the Scottsboro Boys took place with Blacks and Whites marching side-by-side. A mantra of the movement became the chant of "Black and White, Unite and Fight."

Chapter 15

Saving the "X" for Last

While some writers employ a strategy of saving the best for last, we've altered that approach and adopted a new literary technique of saving the "X" for last. And if it also happens to be the best, then we have a double winner on our hands. Please allow us to clarify.

Let's face it, any serious attempt to conduct a thorough review of the history of Black humor is going to become a failed attempt if it is forced to stay within the confines of a G-rated agenda. In order to maintain the integrity of the artists' work, we have used the words they chose to use during their original performances, including sex and profanity.

That being said, we did choose to cushion sensitive ears when appropriately possible. At this stage of the game however, we're going to let the mofo's fall where they may. At this point if we were doing a book on White comedy the perfect segue would be to site George Carlin's classic shtick about the "Seven Words You Can't Say On TV." What the hell, let's do it anyway. Would all you folks please join us in a chant of, "Shit, Piss, Fuck, Cunt, Cocksucker, Motherfucker and Tits!" If that felt really good, feel free to repeat it one more time. Then thank Carlin for getting his seven words in edgewise, and prepare yourself to move on with The Kings of Comedy.

THE KINGS OF COMEDY

From 1997 through the year 2000 one of the most unique tours in comedy history hit the road. What was so unique about it? Never before or after had four comedians of this stature combined forces to tour as a single collective entity. It was Steve Harvey, Cedric the Entertainer, D.L. Hughley, and Bernie Mac who combined forces to comprise The Kings of Comedy.

The tour broke the record for the highest gross, making $18 million in its first year, and then broke its own record by taking in $19 million the following year. Ka-ching! The format of the show was that Steve

Harvey served as an emcee host who introduced the three other comedians and tied the whole thing together.

When the landmark production came to an end in 2020, the decision was made that something big must be done to document the show for all eternity. So Spike Lee was called in to be the producer, and the final two shows of the tour were recorded at the Coliseum in Charlotte, N.C. on February 26 & 27, 2000. Lee subsequently combined the best footage from both nights to create the comedy film which would be released as *The Original Kings of Comedy*.

> *Joining forces for one joint attack*
> *Was a line-up all-star and all-Black*
> *Hughley, so funny*
> *Cedric on the money*
> *With Steve Harvey and that Bernie Mac*

CEDRIC THE ENTERTAINER (1964 -)

After growing up in Missouri, Cedric Antonio Kyles left the Midwest for the Big Apple in the early 1990's seeking showbiz fame and fortune as Cedric the Entertainer. During the 1993-1994 season he hosted the BET network's *ComicView* series. From there he moved on to HBO where he hosted *Def Comedy Jam* in 1995.

His next big break came later that year when he was cast as The Cowardly Lion in a stage revival of the 1978 film *The Wiz*. The following year he began a six-year run in the sitcom *The Steve Harvey Show,* lasting from 1996-2002.

It was in the midst of this series that The Kings of Comedy tour hit the road from 1997-2000, and the success of the movie version of that show further elevated Cedric's stature. Cedric has starred in 55 movies to date and in perusing various polls, three titles that always ranked high are:

* Big Mama's House (2000)
* Barbershop (2002)
* The Honeymooners (2005)

Here's a sampling of Cedric's humor…

* [My tour] started in D.C. where I had to go to the African American Museum of History. Had to do it. One, I'm African American, a lot of you didn't know that, (crowd laughs at the obvious) so I had to go. It's a requirement if you're there. Now [the museum] was nice, don't get me wrong, but it was the usual thing you know. Of course there was a lot on slavery, you knew that was gonna happen, a lot on slavery. They had Martin Luther King, you knew that was gonna happen. I was like where's the stuff I want, ya know. I wanna see Little Richard's curling iron, like little shit. Like the formula for the jheri curl. Who was the first people to decide it was okay to eat chitlins? You know they stink like hell, but if we cook 'em long enough and put some hot sauce on 'em, be like well shit [we can eat these] for years. [That's the kind of stuff I want to see.][1]

* I love Halloween, that's one of my favorite holidays. But I don't know what I'm gonna be this year. I know my favorite costume was a few years ago, remember when the housing crisis was on and everyone was goin' through foreclosure? I dressed up as a foreclosure sign, and just be standin' in people's yards when they come back from trick-or-treatin'. (Extending both arms fully to the sides as if putting his foreclosure sign costume on full display) Lady comes home, goes, "Oh Lord Jesus!"
I'm like, "No, I'm sorry Mam, it's just a costume, it's fine." Scared the shit out of people.[2]

* I stopped trustin' politicians a long time ago 'cause I live in California. As soon as they made Schwarzenegger the governor I was like, "Okay, don't nobody know what they doin' right now." That's obvious, especially when he had a little baby by the maid. I can't believe y'all wasn't suspicious, that wasn't nobody suspicious when that little strong-ass baby was walkin' around the house. Okay, there ain't no way that damn baby gonna be movin' his own crib sayin', "Just slidin' it in front of the TV, Mama, so I can see." Baby got his own car seat, say, "I got it, Mama, don't worry about it (picks up his stool and carries it like car seat.) You get my baby bag, I got this." Strong-ass, little god damn baby.[3]

STEVE HARVEY (1957 -)

Steve Harvey was born in West Virginia in 1957 and his family moved to Cleveland where he grew up and graduated from high school. His move to comedy was by no means immediate, as he spent the decade after high school in a series of menial jobs ranging from carpet cleaner to mailman. His first stand-up performance occurred at a club in Cleveland in 1985 at the age of 28.

And success did not exactly swoop in on Harvey immediately upon taking the stage. After that '85 debut, Harvey would spend three homeless years in the late 1980's living in his '76 Ford. He made due, traveling between gigs taking advantage of whatever means were available to keep himself clean and fed. It does help to know that there will be a happy ending to this story.

The breakthrough came in 1990 at the Johnnie Walker National Comedy Search. His successful appearance at this event led to a seven-year stint hosting the syndicated show *It's Showtime at the Apollo*. During this time the WB network launched the self-titled sitcom *The Steve Harvey Show* which ran from 1996-2002.

From 1997-2000 Steve Harvey also participated in the Kings of Comedy tour, one of the most successful of all time, as we have stated. Of the four "Kings" who participated in the tour, it is Steve Harvey who has probably gone on to achieve the greatest notoriety.

Since 2000, he has been the host of a weekday morning radio program, *The Steve Harvey Morning Show*. He's hosted the Miss Universe Pageant from 2015-2022. He is currently the host of the game shows *Family Feud* and *Celebrity Family Feud*. He has also authored four books and his trophy case features six Emmy Awards and 14 NAACP Image Awards.

Here is a sampling of Harvey's comedy…

* (On the people who become bank robbers)
Let's look at this closer. First of all, who amongst us is the holdup man? It is the uneducated 'cause see, if you got an education you know good and well that it's not a good-ass idea to hold up a liquor store at 2:30 in the mornin' tryin' to raise money. You got better sense than that but

now, if you ain't got no education, your ignorant ass think, "Hey, I can make a livin' robbin' liquor stores."⁴

One time I was up in Cleveland, at 2:30 in the mornin', and I was in this 7-11 gettin' some bread when these four brothers come in and, okay, I ain't sayin' that all Black people steal, you know that ain't true. But that night there were four of 'em. They come in and they got that look... you know how they look when they fixin' to do somethin'. They heads be snatchin' around real quick you know. I was standin' there goin', "Hell no, I ain't got no business in here at no two o'clock in the morning lookin' for bread!"⁵

* Bill collectors were always callin' me. They call so much I developed routines. They say, "When can we expect payment?" I say, "You can *expect* it anytime you want, *gettin'* it is gonna be your problem."⁶

* I can't go to jail, not with this soft skin and these boyish good looks. I'll be snapped up before the first lights out!⁷

BERNIE MAC (1957-2008)

Bernie Mac's big time entertainment career actually got off to a rather late start. He grew up in Chicago, graduating from high school in 1975 and he spent the next 15 years shuffling through a surprisingly long list of random jobs while working comedy clubs on the weekend.

Mac's big break would turn out to be when he won the Miller Lite Comedy Search in 1990. That exposure earned him a spot in HBO's *Def Comedy Jam* in 1992 paving the way for him to become a sought-after actor and stand-up comedian. Media websites' consensus on his three best movies are:

* Ocean's 11 (2001)
* The Player's Club (1998)
* Friday (1995)

After participating in the Kings of Comedy tour from 1997-2000, Mac was ready to head to TV Land. *The Bernie Mac Show* sitcom debuted on Fox in 2001 and ran through 2006. In the show Mac essentially played himself in a scenario where his sister had entered rehab leaving him to take care of her three children. The sitcom's secret to success was its motif of allowing Mac to break the fourth wall, enabling him to take advantage of his comedic roots as a stand-up.

Just to explain that "fourth wall" convention, the typical TV approach assumes there is an invisible wall between the actors and the audience. While the audience sees the actors through this wall, the assumption is that the actors cannot see them back. The production technique whereby the actor looks directly at the camera and speaks to the audience is known as "breaking the fourth wall." *The Bernie Mac Show* was known for its effective use of that technique.

Bernie Mac's death was emotional as he was taken in 2008 at the relatively young age of 50. During his final years he had acknowledged that he was afflicted with sarcoidosis, a disease which causes tissue inflammation. Amongst the 7,000 people in attendance at his funeral were the other three Kings of Comedy, as well as Chris Rock, Ashton Kutcher, and Samuel L. Jackson. Mac's friend, D.L. Hughley delivered the particularly passionate remembrance which brought many in attendance to tears. We'll use that as a segue and pass the Comedy King baton on to Hughley.

D. L. HUGHLEY (1963 -)

D.L. Hughley grew up in South Central LA and fell victim to some of the typical hazards inherent to that habitat. He was expelled from San Pedro High School and wound up a member of the scandalously renowned street gang "The Bloods." To his credit he was able to extricate himself from that environment, obtain his GED, and launch a career in comedy.

Hughley's first high profile gig was landing the role of host on the BET series *ComicView* in 1992. In 1993 he added the first sitcom line to his résumé playing Will Smith's friend in *Fresh Prince of Bel Air*. His biggest sitcom success would of course be the ABC/UPN series *The Hughleys* which ran from 1998-2002. The show had a "movin'-on-up" premise which has the family relocating from a poor inner city LA environment to a ritzy suburb.

It would be in the midst of that sitcom run when *The Kings of Comedy* would be released and here's a sampling of Hughley's humor from that film…

* (regarding bill collectors) They done fucked up and gave Black folks caller ID. Now, first thing we do is run over and check the display and say, "Wait a minute; let that motherfucker ring now. I ain't got no friends with 800 numbers, fuck that, man."[8]

* White folks do shit for excitement we don't do. They go sky divin' bungee jumpin', skiin'. Black folks don't never bungee jump; it's too much like lynchin' for us. So, I'm gonna let you put a rope around me and push me off a bridge? You must be outcha god damn mind![9]

* White folks, I'm tired of y'all and we're going to help you out. If you know anybody who lives in a hurricane area in a trailer park, let them know that if your house is on wheels, and the hurricane is comin', drive the fuck off, drive off, just pull away. Black people, we get the hell out when a hurricane comin'; we say we hope it blows on the first day when we gonna have to pay rent. We say, "I'm not payin' for this house that ain't here no more. You see it?" White people won't run. They say, "I'm not gonna run. Give me some nails and some wood."[10]

* Stuff happens to White folks, don't happen to nobody else. I live in Southern California and two people were mauled by mountain lions. I knew right away they wasn't Black people, 'cause we don't hike. Only way a mountain lion gonna ever get Black people is if it learn how to pick a lock.[11]

WHOOPI GOLDBERG (1955 -)

A certainly fun fact about Whoopi Goldberg is that she is one of the sweet sixteen members of perhaps entertainment's most prestigious club. Only sixteen people have won what is sometimes referred to as an EGAT! Egads, what's an EGAT? The acronym is indicative of the fact that she has won an Emmy Award, a Grammy Award, an Academy Award and a Tony Award. She and 15 others are in that rarified air.

Her first movie appearance came in 1982's *Citizen: I'm Not Losing My Mind, I'm Giving It Away*. Her next big step came when Director Mike Nichols discovered her performing her one-woman act called *The Spook Show* in New York City in 1983. Nichols brought Whoopi's show to Broadway where it debuted on October 24, 1984 and ran for five months.

Here she was noticed by Steven Spielberg, leading to her next big step up the entertainment ladder. Spielberg cast her in a feature role in his next film *The Color Purple* which was released in 1985. Whoopi absolutely killed it with her portrayal of Celie, a Black woman in the early 1900's who endures extraordinarily egregious strife in her struggle for survival, and ultimately happiness. Her performance earned her a Golden Globe Award for Best Supporting Actress. Let's go to a bullet list and we'll outline the details on her EGAT Award.

* Emmy Award (2) – portraying Hattie McDaniel in a special (2002) and *The View* (2009)
* Grammy Award – *Whoopi Goldberg: Original Broadway Show Recording* (1986)
* Academy Award – *Ghost* (1990)
* Tony Award – *Thoroughly Modern Millie* (2002)

> Grammy, Tony, Oscar I can do
> Emmy Awards, of those I've got two
> It's been a great ride
> My cred is bonafide
> All I need is a room with The View

After her appearances in 1992's *Sister Act* and 1993's sequel *Sister Act 2: Back in the Habit*, she established herself as Hollywood's highest-paid actress. She has hosted the Academy Awards on multiple occasions and has been a moderator on the daytime talk show *The View* since 2007.

Here's a sampling of Whoopi's humor…

* (On God) Cats are talkin' 'bout religion, got all this bullshit happenin' and stuff, 'cause you can always tell when God is talkin'. God is really direct. Got those commandments; don't matter what language you speak

or what religion you're in, the commandments are the same... Don't lie, 'cause you ain't never gonna remember the bullshit you said the night before... Don't fuck your neighbor's wife, 'cause you're gonna be mad as hell when he's fuckin' your wife... Honor your mother and father, 'cause you're gonna need childcare soon. Simple shit, you know. God said, "He who is without dog shit on your sneaker take the first step on the white rug."[12]

* (on Jimmy the Greek)

Reporter: "Jimmy can you tell us why there are so many, how shall I say it, Black athletes?"

And Jimmy said: "'Cause that's what there is. That's the way it's been set up, that's how it's been from the beginning. We brought big Black bucks and bred them to big Black gals, and made big Black babies who was fast."

(Whoopi's analysis:) Now where is the oh-fense? What's oh-fensive 'bout that? It ain't a lie. He told the goddamn truth. What happens to you on network TV when you tell the truth is "vroom," you gone. Faster than a fart in a dust storm, Jimmy the Greek was outta there.[13]

* (on White people's reactions to Rock Hudson's AIDS diagnosis) When Rock Hudson came out as gay, it was like John Wayne fucked his horse.[14]

PAUL MOONEY (1941-2021)

Paul Mooney actually passed away during the time we were writing this book. So as we're going through right now and changing "is" to "was" in some of the following passages we're promising ourselves as well as you, our readers, to compose a salute to the man that we hope will have him smiling down from heaven.

As we prepare this book for publication, out last addition is this paragraph where we are able to add that we genuinely feel like we succeeded in our goal stated in the previous sentence. After forwarding a draft of our book to the Paul Mooney World Legacy Team, all three of his children wanted to contribute the following additional thoughts on their father...

* Spring Mooney, his daughter, wrote about the book, "I'm with it! Look's cool!" and about her father she wrote, "He was the recipe to comedy not just the cake. Fearless in his delivery while giving you precious ingredients!! Cut from a different cloth indeed."

* Daryl Mooney, his son, wrote, "Paul Mooney was not only a comic he was an educator. He taught the world through humor about racism and Black Greatness."

* Dwayne Mooney, his son, wrote, "Paul Mooney gave comedians courage to speak their truth."

The Paul Mooney World Legacy Team collectively wrote, "Thanks again for everything! It's a beautiful tribute. Thank you! Would love to see links of the TV show interviews when done. Chat soon,
Mooney World Legacy Team.

Mooney managed to comfortably wear many hats. He was a writer, comedian, actor and social critic. His most famous writing credits were for Richard Pryor, including penning his material for *Saturday Night Live*, multiple cable specials and *The Richard Pryor Show*. Mooney also wrote for Redd Foxx's *Sanford and Son* and *Good Times*, and was the lead writer for Fox's *In Living Color*.

He also contributed to *Chappelle's Show* as a writer and performer. A memorable segment from this was Negrodamus, a Black parody of Nostradamus where Mooney answered questions about life's most unsolvable mysteries. Here's an example…

Q: Why do White people love Wayne Brady?
A: Because Wayne Brady makes Bryant Gumbel look like Malcolm X.[15]

Here's a quote from Mooney that seems to sum up his feeling about where he falls within the racial framework of America. "Whatever that thing is that White people like in Blacks, I don't have it. Maybe it's my arrogance or my self-assurance or the way I carry myself, but whatever it is, I don't have it."

Here is a celebratory sampling of Mooney's humor…

* You White folks see UFO's in your dreams. There's no Martians in Harlem.[16]

* I don't want affirmative action. Too much affirmative, not enough action.[17]

* A new broom can sweep the floor. An old broom knows where the dirt is.[18]

Here's a sampling of Mooney comedy vignettes…

"The American Revolution"

Thank God Paul Revere was White, or we wouldn't be sittin' here now. 'Cause if he'd a been Black, somebody would have shot that nigger, "Oh that nigger stole that horse." They'd a shot Paul Revere.

Hey, who do the White people say sewed the flag? Betsy Ross… ain't that a bitch. Now come on, they had slaves. That bitch was asleep at six. You know some big Black fat Aunt Jemima was up all night sewin' that flag.[19]

"Blame-a-Nigger"

They don't want to give us any credit. They just want to blame everything on niggers. Didn't some White man in Boston shoot his pregnant wife and then shot hisself, talkin' about, "Oh niggers did it." Always trying to blame some niggers…

That's why I'm gonna start a new ad, 1-800-Blame-a-Nigger. So when White folks get in trouble, they just call my agency.

"Hello, Blame-a-Nigger? I just pushed my mother-in-law down the stairs and she may be dead. I don't want to go to jail. Send a nigger over here!"

"Alright, I got one on parole. I'll send him right over sir."[20]

"Nigger Raisins"

(Referencing the California Raisons advertising campaign) White folks' favorite TV commercial is that little, wrinkled, black, shriveled-up raisin. Little nigger raisin with a hat, they think that shit is cute, singin', "Heard it through the grapevine." ♫ All Marvin Gaye and shit. They think that shit is cute.

"Oh, look at the cute nigger raisin."

"Heard it through the grapevine." ♫

They gone nigger fuckin' raisin crazy. They made Ray Charles a raisin. Oh fuck him, he's blind [singing] "What I Say?"♪ Then I looked up one morning and Michael Jackson was a goddamn raisin.

I said, "They gone nigger fuckin' raisin crazy." And the shit ain't cute. I bet if I got me some marshmallows and put some arms and legs on them goddamn marshmallows and let 'em sing "Surfin' USA,"♪ they won't think that shit's so goddamn cute. [21]

> *Marvin Gaye, as a raisin he bellows*
> *Paul Mooney responds saying, "Hell knows*
> *The stars will align*
> *And revenge will be mine*
> *With the Beach Boys dressed up like marshmallows"*

We'll close with a funny story that we're sure will splash a final smile upon the face of Paul Mooney as he looks down upon us from heaven…

Well, there was this man who came to a bar, and he was there with all the other people. And they were standing around him, and all of the sudden, he pulled out of his pocket a little piano. He put the piano on the bar, and they said, "Oh, that's an interesting little piano. Where did you get that little piano there?"

He said, "Oh, I have somethin' even more amazing than that." And he reached into his pocket and he pulled out this little man – no more than 15 inches tall, and he put the man down, and the man started playin' the piano.

And they said, "This is amazing. How did you do this?"

"Well, I got it out of a bottle," he said. "You wanna see the bottle?"

Everybody said, "Yeah."

So he pulled out the bottle, and they said, "How did you get that? How did you get the piano and the man?"

He said, "Well, this genie in the bottle told me that if I wanted to make a wish, I could, you know, have my wish."

So one of the men said excitedly, "Well, can **I** try this?"

So this man sitting next to him told the genie, "I want a million **bucks**," and the genie responded and, all of the sudden, there were a million **ducks** flying overhead!

The man said, "I didn't ask for a million **ducks**, I said a million **bucks**."

And the man who originally brought the piano in said in a dejected voice, "Man, I know how you feel. Do you really think I asked for a 15-inch **pianist?**"[22]

ADDENDUM 1
THE SCOTTSBORO BOYS

For those of you interested in a more individualized look at the nine Scottsboro Boys, we have put together this concise overview for you. We debated whether or not to include this information in the Scottsboro component earlier in the book and came to the conclusion that the impact of the drama may have bogged down in the onslaught of TMI.

Subsequently, we decided on this addendum approach and if we've piqued your interest to the point where you're still with us, read on…

HAYWOOD PATTERSON – Patterson was probably the most famous of the Scottsboro Boys for a few reasons which we'll cover in this component. He was born in Georgia in 1913, the son of a sharecropper, and his family eventually moved to Chattanooga, Tennessee. He left school after third grade and, following a short stint working as a delivery boy, he began hoboing across the country looking for work. On that fateful day of March 25, 1931 Patterson was the first Black to become involved in the altercation with the Whites on the train when one of them stepped on his hand.

Patterson was 18 and illiterate when he entered the jail in Scottsboro but less than a year later, he was reading and writing and playing trivia games with the guards. He proved his prowess by having the guards name any state in the country and demonstrating that he could name that state's capital.

When the last round of trials began, the boys were tried individually and Patterson was tried first because he seemed the most likely to draw a guilty verdict. He was the biggest and he did have a glare about him.

After his fourth conviction in 1937 he was sentenced to 75 years and he was the last Scottsboro Boy interred in Alabama when he escaped on July 17, 1947. Initially he led an interesting underground life, hiding from the law, where he connected with Scottsboro sympathizers and was supported in writing a book about his experience called *The Scottsboro Boy*. He was finally tracked down in Michigan in 1950, but after a nationwide letter-writing campaign was mounted on his behalf, the governor there refused to extradite him back South.

Haywood Patterson stabbed someone in a bar fight in 1951 and went to jail in Michigan on a manslaughter conviction. He died there of cancer at the age of 39 on August 24, 1952.

OZIE POWELL ~ Powell was born in Georgia in 1915 and only had one year of schooling. He was considered to be a shy boy who had been working at a lumber camp prior to his Scottsboro arrest at the age of 16, and he did not know any of the other boys prior to their arrests.

After testifying at Haywood Patterson's trial in February of 1936, Powell was being transported in a car with fellow Scottsboro Boys Clarence Norris and Roy Wright. During the transport Powell got in an argument with a deputy and slashed his throat with a knife. Another deputy responded by shooting Powell in the head, which resulted in permanent brain damage. He was paroled in 1946 and died in Atlanta in 1974.

CHARLIE WEEMS ~ Weems was born in Georgia in 1912 and endured a difficult childhood. His mother, who had eight children, died when he was just four and he was one of just two siblings to survive to adulthood. His education lasted just through fifth grade when he went to work at a pharmacy in Atlanta. Upon his arrest, he was the oldest of the Scottsboro Boys at the age of 19.

After the trials, Weems ended up with a sentence of 105 years but after maintaining a clean record in prison he was paroled in 1943, after serving 12 years. He suffered permanent damage to his eyes after being tear gassed in the prison for reading Communist literature that had been sent to him, but he did move to Atlanta and get married after his release. He worked in a laundromat for a year before dying of tuberculosis.

ANDY WRIGHT ~ Andy Wright was born in Chattanooga and attended school through sixth grade when his father died. At that point he took a job with a local produce distributor to help support the family. Along with his brother Roy, Heywood Patterson and Eugene Williams, Wright boarded the train that fateful day after hearing that logging jobs on the Mississippi River might be available in Memphis. Unfortunately, the Mississippi River would not find a place in Wright's future.

He was 19 at the time of his arrest and while a 1937 *Time* magazine article referred to him as the best natured of the Scottsboro Boys, he was a bit of an enigma. His time during the ordeal was characterized by conflict with both the guards and the rest of the boys, so perhaps he was on his best behavior during the *Time* interview.

In January of 1944 he was paroled and later that year married. After driving a truck for two years, he violated his parole by leaving Alabama in 1946. He was in and out of jail in Alabama for the next four years before being freed for good in 1950.

In 1950 Wright moved to New York where, in 1951, he was once again arrested for rape in a somewhat twisted scenario where the accuser was the daughter of a woman he was dating. He was acquitted of that charge. He kept in touch with Clarence Norris and at one point in 1959 he had orchestrated a reunion with Norris and his younger brother Roy, but when Roy died, so did any plans of a reunion.

At that point Wright returned to Chattanooga to aide his ailing mother and there he died sometime in the 1960's. Indicative of how the Scottsboro Boys' notoriety continued to fade, the only confirmed fact from the last years of his life is that he was buried in an unmarked grave, beside the gravestone of his brother Roy, whose story we tell below.

CLARENCE NORRIS ~ Norris was one of eleven children born to sharecropper parents in Georgia in 1913. His education lasted only through second grade when he left school to work the cotton fields. After a stint working at a Goodyear plant, he began to ride the rails as a hobo looking for transient labor.

Norris was 18 when he was arrested at Scottsboro and by the time the initial wave of trials had played out in 1937, he was the only defendant with a death sentence still hanging over his head. In 1938 the governor of Alabama commuted that sentence to life in prison. Granted parole in 1944, he jumped that parole and headed for New York where he was caught and returned to Alabama. He was finally paroled for good in 1946.

It was Norris who led the most successful life of the boys after the Scottsboro saga. He was gainfully employed, got married, and raised a family. In 1976 Alabama Governor George Wallace invited him to the State House in Montgomery and granted him an official pardon. In 1979 he released his autobiography which was titled *The Last of the Scottsboro Boys*. As the title implies, he was the last survivor, passing away from Alzheimer's in January of 1989.

OLEN MONTGOMERY ~ Montgomery was born in Monroe, Georgia in 1914 and his education lasted through fifth grade. He was extremely nearsighted and virtually blind in one eye. Throughout the entire ordeal, Montgomery consistently stuck to his story that he was riding alone in a car near the end of a train during the entire time of the Black/White brawl and subsequent alleged rape.

By the time the whole travesty began to unravel in 1937, Montgomery was in the group of four that was first released. He had been 17 at the time and was on the train hoping to find work to buy a new pair of glasses. As semblances of sanity began to creep into the case, prosecutors agreed that there was no way he was guilty.

Montgomery aspired to a career in music or vaudeville after his release, but these aspirations never came to fruition. From the late-40's through 1960 he split time between New York and Georgia bouncing back and forth through various jobs and locations. He settled in Georgia where his drinking problem became more severe with time and he passed away in 1975.

EUGENE WILLIAMS ~ Williams was born in Tennessee in 1918 and it is known that he worked in Chattanooga as a dishwasher prior to boarding the Southern Railroad train with his friends, Andy & Roy Wright and Haywood Patterson in March of 1931 at the age of just 13. The aforementioned *Life* magazine article of 1937 cast a negative light upon Williams describing him as "a sullen, shifty mulatto who tries to impress interviewers with his piety."

Williams was also one of the first four released in July of 1937 based upon the fact that he was only 13 at the time of the incident. At that time, he went to St. Louis where he had family who hoped that his passion for religion would lead him to enroll in a Baptist seminary school. His future from this point on is the murkiest of all with there being no record whatsoever of what transpires after his return to St. Louis.

WILLIE ROBERSON - Roberson was born in 1915 in Columbus, Georgia and while things would only get worse, a lot of bad shit had already gone down for him before he was herded off the train and arrested in Scottsboro for the rapes of Victoria Price and Ruby Bates.

At the time of the arrest, Roberson was 17-years old and suffering from a case of syphilis so severe his genitals were covered with sores; he could only walk with the assistance of a cane, and he was nowhere near the scene of the alleged crime. These circumstances served to push him to the top of the list of details Price was clearly lying about. As such, Roberson was included amongst the group of four that were first pardoned by the state of Alabama.

After his release, Roberson lived and worked in New York City where he died of asthma in 1959.

ROY WRIGHT - Wright was born in Chattanooga in 1918 and had never left home before embarking upon the fateful Scottsboro train trip with his older brother Andy. Only 13 at the time of the arrests, Wright kept a bible with him at all times and frequently wrote home to his mother with a sample excerpt reading, "I am all lonely and thinking of you. I feel like I can eat some of your cooking, Mom."

Wright potentially could have had the most successful post-Scottsboro story of any of the boys, but alas it was not meant to be. After being one of the first four released in 1937, he married and also had a successful career, initially in the U.S. Army and later in the Merchant Marines. While on an extensive tour in 1959, Wright became convinced that his wife had been unfaithful to him.

Upon his return home, he shot and killed her before turning the gun upon himself. He was found dead with his bible by his side. He is buried in an unkept Chattanooga grave, but at least he does have a tombstone as opposed to his brother Andy, who was buried next to him in an unmarked grave as we described above.

ADDENDUM 2
SPORTS TIMELINE

Welcome to the Sports Addendum of our book. Here we have compiled a chronological overview of the most significant Black "Firsts" in the history of sports. Please forgive us for any perceived omissions. Anytime you tackle a project of this proportion there are borderline calls.

You can't include every accolade ever achieved as you reach a point where more becomes less. Before we give you our closest borderline example, please allow us to share the funniest "extreme" example we uncovered in our research. At one point we even found an article describing the first foul ball caught in the air by a Black man at Yankee Stadium! Interesting story, but way too obscure for inclusion here.

Next, we'll share with you our closest borderline call, while simultaneously revealing the fact that we are blatant cheaters. What do we mean by that? Our stealthy maneuver of including our close call here in the intro is that we've totally circumvented the fact that we didn't include it below. Not only that, we've elevated one of our favorite athletes from the status of not being mentioned at all, to being the very first guy mentioned in the timeline component of our book.

Who is the benefactor of our conniving conspiracy? That would be Yankee catcher Elston Howard who, in 1963, became the first Black player to win the American League's Most Valuable Player Award. Jackie Robinson had won the National League MVP in 1949 and that milestone is included in our timeline below. So the question facing us was, if a professional sport is divided into two separate but equal leagues and we've already mentioned the first overall winner, do we also include the first winner in the "other" league?

Our original answer was no, but as you've seen above, we managed to abide by our original decision while still taking care of our man, Elston Howard. With our ground rules established let's fire the starter's gun, kick off our countdown, and throw out the first pitch.

FIRST PROFESSIONAL ATHLETE

1872 ~ John W. "Bud" Fowler became the first professional Black athlete and baseball player, at the age of just 14, when he played for an all-White professional minor league team based out of New Castle, Pennsylvania in 1872. In 1878 Fowler became the first Black pitcher to defeat a major league team when his minor league Chelsea Picked Nine defeated the Boston Red Caps (now the Atlanta Braves) who were champions of the National League in 1877. (Note: We would like to hereby add "Chelsea Picked Nine" to our list of favorite baseball team names ever.)

FIRST PROFESSIONAL JOCKEY

1875 ~ Isaac Burns Murphy became the first Black American Thoroughbred horse racing jockey. He achieved his first win at the Clark Handicap in 1879 and he would also win the Kentucky Derby three times, in 1884, 1890 and 1891. He won 530 of his 1,538 starts, giving him a 34% win rate, the highest of all time.

Hall of Fame jockey Eddie Arcaro has said, "There is no chance that his record of winning will ever be surpassed." Murphy was the first inductee into the National Museum of Racing and Hall of Fame which was created in 1955 in Saratoga Springs, New York.

In 1967 his body was exhumed and reinterred at the entrance to the Kentucky Horse Park right next to Triple Crown winner Man o' War. Since 1995 the Isaac Murphy Award has been given to the North American jockey with the highest winning percentage.

FIRST MAJOR LEAGUE BASEBALL PLAYER

1879 ~ This one comes with a caveat because the guy only played one game. On June 21, 1879 William Edward White played one game for the Providence Grays of the National League. The team's regular first baseman suffered an injury and at that time White was the starting first baseman for the Brown University team which is the Ivy League college located in Providence. While details on the specifics of this are not very thoroughly documented, it seems that the Grays plucked White from the local college team as a one-game substitute. In the game, which the Grays won 5-3, White went 1 for 4 and scored a run.

FIRST "REGULAR" MAJOR LEAGUE BASEBALL PLAYER

1884 ~ The first African American to play major league baseball on a regular basis was Moses Fleetwood "Fleet" Walker who hit the big leagues on May 1, 1884. Starting as catcher for the Toledo Blue

Stockings, Fleet Walker played in the then-major league American Association. The 26-year-old hit a respectable .263 in 42 games. Despite the fact that catchers had begun wearing gloves in the late 1870's, Walker eschewed that luxury and caught barehanded.

Obviously Walker was a curiosity from a racial perspective. Take a look at this quote when Toledo played the Washington Nationals in a game in June. The *Washington Post* reported that Toledo's catcher "is a colored man, and no doubt many will attend the game to see our 'colored brother' in a new role." Toledo won the game and in the next day's paper Walker was said to have "played in fine style, catching star pitcher Tony Mullane."

Weldy Walker, Fleet's brother, joined the Blue Stockings in July as an outfielder. Of course history forewarns us that this is not about to become a groundswell of racial equality in American sports. The Toledo franchise did not compete in the American Association in 1885 and it would be 62 years later that the next Black would play major league baseball with the White guys.

FIRST PROFESSIONAL SPORTS TEAM

1885 ~ The first Black professional baseball team was formed in New York City in 1885 by a White promoter named Walter Cook, and they adopted the name of the Cuban Giants. The story on the name is interesting because there were no Cubans on the team. During that era, the manner in which a professional team would have made the money to pay its players was through barnstorming. The team would travel around looking for other teams to play with the goal being to draw enough paying customers to cover travel expenses and salaries.

During the winters of 1885-86 and 1886-87, the Giants barnstormed through Cuba, so that was half of the impetus for the nickname. The story on the other half is great. Cook decided that the Cuban Giants moniker could help attract fans so he conceived a unique shtick to facilitate that goal. The team developed a gibberish they would speak amongst themselves during the game which actually meant nothing, but was spoken in a manner that sounded like Spanish.

The Cuban Giants not only had a gimmick, they were good. In 1886, the team would win their first 40 games before losing to the St. Louis Browns who were a White major league team playing in the American League (currently the Baltimore Orioles franchise). They also defeated major league teams on multiple occasions in exhibition games. They were World Colored Champions of 1887 and 1888. The Cuban Giants were a dominant force in baseball until the team disbanded in 1915.

FIRST PROFESSIONAL SPORTS LEAGUE

1885 ~ On June 16th, the Southern League of Colored Base Ballists celebrated Opening Day of the first pro Black sports league. Despite the most super-cool retro name ever, the league dissolved in August.

FIRST PROFESSIONAL BOXING CHAMPION

1888 ~ Cool milestone here. This would be the year that the first Black athlete would ever win a world championship in any sport. Our winner would be George Dixon, a Canadian boxer who defeated Tommy "Spider" Kelly for the bantamweight title on May 10th of that year. After gaining a little weight, Dixon went up to the featherweight classification and won that world title in 1891.

Dixon's accomplishments are lauded in boxing history. *Ring Magazine* ranked him as the #1 featherweight of all time. He was inducted into the Canadian Sports Hall of Fame in 1955 and the Boxing Hall of Fame in 1990.

George Dixon has inadvertently provided us with an early opportunity to explain the terminology we will use to describe people of color in this timeline. This concept has undergone an interesting transition even within our lifetimes. Of course, the "N-word" has always been offensive. But the inoffensive parallel thereof has evolved from Negro to Colored to Black to African American. There are no official dates for these changes; it's not like there's a committee that decides when to change the names.

But even in looking at a few early entries in this series, we described Fleet Walker as African American and George Dixon as Black. If you think about it, the term Black is a more inclusive umbrella expression. There are people of color who are not American. Case in point, George Dixon would be, for the record, "African Canadian" which doesn't roll right off of anybody's tongue. So, we're not going to get hung up on the terminology but focus our attention on the storytelling.

FIRST HORSE OWNER TO WIN KENTUCKY DERBY

1891 ~ The appropriately-named Jacobin Stables became the first Black to co-own a horse that won the Kentucky Derby. That horse, named Kingman, was ridden by the aforementioned Black jockey Isaac Murphy.

FIRST COLLEGE ALL-AMERICAN FOOTBALL PLAYER

1892 ~ William H. Lewis, from Harvard University, became the first Black named to a college football all-America team. Lewis went on to become a pioneer with multiple accomplishments in the fields of law and politics.

FIRST CYCLING CHAMPION

1899 ~ It's a good thing that we just went through that whole terminology discussion a few entries above. With that in mind, if you take Black Canadians out of the mix, the first African American to achieve a world championship in any sport was Marshall Walter "Major" Taylor. From August 9-11, 1899, Taylor competed in and won the gold medal at the Track Cycling World Championships in Montreal. He was also the U.S. national sprint champion in 1899 and 1900.

FIRST AMERICAN BOXING CHAMPION

1902 ~ Joe Gans became the first Black American boxing champion when he won the lightweight title, which he held from 1902-1908. Nicknamed the "Old Master," *Ring* magazine named him the Greatest Lightweight Boxer of All-Time and he was inducted into the International Boxing Hall of Fame in 1990.

FIRST PROFESSIONAL BASKETBALL PLAYER

1902 ~ The distinction of being the first Black professional basketball player goes to Harry Lew who played in the New England Professional Basketball League. Harry's hoop history began in 1898 when he joined his local YMCA "Young Employed Boys" basketball team which won the Massachusetts State Championship four years in a row.

Riding that wave of success, he joined the city of Lowell's "Pawtucketville Athletic Club," a professional team competing in the aforementioned NEPBL. What was Harry Lew's forte? In the era before which the practice had become illegal, Lew was considered the best double dribbler in the league; apparently he had a great ability to start and stop. Looking almost a half a century ahead, we'll highlight the first Black NBA player when we get to 1948.

Basketball was a much different game at the turn of the 20th century, and we'll let Harry Lew put it in his own words. About his game, Lew stated in a later interview, "Of course we had no backboards in those days, and everything had to go in clean. Naturally there was no rebounding, and after a shot there was a brawl to get the ball. There were no out-of-bounds markers. We had a fence around the court with nets hanging from the ceilings. The ball was always in play and you were guarded from the moment you touched it. Hardly had time to breathe, let alone think about what you were going to do with the ball."

Lew also had a very interesting family history in the Massachusetts area. His great-great grandfather, Barzillai Lew, who was not a slave, fought in the American Revolution and there is a record of him serving as a fifer at the Battle of Bunker Hill on June 17, 1775. Jazz musician Duke Ellington even wrote a song about him where he slightly altered the name to "Barzillai Lou."

His great-great-aunt, Lucy Lew and her husband Thomas Dalton were civil rights activists and the home of his grandparents, Adrastus and Elizabeth Lew, was a station on the Underground Railroad. Finally, his father William Lew was a delegate to the 1891 Equal Rights Convention which was held in Boston, Massachusetts. Quite the family legacy.

FIRST PROFESSIONAL FOOTBALL PLAYER

1902 ~ Playing for the Shelby Blues of the Ohio League, Charles Follis became the first Black professional football player. Known as "The Black Cyclone," Follis played for Shelby from 1902-1906. Their best year was 1904 when Follis starred as a running back on a team that went 8-1-1 and finished in second place in the Ohio League. An injury on Thanksgiving Day 1906 ended Follis' career.

FIRST BASEBALL PERFECT GAME PITCHED

1903 ~ Dan McClellan became the first Black pitcher to throw a perfect game as his Cuban X-Giants defeated the Penn Park Athletic Club of York by a score of 5-0.

FIRST OLYMPIC MEDAL WINNER

1904 ~ The modern Olympics were initiated in 1896 with the first games being held in Athens, Greece, paying tribute to the ancient Olympics. The 1900 games were held in Paris and it would be the 1904 games in St. Louis where the first Black would win a medal.

George Poage was a student athlete at the University of Wisconsin where he became the first Black to win individual Big Ten track championships, doing so in multiple events in June of 1904. He went on to compete in the Olympics that July and won the bronze in both the 200-yard and 400-yard hurdles.

FIRST OLYMPIC GOLD MEDAL

1908 ~ This accolade was achieved by John Baxtor Taylor at the 1908 summer games in London where he ran the third leg of the men's medley relay which took home the gold. Taylor had been a talented Ivy League student and athlete at Penn, and had graduated from Penn's School of Veterinary Medicine. Unfortunately, Taylor did not have much time to enjoy his gold medal or veterinary degree. He died of typhoid fever just five months after the Olympics in December of 1908.

FIRST ROSE BOWL APPEARANCE

1916 ~ This is the first of three Fritz Pollard shout-outs in this timeline. Back in the era when Ivy League schools could go to the Rose Bowl, Brown University was the team invited from the east to take on Washington State in 1916. Pollard had become the first Black player for Brown that year, and followed that up by becoming the first Black to play in the Rose Bowl. Washington State won the game 14-0, after which Pollard would go on to a successful career playing and coaching professional football. See the 1920 entry below.

FIRST WOMAN TO WIN A MAJOR SPORTS TITLE

1917 ~ Tennis would be the sport to see the first Black woman win a major sports title. In 1917 when the new American Tennis Association held its first tournament, it was won by Lucy Diggs Slowe. She would go on to add a few more non-sports firsts to her résumé. She was the first Black woman to serve as a college dean which she did at Howard University, and she formed the first Black sorority Alpha Kappa Alpha, also at Howard.

FIRST SUCCESSFUL BASEBALL LEAGUE

1920 ~ The first successful Black league, the National Negro Baseball League, was formed by Rube Foster, a former pitcher. The league's original run would last through 1931 when it folded. After just one year off, the National Negro Baseball League would reform and operate from 1933-1948.

FIRST PLAYERS IN THE NFL

1920 ~ When the NFL formed in 1920 there were two Black players in the league, Fritz Pollard of the Akron Pros and Bobby Marshall of the Rock Island Independents. The early NFL was such a different animal than the current version, it's actually a bit difficult to wrap your brain around it. The league was essentially just a loose collection of teams from around the country. There was no set schedule and you could play anyone you wanted to. There were no playoffs. Some people played for more than one team. Things were really all over the place.

That being said, the first Black NFL players need to be viewed in a different context than Jackie Robinson breaking the color barrier in baseball. In Robinson's case the league already existed and he was a new man joining a new team. In the case of Pollard and Marshall, they were playing for the same team in 1920 that they'd played for in 1919; their team had just joined a league. By 1933 all Blacks would be out of the NFL, so we will have a Jackie Robinson-type moment coming up in 1946 when Blacks rejoin the league.

FIRST NFL COACH

1921 ~ We just can't get enough of our man Fritz. In 1921 the Akron Pros appointed Pollard to be their player/coach making him the first Black coach in NFL history. Pollard, along with all nine of the league's Black players, were purged from the NFL after the 1926 season and there would not be another Black NFL head coach until 1989. There were a few random appearances of Black players in NFL games until 1933 when the league became fully segregated.

FIRST ICONIC BASKETBALL TEAM FOUNDED

1923 ~ The New York Renaissance basketball team was organized by Bob Douglas who also served as their coach. The "Rens," as they were called, would collectively come to be the first Black inductees into the Basketball Hall of Fame.

FIRST INDIVIDUAL OLYMPIC GOLD MEDAL

1924 ~ At the 1924 Summer Olympics in Paris, DeHart Hubbard became the first Black to win an individual gold medal, doing so in the long jump event. He subsequently set a world record in the long jump in 1925, and in 1926 he tied the world record in the 100-yard dash.

FIRST NEGRO LEAGUE WORLD SERIES

1924 ~ In baseball, the first organized Black league was the Negro National League (NNL) which formed in 1920. When the Eastern Colored League (ECL) formed in 1923, a positive ramification of that scenario was that the two Black leagues could stage their own World Series like the White leagues did. That goal came to fruition in 1924.

The first Colored World Series pitted the Kansas City Monarchs of the NNL against the Hilldale Club of the ECL. For the record, Hilldale is just west of Philadelphia. The series was played in a best of nine format and Kansas City won the 1924 event 5 games to 4. The 1925 series saw a rematch of the same two clubs with Hilldale avenging the previous season's loss, winning 5 games to 1. The original Colored World Series ran from 1923-1927 when the ECL folded.

After a 15-year hiatus the Colored World Series was revived from 1942-1948 with the formation of the Negro American League. After Jackie Robinson broke the color barrier in 1947, the purpose of the Negro Leagues was diminished. As Blacks came to achieve full acceptance into previously White Major League Baseball, the Negro League teams gradually folded and ceased operations.

FIRST SPORTSCASTER

1929 ~ It was at radio station WNJR in Newark, New Jersey that Sherman "Jocko" Maxwell began his sportscasting career with a 5-minute sports newsreel. His multifaceted career would span the next four decades. In terms of broadcasting, Maxwell covered Negro League baseball and had a variety of interview and sports shows on various radio stations in the New York City area. During the 1950's and 1960's he also wrote articles about Black athletes with Negro League baseball providing his primary point of emphasis.

FIRST ASSOCIATED PRESS ATHLETE OF THE YEAR

1935 ~ Joe Louis, nicknamed the "Brown Bomber," actually won the Associated Press Athlete of the Year even before he won the heavyweight title. As he worked his way toward his first title fight, his reputation of modesty and humility had enabled him to develop a considerable fan base. During the pre-WW II era, with anti-Hitler sentiment running high, Louis also benefitted from the fact that his primary opponent in the early part of his career was the German Max Schmeling who was viewed as a puppet of the Hitler regime.

After losing his first fight to Schmeling in 1936, Louis won the championship in 1937 and also defeated Schmeling in their high-profile rematch. Joe Louis would reign as heavyweight champion from 1937-1949, successfully defending his championship 25 times. No heavyweight ever retained the title for a longer period of time and he is in the discussion as to who was the greatest fighter of all time.

His social impact was also significant. No Black person before him had ever achieved the nationwide hero worship that was duly afforded to Joe Louis. The "Brown Bomber" left a legacy to be loved.

FIRST TO WIN FOUR GOLD MEDALS AT THE OLYMPICS

1936 ~ It was Hitler's greatest nightmare. Amidst spreading his myth of Aryan German supremacy, during the 1936 Summer Olympics at Berlin presided over by Hitler, the most stellar accomplishments of the games were achieved by a Black American. Jesse Owens won four gold medals, those being for the 100- and 200-meter dashes, the long jump and the 4×100-meter relay.

After the first few days of the games when it was noticed that Hitler was shaking only the hands of the White gold medal winners, the International Olympic Committee issued a dictum. Hitler was to shake the hands of all winners, or no winners at all. Hitler opted to keep his hands in his pockets for the rest of the games.

We'll share one other Jesse Owens story. At the 1935 Big Ten track meet held at the University of Michigan, Owens set three world records and tied another in a short span of time which has been referred to as "the greatest 45 minutes ever in sports."

In the ESPN SportsCentury Greatest Athletes list of the Top 100 athletes of the 20th century, Jesse Owens came in at #6; Hitler did not make the list.

FIRST WOMAN IN THE OLYMPICS

1936 ~ Tidye Pickett became the first Black woman to compete in the Olympics when she qualified for the 80-meter hurdles. She was eliminated in the semi-final heat.

FIRST POST-WORLD WAR II NFL PLAYER

1946 ~ As covered earlier in this timeline, when the NFL formed in 1920 there were two Black players. Nine Blacks had played in the league by the time all rosters were purged of Blacks in 1926. Between that date and 1933 there were a few sporadic appearances by Blacks with total segregation becoming the policy in that year. From 1933-1945 no Blacks played in the NFL.

That policy was finally put aside in 1946 when running back Kenny Washington joined the Los Angeles Rams. There were a few factors at play in the league decision to allow Washington's signing. The Rams had just moved to LA from Cleveland and the team would be playing their home games at the Coliseum which was a publicly owned venue. Some made the argument that since both Black and White tax dollars had been used to construct the building, the team should be integrated. Sometimes people just need an excuse to do the right thing.

An irony of Kenny Washington's sports career is that he was a teammate of Jackie Robinson on both the baseball and football teams at UCLA. Some people actually thought Washington was a better baseball player than Robinson. One thought that occurred to us is what the storyline of these two men shows about the relative popularity of baseball and football in the late 1940's.

Washington actually broke the color barrier one year before Robinson but compare their legacies. Jackie Robinson has his number 42 retired across all of baseball, except of course on Jackie Robinson Day, when his number is worn by literally every player on every team. Kenny Washington on the other hand, is a virtual unknown.

FIRST BASKETBALL ALL-AMERICAN ~ OLYMPIAN ~ NBA ALL-STAR

1947 ~ The first Black man to be named a college first team All-American basketball player was Donald Barksdale who played for UCLA. He was also the first Black to play on the U.S. Olympic basketball team in 1948 and the NBA All-Star team in 1953. Barksdale was inducted into the Basketball Hall of Fame in 2012.

FIRST MODERN-ERA MAJOR LEAGUE BASEBALL PLAYER

1947 ~ When Brooklyn Dodgers owner Branch Rickey decided it was time for baseball to break the color barrier, he knew he needed a man with command of the two T's. What would those T's be? Talent and temperament. After graduating from UCLA in 1941, Jackie Robinson spent the next four years in the Army during WW II. After the war, Robinson signed a contract with the Negro League Kansas City Monarchs.

Clearly demonstrating that he still had his baseball talents intact, Robinson was called in on August 28, 1945 for a three-hour interview with Branch Rickey. The goal of the interview was for Rickey to determine if Robinson would be able to withstand the pressure of the racial prejudice he would be destined to face.

Rickey asked Robinson if he could face the racial taunts without taking the bait and reacting with anger. There was a reason the interview took three hours because there were back and forth opinions that needed to be exchanged. When initially asked about controlling his anger, Robinson was aghast and replied, "Are you looking for a Negro who is afraid to fight back?"

"No," Rickey replied, "I'm looking for a Negro with guts enough not to fight back." The two men came to a meeting of the minds and, as the future played out, Robinson did an incredible job of carrying himself with grace and dignity throughout his major league career with the Dodgers.

Robinson played the 1946 season for the Dodgers AAA affiliate, the Montreal Royals, which served the dual purpose of giving him a year to hone his skills for the majors while also serving notice to the baseball world that, like it or not, the Dodgers AAA star was destined to make his major league debut the following year.

In that initial 1947 season, Jackie Robinson won the Rookie of the Year award. During his illustrious 10-year career he played in six All-Star Games, six World Series, and became the first Black player ever to win the Most Valuable Player award in 1949.

In 1962 Robinson was elected into the Baseball Hall of Fame and in 2004 baseball established Jackie Robinson Day. His number 42 was retired across all of baseball except for every April 15. On that day, every player in Major League Baseball wears #42 in honor of Jackie Robinson.

FIRST AMERICAN LEAGUE PLAYER

1947 ~ On July 5th, Larry Doby became the first Black to play in an American League game when he pinch hit for the Cleveland Indians against the Chicago White Sox. Doby and teammate Satchel Paige were the first Blacks to play in, as well as win, the World Series with the Indians in 1948. He finished second in the American League MVP voting in 1954 when he led the league in home runs and RBI's.

FIRST MAJOR LEAGUE PITCHER

1947 ~ Later in 1947, the Dodgers added pitcher Dan Bankhead to their roster and on August 26th he became the first Black to pitch in a Major League game and also the first to hit a home run in his first at bat!

FIRST MAJOR LEAGUE CATCHER

1948 ~ The next season Roy Campanella became the first Black Major League catcher, also playing for the Brooklyn Dodgers.

FIRST WOMAN OLYMPIC GOLD MEDAL WINNER

1948 ~ Alice Coachman was a track and field athlete who totally dominated her sport for a decade beginning around 1940 before becoming the first Black woman to win an Olympic gold medal, doing so in the 1948 London games in the high jump event. After returning to the United States following the Olympics, Coachman found herself to be a somewhat reluctant celebrity.

She was invited to meetings with President Harry Truman and former First Lady Eleanor Roosevelt. Renowned jazz musician Count Basie threw her a personal party and she was honored with parades from Atlanta to Albany. Added to her list of "firsts" was that she became the first Black to become a spokesperson for a major company when Coca-Cola signed her in 1952.

In the category of "what could have been" Coachman's career résumé is absolutely compromised by the fact that the peak of her athletic prowess precisely coincided with WW II. During an era, from 1939 through 1948, when she won the AAU high jump championship for ten years straight, the Olympics were canceled in 1940 and 1944.

Track and field is one of those sports where, if somebody is going to get famous, it's probably going to be through the Olympics and Alice Coachman was deprived of the best opportunities during the prime of her career. She also excelled in multiple other track and field events and had those two cancelled Olympics actually occurred, she may have become the most decorated female Olympic athlete in history.

FIRST TO DESIGN AND CONSTRUCT A GOLF COURSE

1948 ~ Okay let's head for the links and play some of that game where you yell fore, shoot six, and write down five. Bill Powell was an entrepreneur who became the first Black to design, construct and own a golf course. The course he created, which is still located in East Canton, Ohio, is called the Clearview Golf Club.

Powell played golf in high school and college in the Canton area before serving in the Air Force during WW II. After returning to the states, Powell sought to continue his passion for golf but found himself banned from the segregated golf courses. At that point he decided to build his own, but again segregation kicked in causing a needed bank loan to be rejected. Finally, with the financial support of two Black doctors and his brother, Powell bought an 80-acre farm in East Canton, Ohio in 1946.

Then the work began. With the help of his wife Marcella, the Powells began the job of landscaping their course. It was a labor of love which resulted in the opening of a fully integrated golf course in 1948. Three decades later in 1978, the course was expanded to 18 holes. The course, which is still operating today, was designated as a national historic site in 2001. We'll close with the one quote that Bill Powell was most noted for, "The only color that matters is the color of the greens."

FIRST MAJOR LEAGUE ALL-STARS

1948 ~ Brooklyn Dodgers Jackie Robinson, Roy Campanella and Don Newcombe became the first Blacks to play in the Major League All-Star Game.

FIRST NBA PLAYER

1950 ~ When the NBA formed in 1950 there were three Black players on different teams which were in the league. So it was actually because of the order in which the teams' season openers fell that Earl Lloyd of the Washington Capitols became the first Black to play in an NBA game. The game was played on Halloween night, October 31, 1950 at the Edgerton Park Arena, the home of the Rochester Royals. Lloyd would go on to play 560 games in a nine-year NBA career.

The other two Blacks to appear on season-opening rosters and play in the NBA that year were Charles Henry Cooper (Boston Celtics) and Nat "Sweetwater" Clifton (New York Knicks).

FIRST MAJOR LEAGUE HOME RUN LEADER

1952 ~ The Cleveland Indians' Larry Doby became the first Black to lead his league in home runs with 32 round-trippers topping the American League.

FIRST NBA ALL-STAR

1953 ~ Don Barksdale became the first Black to play in the NBA All-Star Game, representing the Baltimore Bullets (currently the Washington Wizards franchise).

FIRST NASCAR DRIVER

1953 ~ Because of the Good Old Boy Mentality of the Deep South where NASCAR was originally most popular, breaking into that sport bore additional challenges. The first Black to attain his NASCAR license was Wendell Scott in 1953. He also became the first Black driver to win a NASCAR race, doing so at Speedway Park in Jacksonville, Florida on December 1, 1963. Scott fought the racism to which he was exposed in admirable fashion achieving a great deal of respect amongst his fellow racers, as well as legions of fans, both Black and White. He was inducted into the NASCAR Hall of Fame in 2015.

FIRST WIMBLEDON TENNIS CHAMPION

1953 ~ Althea Gibson became the first Black to win a Wimbledon title when she captured the doubles championship, playing with Brit Angela Buxton. Note the follow-up successes in her 1957 entry.

FIRST POST-WORLD WAR II NFL QUARTERBACK

1953 ~ Constituting perhaps the most appropriate name on the list, the first Black quarterback of the modern era was the Chicago Bears' Willie Thrower.

FIRST MAJOR LEAGUE NO-HITTER

1955 ~ The Chicago Cubs' Sam Jones became the first Black pitcher to throw a no-hitter in a Major League baseball game.

FIRST WOMAN TO WIN A GRAND SLAM TENNIS TOURNAMENT

1956 ~ Althea Gibson was one of the first women to break the color barrier in international tennis and in 1956 she won her first Grand Slam tournament, taking the French Open. In 1957 she added Wimbledon and the U.S. Open to her Grand Slam win list, and she would go on to win 11 Grand Slam tournaments in all. She was a great all-around athlete who also competed on the Women's Professional Golf Tour.

Here are some thoughts on Gibson from tennis star Venus Williams, "I am honored to have followed in such great footsteps," she wrote. "Her accomplishments set the stage for my success, and through players like myself and Serena and many others to come, her legacy will live on."

FIRST BASEBALL PITCHER TO WIN THE MVP & CY YOUNG AWARDS

1957 ~ Don Newcombe was a star pitcher whose baseball career spanned from 1949-1960, primarily with the Brooklyn Dodgers. His résumé contains an impressive list of firsts. He was the first Black pitcher to start a World Series game (1949), the first to win 20 games in a season (1951) and the first to win the Rookie of the Year, Most Valuable Player, and Cy Young Awards during his career. Those last two accolades were both achieved in 1957.

FIRST FEMALE ATHLETE OF THE YEAR

1957 ~ As mentioned above, Althea Gibson won both Wimbledon and the U.S. Open in 1957. These accomplishments enabled her to become the first Black woman to win the Associated Press Female Athlete of the Year. Adding to her accolades, Gibson won Wimbledon and the U.S. open again in 1958 when she was also named the Associated Press Female Athlete of the Year for a second consecutive year.

"She is one of the greatest players who ever lived," said Bob Ryland, first Black professional tennis player and former coach of Venus and Serena Williams. See Ryland entry below.

FIRST MALE PRO TENNIS PLAYER

1958 ~ In March of 1958 Bob Ryland became the first professional Black male tennis player when he competed in the World Pro Championships in Cleveland. Ryland went on to have an interesting tennis career in teaching as well as coaching. In the early 1960's when he was based in Washington, DC, he actually gave tennis lessons to John F. and Bobby Kennedy. In 1963 he moved to New York City and while there instructed an impressive list of celebrities including Eartha Kitt, Mike Wallace, Tony Bennett, Bill Cosby, Barbra Streisand and Dustin Hoffman.

FIRST WOMAN TO WIN THREE GOLDS AT ONE OLYMPICS

1960 ~ Wilma Rudolph made her first big sports splash at the 1956 Olympics at Melbourne, Australia where she competed in the 200-

meter dash and won the bronze in the 4 × 100-meter relay. Four years later in Rome she won Olympic gold in the 100-meter and 200-meter dashes and the 4 x 100-meter relay. She was one of a handful of Black athletes who became icons after competing in the 1960 Olympics with others including Cassius Clay (Muhammad Ali), Rafer Johnson and Oscar Robinson.

FIRST TO HIT FOUR HOME RUNS IN A GAME

1961 ~ On April 30 Willie Mays became the first Black to hit four home runs in a single game. Nicknamed "The Say Hey Kid," Willie Mays spent most of his 22-year career with the New York/San Francisco Giants, before finishing his career with the New York Mets. He retired in 1973 as the second most prolific home run hitter in history and was inducted into the Hall of Fame in 1979. *The Sporting News* "List of the 100 Greatest Baseball Players" placed Mays as #2, behind only Babe Ruth.

FIRST HEISMAN TROPHY WINNER

1961 ~ The Ernie Davis story is one of the most tragic in sports. After a stellar college career at Syracuse, Davis won the Heisman Trophy and was the #1 pick in the NFL draft. One football tradition in place at that time was the College All-Star Game where the best senior players would play an exhibition game against the reigning NFL champions. Davis was in Chicago during the summer of 1962 preparing to play in that game against the Green Bay Packers when he woke up one morning with a swollen neck which was eventually diagnosed as leukemia. Ernie Davis died on May 18, 1963 without ever having played a professional game.

FIRST TO JOIN THE PGA TOUR

1961 ~ The first Black to achieve major success in the sport of golf was Charlie Sifford who joined the PGA Tour in 1961. His tour victories included the Greater Hartford Open in 1967 and the Los Angeles Open in 1969. After moving on to the Seniors Tour, he won the PGA Seniors Championship in 1975. Lee Trevino once referred to Sifford as the "Jackie Robinson of golf," and Tiger Woods also acknowledged that "Charlie Sifford paved the road to my career." Sifford was inducted into the Golf Hall of Fame in 2004.

FIRST TO SCORE 100 POINTS IN AN NBA GAME

1962 ~ On March 2, Wilt Chamberlain scored 100 points leading his Philadelphia Warriors to a 169-147 victory over the New York Knicks in a game played at the Hershey Sports Arena. It's a record that still stands with the #2 performance being Kobe Bryant's 81-point game. Chamberlain led the league in rebounding 11 times and scoring 7 times. We're still looking for challengers to take on his claim of having slept with 20,000 women.

FIRST BASEBALL HALL OF FAMER

1962 ~ Jackie Robinson became the first Black inducted into the Baseball Hall of Fame.

FIRST BASKETBALL HALL OF FAME INDUCTION

1963 ~ The New York Renaissance was inducted into the Basketball Hall of Fame as a team. Here's their story. The "Rens," as they were called, were an all-Black team organized and coached by Bob Douglas which played its home games at the Renaissance Casino and Ballroom which was located at 138th Street and Seventh Avenue in Harlem. Between 1923 and 1949 the team compiled an overall record of 2,588 wins and just 539 losses. In 1932-33 the Rens compiled a record of 120-8 including an all-time pro record of winning 88 games in a row.

FIRST MAJOR LEAGUE BASEBALL COACH

1963 ~ Buck O'Neil was a first baseman for the Negro League's Kansas City Monarchs. He also managed that team and in 1963 became the first Black Major League Baseball coach for the Chicago Cubs. In his later years he shone as a charismatic and articulate spokesman for the Negro Leagues and was one of the driving forces in establishing the Negro Leagues Baseball Museum in Kansas City.

FIRST GOLFER IN THE LPGA

1963 ~ If you've missed Althea Gibson since we left her back in the world of tennis in our 1957 timeline milestone, good news... Althea is back. In 1963, at the age of 36, she became the first Black member of the Ladies Professional Golf Association (LPGA). Between 1963 and 1977 she played in 171 events. The brilliance of her golf career, however, was not based upon her results. It was her goal to break new barriers, a goal which she certainly achieved.

Gibson's best finish was a second-place tie at the Buick Open in Columbus, Ohio in 1970. What was her take for that #2 finish? She made $3,633. Over the course of her 14-year golf career, she earned a grand total of $19,250 or, you do the math, a little over a thousand dollars a year. She was able to pursue her passion and cause with sponsorship deals and the support of her family.

"If I made it, it's half because I was game enough to take a lot of punishment along the way and half because there were a lot of people who cared enough to help me," she wrote in her autobiography *I Always Wanted to Be Somebody.*

FIRST WORLD SERIES MVP

1964 ~ Bob Gibson was one of the greatest baseball pitchers of all time, spending his entire career from 1959-1975 with the St. Louis Cardinals. He became the first Black player to win the World Series MVP when the Cardinals defeated the Yankees in 1964. He again won that honor when the Cardinals defeated the Red Sox in 1967. In 1968 he won both the MVP and Cy Young Awards in the National League. Bob Gibson was elected into the Baseball Hall of Fame in 1981.

FIRST TO PLAY IN NFL PRO BOWL EVERY YEAR OF HIS CAREER

1965 ~ When Jim Brown retired from the Cleveland Browns, he ended a career where he became the first (and still the only) NFL player to be invited to the NFL Pro Bowl (all-star game) every year of his career. In 8 out of his 9 seasons he was the NFL's leading rusher. *The Sporting News* named him the "Greatest Professional Football Player Ever."

FIRST NCAA BASKETBALL CHAMPS WITH ALL BLACK STARTERS

1966 ~ It was March 19, 1966 when the underdog Texas Western Miners upset powerhouse Kentucky to become the first team to win the NCAA college basketball championship with an all-Black starting lineup. You may be wondering how this college, Texas Western, won a national championship and then became totally unknown. Well, they didn't actually; they just changed their name. It's now the University of Texas at El Paso (UTEP). The 1966 team, as well as its coach Don Haskins, has been inducted into the Basketball Hall of Fame.

FIRST UMPIRE IN MAJOR LEAGUE BASEBALL

1966 ~ On April 11, Opening Day of the '66 season, Emmett Ashford became the first Black MLB umpire as the Cleveland Indians defeated the Washington Senators 5-2.

FIRST BASEBALL TRIPLE CROWN

1966 ~ The "Triple Crown" is a term of significance in both baseball and horse racing. But since our series is focusing solely on Black human athletes, and totally ignores the color of the horses, we're clearly headed to the baseball diamond for this one. Frank Robinson was one of the great baseball players of all time and we will share a few of his accomplishments in this component, in addition to the fact that he became the first Black to win baseball's Triple Crown. Playing for the Baltimore Orioles in 1966 he led the American League in home runs, RBI's and batting average.

Robinson split most of his brilliant career between the Cincinnati Reds and Baltimore Orioles. After winning the National League MVP with the Reds in 1961, his 1966 MVP with the Orioles made him the first player ever to win that award in both leagues. A 14-time all-star, Robinson retired as the fourth-most prolific home run hitter behind only Hank Aaron, Babe Ruth and Willie Mays. Look forward to his upcoming appearances in our timeline as first Black manager and first Black to have his number retired for three different organizations.

FIRST NFL ANNOUNCER ON NATIONAL BROADCAST

1966 ~ Lowell Perry became the first Black announcer on a nationally telecast NFL football game. Perry had previously played football in college at the University of Michigan and professionally for the Pittsburgh Steelers. He was a two-way player who was a safety on defense, an end on offense and also a kick returner. Perry was hired by CBS to provide color commentary on Pittsburgh Steelers games.

FIRST NBA HEAD COACH

1966 ~ Mentally, as well as physically, Bill Russell was a basketball machine. When he became the NBA's first Black head coach in 1966, he was still one of the league's best players. Russell would be one of the last men to serve in the role of player/coach and he would be the last to ever win an NBA championship in that capacity.

Winning was in his bloodstream. He won two NCAA championships with the University of San Francisco Dons in 1955 and 1956, also winning an Olympic gold medal in that latter year. Then he went on to the NBA where he was the centerpiece of a Boston Celtic dynasty that won 11 championships in 13 years. He was inducted into the Basketball Hall of Fame in 1975. In 2011, Barack Obama awarded Russell the Presidential Medal of Freedom for his accomplishments on the court and in the civil rights movement.

FIRST PRO FOOTBALL HALL OF FAME INDUCTEE

1967 ~ Emlen "The Gremlin" Tunnell, who played defensive back for the New York Giants and Green Bay Packers became the first Black inducted into the Pro Football Hall of Fame. As a side note, he was also the first HOF inductee, of any race, who played only defense.

FIRST GRAND SLAM TENNIS WINNER

1968 ~ On September 9, 1968 Arthur Ashe became the first Black man to win a Grand Slam tennis tournament when he captured the U.S. Open in New York City. He was also the first Black selected to the U.S. Davis Cup team and also the only Black to win three of the four Grand Slam events, eventually adding Wimbledon and the Australian Open to his résumé. His ATP ranking reached as high as #2 in 1976.

Tragically Ashe's legacy would become double-edged when he contracted AIDS during heart surgery in 1983. His battle with the disease prompted him to found the Arthur Ashe Foundation for the Defeat of AIDS and he also established the Arthur Ashe Institute for Urban Health before his death from AIDS-related pneumonia in 1993. He was awarded the Presidential Medal of Honor for both his work on the court and in the community.

FIRST OLYMPIC MEDAL CEREMONY PROTEST

1968 ~ This occurred during a medal ceremony in the Olympic Stadium in Mexico City on October 16, 1968 when Tommie Smith and John Carlos had come in first and third in the 200-meter dash. During the playing of the national anthem, each raised a black-gloved fist in what has certainly become one of the more iconic moments in Olympic history.

A couple interesting side stories… Both men, along with Australian silver-medal winner Peter Norman, wore human rights badges on their jackets. The Australian also joined the Smith/Carlos initiative with another contribution. While the Americans had planned a double right-handed-glove salute, John Carlos discovered upon approaching the medal stand that he had forgotten his gloves. It was Norman who suggested that Smith and Carlos share the one pair of gloves they had and that would be the explanation behind why the two American men sported gloves on opposite hands.

FIRST STARTING PROFESSIONAL QUARTERBACK

1968 ~ During his rookie season, the Denver Broncos had planned for Marlin Briscoe to play cornerback but ironically those first two syllables shifted from "corner" to "quarter." As the season unfolded, Briscoe came to find himself surprisingly cast in the role of being the first Black starting quarterback in pro football history. Injuries and inconsistent quarterback play had gotten the Broncos off to a rough start and they were willing to take a gamble. Briscoe had played quarterback in college at Omaha, so he was inserted as an emergency starter. And it worked, at least for a little while.

After an 0-3 start, the Broncos rallied to win four of their next five games with Briscoe starting at QB. Things, however, went downhill after that as Denver finished with a 5-9 record. Briscoe was informed that he would not be starting at QB the following year, and during the off-season he was traded to the Buffalo Bills. Marlin Briscoe never played quarterback again, but did go on to enjoy a successful pro career as a receiver. He led the Bills in receptions during his first three years with the team.

FIRST TO WIN ALL THREE NBA MVP'S IN A SINGLE YEAR

1970 ~ In any given season there are three MVP awards given out by the National Baseball Association. They are, in order, for the All-Star Game, the regular season, and the NBA finals. During the 1969-70 season New York Knicks star Willis Reed became the first Black player to win all three of those awards. Reed spent his entire 11-year career with the Knicks, was inducted into the Basketball Hall of Fame in 1982, and was voted one of the "50 Greatest Players in NBA History" in 1996.

FIRST FEMALE JOCKEY

1971 ~ Cheryl White became the first Black woman jockey in the U.S. She would come in 11th in her first race in June of 1971 but notched her first victory on September 3rd of that same year. She would go on to a stellar career in which she had 226 wins while earning $762,624.

FIRST INDIVIDUAL INDUCTED INTO BASKETBALL HALL OF FAME

1972 ~ Bob Douglas, who organized and coached the New York Renaissance basketball team became the first individual Black to be inducted into the Basketball Hall of Fame. The "Rens," as a team, had been inducted in 1963.

FIRST TO BREAK MAJOR LEAGUE BASEBALL CAREER HOME RUN RECORD

1974 ~ It was April 8, 1974 when a crowd of 53,775 assembled at Atlanta-Fulton County Stadium hoping to witness the breaking of the most sacrosanct record in sports history. Their hopes of seeing Hank Aaron break Babe Ruth's home run record were realized when Aaron launched career-home run #714 into the bleachers.

He ended his career with 755 home runs and while that was certainly the loudest part of his legacy, Hank Aaron had a lot of other achievements to keep that one company. He retired with, and still holds, the career record for most RBI's with 2,297. He also leads the majors in career extra base hits and total bases and he ranks in the Top 5 for hits and runs.

In his 23 seasons he made the All-Star team 24 times, a seeming numerical anomaly made possible by the fact that from 1959-1962 Major League Baseball played two All-Star games per year. On its list of the "100 Greatest Baseball Players" *The Sporting News* ranked Aaron fifth, and in 1982 he was inducted into the Baseball Hall of Fame in his first year of eligibility.

FIRST MANAGER IN BASEBALL

1975 ~ By the early 1970's baseball great Frank Robinson had let it be known that he aspired to be the first Black manager in Major League Baseball. That opportunity arose for him when the Cleveland Indians named him player/manager in 1975. It was just a minor gamble on the Indians part, as the franchise had been saddled in mediocrity for decades.

For better or worse, Robinson was able to perpetuate that pattern. In 2+ seasons in Cleveland he compiled an overall record of 166-169 and he was fired on June 19, 1977 after the Indians started 26-31. The experience did prepare him for three managerial stints in the future.

He managed the San Francisco Giants from 1981-84, the Baltimore Orioles from 1988-91 and the Montreal Expos/Washington Nationals from 2002-2006.

FIRST MAN TO QUALIFY FOR THE MASTERS GOLF TOURNAMENT

1975 ~ Back in the 1960's era of our timeline we saw Charlie Sifford qualify for the PGA tour and play in three of the four major tournaments, but Charlie never quite cleared the bar that would have made him eligible to compete in the Masters Tournament. The first Black to accomplish that feat was Lee Elder, who earned his way into the tournament by virtue of his win at the 1974 Monsanto Open. Despite missing the cut at the Masters, Elder's impact had been made.

Elder had first played the PGA tour in 1968, placing 40th on the money list that year. Another legacy he boasts is being the first Black to participate in the South African PGA Championship in Johannesburg, after accepting a personal invitation from Gary Player to play in the 1971 tournament. While apartheid policies were in effect at that time, Elder agreed to participate after the South African government agreed not to subject him or spectators to the usual segregation requirements.

FIRST SUPER BOWL MVP

1975 ~ It took nine Super Bowls for it to happen, but on January 12, 1975 the Pittsburgh Steelers' Franco Harris became the first Black to win the game's MVP award. He ran for 158 yards, establishing a new Super Bowl record in the Steelers 16-6 win over the Minnesota Vikings. Harris played 12 of the 13 years in his Hall of Fame career for the Steelers.

He was also the key figure in one of the most famous plays in pro football history. The play was dubbed "The Immaculate Reception," and it occurred in a 1972 playoff game pitting the Steelers against the Oakland Raiders. With 22 seconds left to play, the Raiders were holding on to a 7-6 lead while the Steelers had the ball in their own territory.

After dropping back, quarterback Terry Bradshaw just got off a pass intended for John "Frenchy" Fuqua. Raiders' defender Jack Tatum broke up the play, driving the ball back toward the line of scrimmage. The football just happened to be driven right into the waiting hands of Franco Harris who scooped it from just off the ground and ran it into the end zone for the touchdown that won the game. Immaculate indeed.

FIRST PLAYER INDUCTED INTO THE BASKETBALL HALL OF FAME

1975 ~ Bill Russell became the first individual Black player inducted into the Basketball Hall of Fame. The New York Rens had been inducted as a team in 1963 and their owner/coach Bob Douglas entered the Hall in 1972.

FIRST BOXER TO WIN HEAVYWEIGHT TITLE THREE TIMES

1977 ~ If you had to pick one Black athlete that had the most dramatic impact upon both sports and society there could be no other choice but Muhammad Ali. In being faithful to our "firsts" motif for this timeline we're landing on this one as being the most significant thing he was the first to accomplish, even though it occurred fairly late in his career.

After winning the Olympic gold in 1960, Ali defeated Sonny Liston to win the heavyweight championship in 1964. After successfully defending his title on multiple occasions, Ali was stripped of his crown in 1968 for refusing to register for the draft during the height of the Vietnam War. By doing so he made himself a voice of the conscience of America, although some realized that only years later, and with reluctance.

Having written extensively about this man in our previous endeavors, we are going to close this component with our three favorite related quotes, two by him and one about him. Our favorite thing said about him was that… At the height of Ali's fame, he had become so well-known that if someone saw the Pope, in full regalia, walking down the street with Muhammad Ali, the average person would be thinking, "Who's that with Muhammad Ali?"

Our favorite two by him are… "It isn't the mountain ahead to climb that wears you out; it's the pebble in your shoe," and "Live every day as if it were your last, because someday you are going to be right."

FIRST BASKETBALL DUNK BY A WOMAN

1980 ~ The first female pro basketball in the U.S. was played in the Women's Basketball League from 1977-1980. While the league only lasted three years before folding, it did manage to feature the first dunking of a basketball by a woman. The star of this story is one Cardte Hicks who had played her college hoops at Long Beach State and Cal State Northridge. Hicks only played in the league's final season accomplishing her groundbreaking dunk as a member of the San Francisco Pioneers.

FIRST TO WIN NBA FINALS AND NBA FINALS MVP IN ROOKIE SEASON

1980 ~ After winning the NCAA Championship with Michigan State in 1979, Magic Johnson hit the ground running in the NBA. His Los Angeles Lakers won the 1980 NBA title and Johnson was named MVP of the finals becoming the first (and still the only) rookie to do so. Other "magical" career achievements include 12 All-Star game appearances, 9 NBA finals appearances, and being the league's all-time leader in assists per game.

FIRST PLAYER IN THE NHL

1981 ~ Drafted by the Detroit Red Wings in 1977, Val James spent four years in the minors before signing with the Buffalo Sabres in 1981. He became the first Black to play in the National Hockey League during the 1981-82 season. James was a left winger known for his physical style of play. He finished his NHL career in the 1986-87 season with the Toronto Maple Leafs.

FIRST NCAA WOMEN'S BASKETBALL DUNK

1984 ~ The first official dunk of a basketball by a woman in an NCAA game was achieved by Georgeann Wells playing for the University of West Virginia in a December 21st game against the University of Charleston. Georgeann was truly a trailblazer as her feat would go unmatched for some time. It would be a full eight years before the next female dunk occurred when the University of North Carolina's Charlotte Smith duplicated the feat.

FIRST PLAYER TO WIN THE STANLEY CUP

1984 ~ In hockey, the '80s were the era of the Edmonton Oilers when the Great One, Wayne Gretzky, dominated the sport. And who was the goalie on those great Gretzky teams? That would be Grant Fuhr who found himself in fine position to not only be the first Black to win a Stanley Cup, he'd also be the first Black to win five of them. He was also a six-time all-star and in 2003 Grant Fuhr became the first Black inducted into the Hockey Hall of Fame.

FIRST COLLEGE FOOTBALL COACH TO BREAK RECORD FOR MOST WINS

1985 ~ With his 324th victory, Grambling State's Eddie Robinson broke the existing record for wins in college football. When he retired in 1997, he left a legacy of 408 wins, 165 losses and 15 ties. He was inducted into the College Football Hall of Fame in 1997.

FIRST FORMULA 1 RACE CAR DRIVER

1986 ~ Willy T. Ribbs became the first professional Black "Indy car" or Formula 1 race car driver and five years later, in 1991, he would become the first to qualify for the Indianapolis 500.

FIRST TO SAIL AROUND THE WORLD

1987 ~ Teddy Seymour became the first Black to sail around the world in 1987. Four years later, in 1991, Bill Pinkney became the first to complete the task following the "Age of Sail" route going around the southern tips of Africa and South America (thus not taking advantage of the Panama and Suez Canals.)

FIRST WOMAN WINTER OLYMPIC MEDAL WINNER

1988 ~ The first time a Black woman would win a Winter Olympic medal for the U.S. would occur at the 1988 games in Calgary when Debi Thomas won the bronze medal in figure skating. Thomas' breakthrough year in the sport was 1986 when she won the U.S. and World Championships. Those achievements led her to win the ABC's Wide World of Sports Athlete of the Year award. She also won the World Professional Championships in 1988, 1989 and 1991.

FIRST QUARTERBACK TO WIN THE SUPER BOWL

1989 ~ The first Black quarterback to start in the Super Bowl also became the first to win the game when the Washington Redskins defeated the Denver Broncos 42-10 in Super Bowl XXII. Doug Williams led the Redskins' victory, passing for 340 yards and four touchdowns. Williams took home the MVP award for his efforts.

FIRST MODERN-ERA NFL COACH

1989 ~ Way back in the early 1920's Fritz Pollard had served as player/coach for the Akron Pros, but it wasn't until 1989 when Art Shell was named head coach of the Los Angeles Raiders that the modern NFL had its first Black coach. Shell had played for the Raiders and would coach there for five years, being named AFC Coach of the Year in 1990. He also went on to coach the Kansas City Chiefs and

Atlanta Falcons, and was inducted into the Pro Football Hall of Fame in 1989.

FIRST MANAGER TO WIN THE WORLD SERIES

1992 ~ Cito Gaston became the first Black manager to reach and win the World Series when his Toronto Blue Jays defeated the Atlanta Braves 4 games to 2. Gaston had played as an outfielder from 1967-1978 primarily for the San Diego Padres and Atlanta Braves. He managed Toronto from 1989 to 1997, then again from 2008 to 2010. During this time, he managed the Blue Jays to four American League East division titles (1989, 1991-93), while winning the pennant and World Series in both 1992 and '93.

FIRST TO WIN MAJOR GOLF CHAMPIONSHIP

1997 ~ After turning pro in 1996, Tiger Woods would have three major golf championships under his belt by the end of 1997, the first of those wins coming at the Masters which he won by a record-breaking 12 strokes. This was the beginning of a marvelous Hall of Fame career for Woods who spent more time ranked as the #1 golfer in the world than any player in history.

Tiger Woods' total of 15 major championships trails only Jack Nicklaus who has 18. He won the PGA Player of the Year eleven times and was the leading money winner ten times. He won 82 PGA events which ties him for the lead with Sam Sneed. In 2019 Tiger Woods became just the fourth golfer to receive the Presidential Medal of Freedom.

FIRST UFC CHAMPION

1997 ~ Maurice Smith became the first Black to win a UFC Championship belt, doing so in the heavyweight division.

FIRST TO WIN 10 NBA SCORING TITLES

1998 ~ On the way to his 6th NBA championship, Michael Jordan became the first man to win 10 NBA scoring titles as he led the league, averaging 28.7 points per game. Additional Jordan accolades include being named to the All-NBA First Team 10 times, winning the MVP award 5 times, and being named to the NBA All-Star team 14 times.

FIRST CENTENNIAL AWARD FROM INTERNATIONAL OLYMPIC COMMITTEE

2000 ~ When its "Sportsman of the Century" honor was awarded by the International Olympic Committee for the first time, it was Carl

Lewis who took home the trophy. Over a span of four Olympiads from 1984 to 1996 he won ten Olympic medals, nine gold and one silver. Lewis was a sprinter and a long jumper who was one of only six athletes to win the Olympic gold four times in the same event, that being the long jump.

FIRST SPORTS ILLUSTRATED GREATEST FEMALE ATHLETE OF ALL-TIME

2000 ~ At the turn of the century, *Sports Illustrated* declared Jackie Joyner-Kersee to be the "Greatest Female Athlete of All-Time." Her Olympic résumé included six medals won over a span of four Olympiads from 1984-1996. Her primary events were the heptathlon and long jump in which she won three gold, one silver, and two bronze medals.

FIRST WOMAN TO WIN A WINTER OLYMPIC GOLD MEDAL

2002 ~ If at first you don't succeed, try again; that's the moral of this story. Vonetta Flowers was a standout member of the University of Alabama at Birmingham (UAB) track and field team. She made multiple attempts to qualify for the U.S. Summer Olympic team as a sprinter and/or long jumper, but never quite made it.

Subsequently, she decided to give the bobsled a shot. She found immediate success as a brakewoman and teamed up with driver Jill Bakken for the 2002 winter games at Salt Lake City. The pair won the gold in the two-woman bobsled, making Flowers the first Black athlete, male or female, to ever win a Winter Olympics gold medal.

FIRST WOMAN TO HOLD #1 OPEN ERA TENNIS RANKING

2002 ~ When she ascended to the #1 ranking in singles on February 25, 2002, Venus Williams became the first Black women to do so since Althea Gibson in 1957. Williams won four Olympic gold medals, one in singles and three in women's doubles with her sister Serena, and she also has a silver medal in mixed doubles. Her having played in 88 Grand Slam tournaments is the all-time high for a man or a woman. In 2010, alongside her sister, Venus Williams also attained the #1 ranking in the world in women's doubles.

FIRST TO BECOME MAJORITY OWNER OF A TEAM IN ONE OF THE FOUR MAJOR SPORTS

2002 ~ Robert L. Johnson became the first Black majority owner of a major sports franchise when the NBA Board of Governors granted him the expansion Charlotte Bobcats franchise.

FIRST WOMAN TO WIN A CAREER GRAND SLAM IN TENNIS

2003 ~ Serena Williams became the first woman to achieve a career grand slam in tennis by capturing the Australian Open. The other three tournaments which comprise the grand slam, and which Williams had earlier won, are the U.S. Open, the French Open, and Wimbledon.

FIRST HOCKEY HALL OF FAME INDUCTEE

2003 ~ Grant Fuhr became the first Black inductee in the Hockey Hall of Fame.

FIRST GOLF HALL OF FAME INDUCTEE

2004 ~ Charlie Sifford became the first Black inductee in the World Golf Hall of Fame.

FIRST INDIVIDUAL WINTER OLYMPIC GOLD MEDAL

2006 ~ By winning the men's 1000-meter speed skating, Shani Davis became the first Black to win an individual Winter Olympic gold medal.

FIRST PRO FOOTBALL HALL OF FAME QUARTERBACK

2006 ~ Following a long and well-traveled football career, Warren Moon became the first Black quarterback inducted into the Pro Football Hall of Fame. After beginning his pro football career in the Canadian Football League with the Edmonton Eskimos in 1978, Moon returned to the states where he began his NFL career in 1984. The greatest years of his career followed during his tenure with the Houston Oilers (1984-1993). He finished with stints playing for the Minnesota Vikings, Seattle Seahawks, and Kansas City Chiefs.

FIRST COACH TO WIN THE SUPER BOWL

2007 ~ There had never been a Black head coach in the Super Bowl before 2007, and then there were two. When Tony Dungy's Indianapolis Colts took on Lovie Smith's Chicago Bears there was one thing for certain. One of those gentlemen was going to become the first Black coach ever to win a Super Bowl. When the Colts beat the Bears 29-17, Tony Dungy was accorded that honor.

FIRST AMERICAN BORN PLAYER TO WIN STANLEY CUP

2010 ~ Dustin Byfuglien became the first American-born Black player to win the Stanley Cup when his Chicago Blackhawks captured the trophy. It was noted earlier that Canadian-born Grant Fuhr had won the Cup earlier with the Edmonton Oilers.

FIRST WOMEN TO HOLD #1 DOUBLES TENNIS RANKING

2010 ~ During this year the Williams sisters ascended to the rank of #1 in women's doubles for the first time. We'll use this entry to offer career shout-outs to this dynamic duo of sisters.

Venus, who became the first Black woman in the Open Era to reach #1 in the Women's Tennis Association rankings in February of 2002, went on to spend 19 total weeks in that position. She has reached 16 Grand Slam finals and her seven singles' titles have her tied for 12th in the all-time list. In the early 2000's she and her sister Serena dominated the sport of tennis in a way no pair of women had ever previously done.

Serena currently holds 23 Grand Slam singles titles, second only to Margaret Court who has 24. She has been ranked #1 in the world by the Women's Tennis Association on eight separate occasions between 2002 and 2017, and has spent 319 weeks ranked as the number one player in the world. Our calculator has that come in at just over six years, certainly confirming Serena William's status as one of the greatest women tennis players of all-time.

FIRST WOMAN TO WIN OLYMPIC GOLD IN GYMNASTICS

2012 ~ Gabby Douglas became America's darling at the 2012 Olympics in London. She won the gold medal in the individual all-around event and the U.S. women's team also brought home the gold. At the 2016 games in Rio de Janeiro, Douglas was on the team that again won the team gold, but she saw the individual gold go to teammate Simone Biles, yet another up-and-coming Black female gymnast.

FIRST GIRL TO PLAY IN THE LITTLE LEAGUE WORLD SERIES

2014 ~ Mo'ne Davis became the 18th girl and first Black female to participate in the Little League World Series in Williamsport,

Pennsylvania. She enjoyed more success than any of her predecessors, becoming the sixth to get a hit and the first to record a win as a pitcher. Cherry on top… not only did she win the game, she pitched a shutout! Okay, we'll give you one more; she also became the first Little Leaguer to appear on the cover of *Sports Illustrated*.

FIRST INDUCTED INTO NASCAR HALL OF FAME
2015 ~ Wendell Scott, who attained the first Black NASCAR license (1953) and was the first to win a NASCAR race (1963), deservedly became the first Black NASCAR Hall of Fame inductee.

FIRST NFL PLAYER TO TAKE A KNEE
2016 ~ Colin Kaepernick dropped to one knee during the playing of the national anthem at the beginning of the San Francisco 49ers' last 2016 pre-season football game as a protest against racial injustice, police brutality and systematic oppression in the United States. Seemed like a disciplined, socially conscious gesture at the time, but who knew?

In 2012 Kaepernick had led the 49ers to the Super Bowl and in 2013 he got them back to the NFC title game so he seemed on course to enjoy a successful NFL career, but after the kneel down, things would never quite be the same again. He continued to kneel during the anthem for the rest of the 2016 season in what became an increasingly polarizing gesture.

Becoming a free agent after that season, Kaepernick went unsigned throughout 2017 and subsequently filed a grievance against the league accusing the owners of collusion to prevent him from playing. A confidential settlement was reached in 2019 but, to this date, no NFL team has been willing to sign him.

FIRST NUMBER RETIRED BY THREE DIFFERENT BASEBALL TEAMS
2017 ~ This will be our third visit with baseball legend Frank Robinson in this timeline. His stellar baseball career led to his becoming the first man to win the MVP award in both the American and National Leagues. Robinson won the award with the Cincinnati Reds in 1961 and the Baltimore Orioles in 1966, the year in which he also became the first Black to win the Triple Crown, leading the league in home runs, RBI's and batting average.

Frank Robinson also went on to become the first Black manager in major league baseball when he assumed that role as the player/manager for the Cleveland Indians in 1975. It's rather interesting that there were decades separating the retirement of his #20 by these three organizations. The Baltimore Orioles retired his number in 1972, the Cincinnati Reds followed suit in 1998, and finally in 2017, the Cleveland Indians retired his number to pay fitting tribute to the fact that he would go down in history as baseball's first Black manager.

FIRST U.S. OLYMPIC HOCKEY PLAYER

2018 ~ The Minnesota Wild's Jordan Greenway became the first Black hockey player named to Team U.S.A., representing his country in the Olympics.

FIRST WOMAN TO WIN 11 OLYMPIC MEDALS

2021 ~ When she won the bronze medal in the 400-meter dash, Allyson Felix established herself as the most decorated woman in Olympic history. Her collection of medals includes 5 gold, 4 silver and 2 bronze. Her appearance in the Tokyo games was her 5th trip to the Olympics, and the first where she would be returning home to her 2-year-old daughter.

ADDENDUM 3
THE TIMELINE

1490's ~ There is documentation of some free Africans living in the Caribbean and South America.

1502 ~ Juan Garrido, a Black African conquistador in the entourage of Ponce de Leon, arrives at the island of Hispaniola. This is the island that currently comprises the countries of Haiti and the Dominican Republic.

1508 ~ Garrido accompanies de Leon on his invasions of both Cuba and Puerto Rico.

1513 ~ Garrido again accompanies de Leon on their first expedition to Florida looking for gold and the Fountain of Youth. This establishes Garrido as the first Black known to have set foot in what would become the United States.

1526 ~ The first free Africans are documented living in the area that would become the United States. It is also during this year that Spanish explorer Lucas Vazquez de Ayllon brings Black slaves from the Spanish colony of Santo Domingo on Hispaniola to the Spanish colony of San Miguel de Gualdape in modern-day South Carolina. The colony flounders with some of the slaves escaping to seek shelter with Native Americans while the remaining slaves are returned to Hispaniola.

1565 ~ Spanish conquistador Don Pedro Menendez de Aviles brings Black slaves with him to assist in the founding of St. Augustine. That Spanish city, the first permanent settlement in the United States, becomes the hub of slave trade in Florida for the next century and a half.

1606 ~ Agustin becomes the first Black, slave or otherwise, whose birth is documented to have taken place in what would eventually become the United States.

1619 ~ Slavery officially enters the future 13 colonies (which would not include the aforementioned Florida scenario and brief attempt in South Carolina). In August of that year, a journal entry records that "20 and odd" Angolans, kidnapped by the Portuguese, arrive in the British colony of Jamestown, Virginia and are then bought by English colonists to work on the expanding cultivation of tobacco.

1664 ~ The colony of Maryland passes the first law banning interracial marriage (referred to as miscegenation) with several other colonies rapidly following suit. Penalties for White people violating this law include imprisonment, exile, and even enslavement.

1721 ~ The slave Onesimus shares the African concept of vaccination with American doctors saving lives during a smallpox outbreak in Boston.

1738 ~ The first free Black community in what is now the United States is formed. Called Gracia Real de Santa Teresa de Mose, the community is formed in the territory of Spanish Florida. The name is subsequently shortened to Fort Mose.

1746 ~ Lucy Terry becomes the first Black to compose a surviving piece of literature. Terry is a slave whose ballad poem "Bars Fight" manages to be passed on through one means or another before finally being published over a century later in 1855 in Josiah Holland's *History of Western Massachusetts*. Some clarification on the poem title is probably appropriate as this landmark piece of literature did not detail a colonial-era barroom brawl. The word "bars" was used to mean "meadow" during that time period and the poem was about an Indian attack on two White families that had occurred on August 25, in Deerfield, Massachusetts.

1761 ~ Jupiter Hammon becomes the first Black to publish a piece of literature. His poem "An Evening Thought: Salvation by Christ with Penitential Cries" is published as a "broadside," or a one-sided sheet of paper, like a poster or announcement. Hammon is also a popular preacher and bookkeeper who goes on to publish numerous works about religion and the evils of slavery.

1767 ~ Clockmaker Peter Hill is born as a slave. After achieving his freedom, he goes on to become the first and only Black clockmaker of the late-1700's and early-1800's.

1768 ~ Wentworth Cheswell becomes the first Black elected to public office when his town of Newmarket, New Hampshire elects him town constable. In addition to fighting in the Revolutionary War, he also serves his town of Newmarket as an assessor, auditor and Justice of the Peace.

1773 ~ Phillis Wheatley becomes the first published Black author in the world. The 12-year-old slave from Boston travels to London for the publication of her book called *Poems on Various Subjects, Religious and Moral*.

1774 ~ The first separate Black congregation forms as Silver Bluff Baptist Church in Beech Island, South Carolina.

1775 ~ Prince Hall becomes the first Black to join the Freemasons. Hall is a leader in the free Black community of Boston and an active abolitionist and advocate for the educational rights of Black children.

1778 ~ The first Black U.S. military regiment is formed as part of the Continental Army. It serves during the Revolutionary War as the First Rhode Island Regiment. It is one of few units to serve throughout the entire war.

1780's ~ The Underground Railroad forms as a loose network of safe houses helping slaves to escape to the North and Canada. The network of stations was supported by abolitionists who favored Black freedom.

1783 ~ James Derham becomes the first Black to formally practice medicine in the U.S. although he actually does not have a degree. He studies medicine in Philadelphia under Dr. John Kearsley Jr. From there he moves to New Orleans where he partners in a medical practice with Robert Dove. Dove eventually provides Derham the financial assistance he needs to open his own practice.

1785 ~ Reverend Lemuel Haynes becomes the first ordained Black Christian minister in the U.S. He is ordained in the Congregational Church which evolves into the United Church of Christ.

1791 ~ A successful slave rebellion in Haiti initiates increased efforts to prevent a similar event from happening in the U.S.

1793 ~ Richard Allen founds the first African Methodist Episcopal Church in Philadelphia, Pennsylvania.

1793 ~ Eli Whitney invents the cotton gin which enables cotton to leapfrog tobacco as the #1 cash crop of the South, a development which also serves to increase the demand for slave labor.

1793 ~ Congress passes the Fugitive Slave Act making it a federal crime to assist an enslaved person trying to escape.

1797 ~ Sojourner Truth is born in Swartekill, New York. In 1826 she would escape to freedom with her daughter and become one of the country's most powerful advocates for abolition, as well as women's rights.

1799 ~ John Chavis becomes the first Black to enroll in an American college, attending Washington and Lee University in Lexington, Virginia, but does not receive a degree. He goes on to become a Presbyterian minister and teacher.

1804 ~ Lemuel Haynes receives an honorary Master's degree from Middlebury College in Vermont. Haynes is a veteran of the Revolutionary War.

1807 ~ John Gloucester founds the first Black Presbyterian Church in the U.S., located in Philadelphia, Pennsylvania.

1817 ~ Frederick Douglass is born in Cordova, Maryland. He goes on to become the most high-profile figure in the abolitionist movement.

1818 ~ Molly Williams becomes the first Black female firefighter in the U.S. serving for the Oceanus Engine Company #11 in Manhattan.

1821 ~ Thomas L. Jennings becomes the first Black to be issued a patent which he receives for his dry-cleaning process.

1822 ~ Harriet Tubman is born in Dorchester County, Maryland. After escaping slavery, she goes on to become extremely active in the Underground Railroad, serves as a scout and a spy for the Union Army during the Civil War, and in her later years becomes active in the women's suffrage movement.

1822 ~ Absalom Boston becomes the first Black captain to sail a whaleship with an all-Black crew. His operation is based out of Nantucket Island in Massachusetts.

1823 ~ Alexander Lucius Twilight becomes the first Black to receive a college degree in the U.S. upon his graduation from Middlebury College in Vermont.

1826 ~ Edward Jones becomes the second Black to receive a college degree in the U.S. upon his graduation from Amherst in Massachusetts.

1827 ~ Reverend Peter Williams Jr. founds the first Black owned-and-operated newspaper. Published in New York City, the paper is called *Freedom's Journal*.

1831 ~ The Nat Turner Rebellion occurs. Beginning with a small band of followers, Turner kills his owners, then assembles a group of around 75 Black people who kill some Whites in a two-day rebellion which ends when a Virginia state militia overwhelms the rebels. Turner is hanged for the insurrection.

1831 ~ William Lloyd Garrison founds the radical abolitionist newspaper *The Liberator* in Boston, Massachusetts.

1832 ~ Pio Pico becomes the first Black governor in what is now the United States. Pico is the governor of the Mexican territory of Alta California until modern-day California is ceded by Mexico to the U.S. in 1848.

1833 ~ Oberlin College is founded in Ohio. From its inception Oberlin is open to Blacks and women and the institution boasts a deep history of support for Black higher education.

1836 ~ Alexander Twilight becomes the first Black elected to a state legislature. He serves in this capacity for the state of Vermont (where he had become the first Black to graduate from a U.S. college in 1823 as noted above.)

1836 ~ Frank McWorter becomes the first Black to found, plan, establish and register a town in the United States. New Philadelphia, Illinois is a biracial town which serves an active role with the Underground Railroad.

1837 ~ James McCune Smith becomes the first Black doctor in the U.S. with a medical degree. Smith gets his degree at the University of Glasgow in Scotland and practices in New York City. He also owns two pharmacies.

1837 ~ Opening as the Institute for Colored Youth, the first Black institute of higher learning is founded in Cheyney, Pennsylvania. The college is now known as Cheyney University and it does not become a degree-granting institution until 1932.

1844 ~ George B. Vashon becomes the first Black to graduate from Oberlin. He subsequently becomes one of the founding professors of Howard University.

1845 ~ Frederick Douglass publishes his first biography *Narrative of the Life of Frederick Douglass, an American Slave*. He then leaves for England and Scotland to escape slave hunters.

1845 ~ Macon Bolling Allen becomes the first Black licensed to practice law in the United States. Allen had passed the bar exam in Boston and becomes the first Black lawyer to argue a case in front of a jury.

1846 ~ English admirers purchase Frederick Douglass' freedom and he returns to the U.S.

1847 ~ Frederick Douglass begins publishing the *North Star*, a weekly newspaper, from his home in Rochester, New York.

1847 ~ Dr. David J. Peck becomes the first Black to graduate from a medical school in the U.S., Rush Medical School in Chicago. He initially practices in Philadelphia, then later in Nicaragua.

1847 ~ Joseph Jenkins Roberts becomes the first African American president of any country in the world. He assumes that position for the country of Liberia which the U.S. had founded to offer freed slaves the opportunity to return to Africa.

1849 ~ Charles L. Reason becomes the first Black college professor at a mixed race institution of higher learning, New York Central College in McGrawville, New York.

1849 ~ Harriet Tubman escapes to Philadelphia and begins working with the Underground Railroad.

1849 ~ Frederick Douglass and Susan B. Anthony meet for the first time when Anthony settles in Douglass' hometown of Rochester, NY.

1851 ~ Sojourner Truth delivers her "Ain't I a Woman?" speech at the Ohio Women's Rights Convention.

1852 ~ Harriet Beecher Stowe writes *Uncle Tom's Cabin*, which details the harsh conditions experienced by enslaved Blacks.

1853 ~ William Wells Brown becomes the first Black to publish a novel. It is titled *Clotel; or, The President's Daughter*.

1854 ~ James Augustine Healy becomes the first Black Roman Catholic priest in the U.S., preaching in Portland, Maine. He would also go on to become the first Black bishop in the U.S.

1854 ~ Ashmun Institute is founded and becomes the first institute of higher learning for Black men. The school, now known as Lincoln University, is located in Oxford, Pennsylvania and future graduates will include Langston Hughes and Thurgood Marshall.

1855 ~ Frederick Douglass publishes his second autobiography, *My Bondage and My Freedom*.

1855 ~ Berea College is founded and becomes the first interracial and coeducational institute of higher learning in the South. The college is located in Berea, Kentucky.

1856 ~ Wilberforce University is founded and becomes the second institute of higher learning solely for Black students. Located in Wilberforce, Ohio, the school becomes a primary stop on the Underground Railroad.

1856 ~ Martin Henry Freeman becomes the first Black president at an institution of higher learning, assuming the position at Avery College in Pittsburgh, Pennsylvania. Avery College closed in 1873.

1857 ~ The Dred Scott decision by the Supreme Court serves to perpetuate the control that Southern slaveholders have over their slaves.

1858 ~ William Wells Brown follows up his 1853 novel by becoming the first Black to publish a play in the United States. It's

called *The Escape; or, A Leap for Freedom*.
1858 ~ Frederick Douglass attends the first Women's Rights Convention at Seneca Falls, New York. The event is organized by Susan B. Anthony and Elizabeth Cady Stanton.
1858 ~ Sarah Jane Woodson Early becomes the first Black female college professor, teaching at Wilberforce College in Ohio.
1858 ~ John Brown stays at Frederick Douglass' home in Rochester while planning to encourage a slave revolt. By the next year, Douglass decides not to support Brown's revolt at Harper's Ferry.
1859 ~ Novelist Harriet E. Wilson becomes the first Black of either gender to publish a book in North America. Despite the typically female first name, Wilson was actually a man. (Note: The 1773 Phillis Wheatley book had been published in England.)
1859 ~ Abolitionist John Brown leads a raid on the federal arsenal at Harper's Ferry, Virginia hoping to obtain weapons to use in a larger initiative against slave owners. They temporarily take the arsenal but are eventually overpowered by state and federal forces. Brown is hung for leading the insurrection establishing himself as a martyr to the abolitionist cause.
1861 ~ Eleven Southern states secede from the union effectively beginning the Civil War.
1861 ~ Frederick Douglass meets with Abraham Lincoln for the first time.
1861 ~ The 1st Louisiana Native Guard of the Confederate Army becomes the first American military unit with Black officers, ironically joining in the fight to preserve slavery.
1862 ~ The 1st South Carolina Volunteers become the first recognized Black American combat unit, also ironically fighting to preserve slavery.
1862 ~ Mary Jane Patterson becomes the first Black American woman to earn a B.A., accomplishing the feat at Oberlin College in Ohio.
1863 ~ Abraham Lincoln issues the Emancipation Proclamation freeing the slaves in the secessionist Confederate states.
1863 ~ Bishop Daniel A. Payne takes over Wilberforce University in Ohio thus making it the first college in the U.S. owned and operated by Blacks.
1864 ~ Rebecca Davis Lee Crumpler becomes the first Black American woman to earn an M.D. Her degree was earned at the New England Female Medical College.

1864 ~ As a week-old infant, slave George Washington Carver is kidnapped along with his mother and sister. Owner Moses Carver hires John Bentley to find them, but Bentley is only able to retrieve baby George who they raise and send to college.

1865 ~ Martin Delany becomes the first Black field officer in the U.S. Army attaining the rank of major by the end of the Civil War.

1865 ~ Orindatus Simon Bolivar Wall becomes the first Black to attain the rank of captain in the U.S. Army.

1865 ~ Frederick Douglass attends Lincoln's second inaugural ball at the White House where Lincoln, to the assembled crowd, describes Douglass as "a man among men."

1865 ~ Robert E. Lee surrenders to Ulysses S. Grant at the Appomattox Courthouse ending the Civil War.

1865 ~ The 13th Amendment officially abolishes slavery. It was the first of three Reconstruction-related amendments to be adopted after the Civil War.

1865 ~ Patrick Francis Healy becomes the first Black American to earn a Ph.D. He earns his degree at the University of Louvain in Belgium.

1866 ~ Cathay Williams becomes the first woman to enlist in the U.S. Army, passing an obviously too lax physical which does not detect her gender. Women could not legally enlist until 1918.

1868 ~ Oscar Dunn becomes the first Black elected Lieutenant Governor in the U.S. He attains this position in the State of Louisiana.

1868 ~ Pierre Caliste Landry becomes the first Black elected mayor of a U.S. city, Donaldson, Louisiana.

1868 ~ The 14th Amendment grants "equal protection under the law" to all persons born or naturalized in the United States.

1868 ~ Howard University becomes the first college to open a medical program for Blacks.

1869 ~ Ebenezer Don Carlos Bassett becomes the first Black U.S. international diplomat when he is appointed as foreign minister to Haiti.

1869 ~ Robert Tanner Freeman becomes the first Black dentist in the country, earning his degree at Harvard.

1870 ~ The 15th Amendment prohibits the federal government and each state from denying a citizen the right to vote based on that citizen's "race, color, or previous condition of servitude."

1870 ~ James Webster Smith becomes the first Black admitted to the U.S. Military Academy at West Point.

1870 ~ Hiram Rhodes Revels becomes the first Black U.S. Senator. He is elected as a Republican from Mississippi.

1870 ~ Joseph Rainey becomes the first Black elected to the House of Representatives. He is elected as a Republican from the state of South Carolina.

1871 ~ Oscar James Dunn becomes the first Black "acting Governor." Dunn serves as Louisiana's Governor from May until August when Governor Henry C. Warmoth is unable to serve.

1872 ~ John Henry Conyers becomes the first Black admitted to the U.S. Naval Academy at Annapolis.

1872 ~ P.B.S. Pinchback becomes the first Black Governor of a U.S. state when Henry C. Warmoth is impeached in Louisiana. The first Black to be actually elected as a Governor is a milestone still to be attained.

1872 ~ Charlotte Ray becomes the first Black lawyer, earning her degree at Howard University in Washington, D.C.

1875 ~ James Augustine Healy, from Portland Maine, becomes the first Black Roman Catholic bishop in the U.S.

1876 ~ Edward Alexander Bouchet becomes the first Black to earn a doctorate degree in the U.S., achieving this accomplishment at Yale.

1877 ~ Henry Ossian Flipper becomes the first Black to graduate from West Point and become a commissioned officer in the U.S. military.

1878 ~ Horatio J. Homer, from Boston, becomes the first Black police officer in the U.S.

1879 ~ Mary Eliza Mahoney becomes the first Black to graduate from a formal nursing school. She earns her degree from a program conducted at the New England Hospital for Women and Children in Boston.

1880 ~ Michael Healy becomes the first Black to captain a U.S. government ship. He commands multiple vessels in what was then the territory of Alaska serving the government in that capacity for over 20 years.

1881 ~ Spelman College becomes the first Black College for women in the U.S., located in Atlanta, Georgia.

1881 ~ Blanche K. Bruce, then serving as the Register of the Treasury, becomes the first Black man whose signature appears on U.S. paper currency.

1881 ~ Booker T. Washington founds the Tuskegee Institute with the 4th of July as the official date of founding.

1882 ~ Virginia State University becomes the first fully state-supported four-year college for Blacks.

1883 ~ Nettie Craig-Asberry becomes the first Black woman to earn a doctoral degree, obtaining her Music degree from the University of Kansas.

1884 ~ John R. Lynch becomes the first Black to chair, as well as deliver the keynote address at, the National Convention of a major political party. He does so at the Republican National Convention at Chicago.

1885 ~ Judy W. Reed becomes the first Black woman to hold a patent which is granted for her dough kneader.

1890 ~ Ida Rollins becomes the first Black woman to earn a dental degree, doing so at the University of Michigan.

1890 ~ George Washington Johnson becomes the first Black to record a best-selling record with "The Laughing Song" and "The Whistling Coon."

1892 ~ Matilda Sissieretta Joyner Jones becomes the first Black to sing at Carnegie Hall.

1893 ~ Daniel Hale Williams performs the world's first successful open-heart surgery. Williams had been a graduate of the Chicago Medical College which is now part of Northwestern University.

1895 ~ W.E.B. Du Bois becomes the first Black to earn a doctoral degree from Harvard University. Du Bois goes on to achieve a diverse and distinguished career as a sociologist, civil rights activist, historian and writer.

1895 ~ Frederick Douglass dies after attending a rally for women's rights. His heart was in the right place to the very end.

1896 ~ Booker T. Washington becomes the first president of Tuskegee Institute, now Tuskegee University, located in Tuskegee, Alabama.

1896 ~ George Washington Carver becomes director of agricultural research at Tuskegee Institute. Carver is a botanist and chemist who does landmark work on a system of crop rotation, as well as developing alternate uses for peanuts, soybeans, and sweet potatoes. Carver teaches at this institution for 47 years.

1896 ~ The Supreme Court's verdict in the "Plessy v. Ferguson" case upholds the Jim Crow laws and the "separate but equal" policies adopted in the South. This decision remains the overriding judicial precedent in civil rights cases until its reversal in the 1954 "Brown v. the Board of Education" case.

1897 ~ Solomon Carter Fuller becomes the first Black psychiatrist in the U.S., graduating from Boston University.

1900 ~ Booker T. Washington, president of Alabama's Tuskegee Normal and Industrial Institute publishes his bestselling book *Up from Slavery* urging Blacks to pursue educational avenues to acquire the skills necessary to achieve economic success.

1901 ~ Booker T. Washington becomes the first Black to be invited to dinner at the White House. The invitation was extended by Teddy Roosevelt who had assumed the Presidency that year following the assassination of William McKinley.

1903 ~ *In Dahomey* becomes the first Black play to hit Broadway. Burt Williams and George W. Walker write and star in the musical revue.

1903 ~ Maggie L. Walker becomes the first Black bank president, doing so at St. Luke Penny Savings in Richmond, Virginia.

1903 ~ Alpha Kappa Nu becomes the first Black male Greek-letter sorority in the U.S., forming at Indiana University.

1904 ~ Mary McLeod Bethune became the first woman to found an institution which would evolve into an HBCU. The school was founded in Daytona and it would eventually morph into Bethune-Cookman University.

1907 ~ Reverend Robert Josias Morgan becomes the first Black Greek Orthodox priest in the U.S.

1908 ~ Alpha Kappa Alpha becomes the first Black female Greek-letter sorority in the U.S., forming at Howard University.

1909 ~ The NAACP is founded on February 12 in New York City. The National Association for the Advancement of Colored People states the goals of abolishing all forced segregation, enforcing the 14th and 15th Amendments, and equalizing education for all students, Black and White. Distinguished members of the founding organizers include W.E.B. Du Bois, Ida B. Wells, and Mary White Ovington.

1909 ~ Matthew Henson, as co-leader of the Peary Expedition, becomes the first man to set foot on the North Pole.

1910 ~ Comedian Bert Williams assumes the lead role in the Ziegfeld Follies, the most successful show on the vaudeville circuit.

1910 ~ Madam C.J. Walker becomes the first Black female millionaire. The businesswoman makes her fortune with a unique line of hair and cosmetic products specifically geared to Black women.

1910 ~ Daisy Tapley becomes the first Black female to make a commercial musical recording. Tapley is a classical singer and vaudeville performer in Chicago.

1912 ~ Trumpeter W.C. Handy who dubs himself "Father of the Blues" publishes the sheet music for "Memphis Blues." While the blues had been around for generations, Handy is the first to publish the genre, effectively bringing it from the rural deltas to the urban cities thus enabling the blues to attain new levels of popularity. Referring to his musical style as "southern rag," he writes his most famous composition "Saint Louis Blues" in 1914. W.C. Handy also goes on to become the first Black performer to have his image grace a U.S. postage stamp when he is so-honored in 1969.

1914 ~ Eugene Jacques Bullard becomes the first Black U.S. military pilot. He is one of just a few Black pilots during WW I.

1916 ~ Charles Young becomes the first Black colonel in the U.S. Army. He is also the third Black West Point graduate and the highest-ranking Black Army officer until his death in 1922.

1917 ~ The Harlem Hellfighters, arguably the most efficient U.S. World War I infantry brigade, are deployed to Europe.

1919 ~ James Wormley Jones becomes the first Black special agent for the FBI.

1919 ~ Georgia Ann Robinson becomes the first Black female police officer, achieving the position in Los Angeles.

1919 ~ Oscar Micheaux becomes the first Black to direct a feature film. *The Homesteader* is the first of over 30 films by Micheaux, whose works included westerns, comedies, musicals and romances.

1920 ~ George Washington Carver delivers his "The Possibilities of the Peanut" speech to the United Peanut Association of America.

1921 ~ Bessie Coleman becomes the first Black woman, as well as the first Native American, to obtain a pilot's license. She is awarded her pilot's license by France's Fédération Aéronautique Internationale, because there are no training options available for her in the U.S.

1921 ~ Georgiana Rose Simpson becomes the first Black woman to earn a Ph.D. in the U.S., receiving her degree in German from the University of Chicago.

1921 ~ Harry Pace becomes the first Black to found a record label which he calls Black Swan Records. The label, based in Harlem, specializes in jazz and blues.

1923 ~ Louis Armstrong makes his first studio recordings with King Oliver for Gennett Records in Chicago. The renowned trumpeter goes on to sign with Okeh Records in 1925 and begin a string of hit recordings including "Saint James Infirmary" and "Basin Street Blues" which would make him a jazz legend. Regarding jazz, music historian Charles Garrett wrote that Louis Armstrong was, "both the music's Holy Grail and its Rosetta Stone."

1926 ~ Charles R. Drew graduates from Amherst College. He goes on to achieve breakthrough lifesaving discoveries in the storage and transfusion of blood.

1927 ~ DeFord Bailey makes his original recording of "Pan American Blues" for Brunswick Records in New York City, a tune which includes the first blues harmonica solo. As of 1928, Bailey is Nashville-bound where he becomes a legendary studio musician. He is one of only two Blacks to be inducted into the Grand Ole Opry and the Country Music Hall of Fame, the other being Charley Pride.

1928 ~ Oscar Stanton De Priest becomes the first Black elected to the U.S. House of Representatives since Reconstruction. De Priest is elected as a Republican from Illinois.

1928 ~ Minnie Buckingham Harper becomes the first Black woman to serve in a state legislature, having been elected in West Virginia.

1930 ~ Son House makes his first recordings for Paramount Records, with follow up recordings made when the Library of Congress sends Alan Lomax to the Mississippi Delta in 1941 to document blues artists. In 1943 House retires from music and moves to Rochester, New York. Decades later, some Rochester record collectors "discover" House working at the train station there in 1964, totally unaware of the fact that his 1941 recordings have made him legendary. House spends the next decade traveling the world and basking in the blues glory he rightly deserves.

1931 ~ William Grant Still becomes the first Black composer to write a symphony performed by a leading orchestra. His *Symphony #1* is performed by the Rochester Philharmonic Orchestra.

1931 ~ Cab Calloway becomes the first Black to sell a million copies of a record when his jazz classic "Minnie the Moocher" tops the charts. Calloway is a multi-talented performer. In the video for

"Minnie" he can be seen singing, dancing and leading the band all at the same time. He continues to perform until his death in 1994.

1933 ~ In a unique storyline, Huddie Ledbetter, better known as Lead Belly, records his first tracks at the age of 45 while still in jail serving time for a variety of miscellaneous crimes. He had been discovered in prison by John and Alan Lomax from the Library of Congress. Lead Belly writes and performs some classic tunes such as "Goodnight, Irene," "Cotton Fields" and "Midnight Special."

1934 ~ The Apollo Theater opens in Harlem. The iconic venue comes to be a symbol of live Black entertainment which is still thriving today.

1935 ~ The Benny Goodman Trio becomes the first interracial jazz group with Black pianist Teddy Wilson joining clarinetist Goodman and drummer Gene Krupa.

1935 ~ Stepin Fetchit becomes the first Black entertainer to make a million dollars.

1936 ~ William Grant Still becomes the first Black to conduct a major U.S. orchestra when he leads the Los Angeles Philharmonic.

1936 ~ Jesse Owens wins four gold medals at the 1936 Summer Olympics in Berlin when Black American athletes are taking the theory of Aryan supremacy and shoving it down Adolph Hitler's throat.

1936-1937 ~ Almost unbelievably, legendary bluesman Robert Johnson only has two recording sessions take place in his entire life, occurring on November 23, 1936 in San Antonio and June 19-20, 1937 in Dallas, Texas. With an entire recorded library of only 29 songs, Johnson's passionate vocals and searing guitar riffs manage to send an impactful wave crashing onto the beach of the future of blues and rock & roll. His list of prominent disciples includes the Rolling Stones, Led Zeppelin, Eric Clapton and Jimi Hendrix, just to mention a few.

1939 ~ The first Black to have their own TV show is Ethel Waters when *The Ethel Waters Show* special airs on NBC on June 14. Ethel Waters would return to television eleven years later as the star of the sitcom *Beulah*. In that show she plays the part of a warmhearted housekeeper.

1940 ~ Booker T. Washington becomes the first Black to be depicted on a U.S. postage stamp.

1941 ~ In January, the first all-Black military aviation program is created at the Tuskegee Institute.

1941 ~ Muddy Waters makes his first recordings when the Library of Congress sends Alan Lomax to Mississippi to record local blues musicians. In 1943 he moves to Chicago and signs with Chess Records where his biggest hits, released in the 1950's, include "Hoochie Coochie Man," and "I Just Want to Make Love to You."

1941 ~ *Time* magazine proclaims George Washington Carver "the Black Leonardo."

1941 ~ Josh White becomes the first Black to give a White House Command Performance. White was a singer, guitarist and songwriter.

1942 ~ Alfred Masters becomes the first Black member of the U.S. Marine Corps.

1943 ~ The first graduates from the Tuskegee air program fly out to join the allied effort in WW II, flying over 3,000 missions against the Germans and Italians. During these missions the Tuskegee Airmen would take out 387 enemy planes and 1,000 enemy railroad cars and vehicles.

1944 ~ The only all-Black WW II women's military unit, the 6888th Central Battalion, is deployed to England, then France, charged with taking over the U.S. Army's disastrous mail delivery system. It is projected that the debacle they inherit will take six months to rectify. The girls get the job done in three months and continue to run the mail system for the remainder of the war.

1944 ~ Camilla Williams becomes the first Black to receive a contract with a major American opera company. She performs as a soprano with the New York City Opera.

1944 ~ Matt Baker becomes the first Black comic book artist by virtue of his work on "Jumbo Comics" #69 (Fiction House). Baker's work during the 1940's and 50's earns his induction into the Comic Book Hall of Fame in 2009.

1944 ~ Harry McAlpin becomes the first Black reporter to attend a U.S. presidential news conference, employed by the National Negro Publishers Association. On the occasion of the February 8th conference, President Franklin Roosevelt greets McAlpin by shaking his hand and saying, "I'm glad to see you, Mr. McAlpin, and very happy to have you here."

1944 ~ Frederick Douglass Patterson founds The United Negro College Fund to raise money for Black colleges, and their students.

1945 ~ Todd Duncan becomes the first Black member of the New York City Opera. He had also starred as Porgy in the original production of *Porgy and Bess* in 1935.
1945 ~ Frederick C. Branch becomes the first Black U.S. Marine Corps officer.
1945 ~ Olivia Hooker becomes the first Black woman to enter the Coast Guard. She is also one of the last survivors of the Tulsa race riot of 1921, also known as the Black Wall Street Massacre.
1946 ~ Booker T. Washington becomes the first Black whose image graces a U.S. Memorial coin when his face appears on the front of a half dollar which was minted until 1951. The back of the coin depicts the cabin in which Washington was born.
1947 ~ *All-Negro Comics* becomes the first comic book series to be produced entirely by Blacks.
1947 ~ Jackie Robinson breaks the color barrier in baseball with the Brooklyn Dodgers.
1948 ~ President Harry Truman issues an executive order integrating the U.S. Armed Forces.
1948 ~ James Baskett becomes the first Black male to receive an Oscar, winning an honorary award for his portrayal of Uncle Remus in the classic Disney film *Song of the South*. It is his voice heard on the legendary original recording of "Zip-a-Dee-Doo-Dah."
1948 ~ William Grant Still becomes the first Black composer to have an opera performed by a major U.S. company. The New York City Opera performed his *Troubled Island*.
1948 ~ Bob Howard becomes the first Black to host a regularly scheduled network television series *The Bob Howard Show*. The show runs for 13 episodes on CBS with Howard singing and playing the piano in 15-minute installments.
1949 ~ Wesley Brown becomes the first Black to graduate from the U.S. Naval Academy. He goes on to serve in both the Korean and Vietnam Wars.
1949 ~ Fats Domino makes his first recordings for Imperial Records. The singer/songwriter and pianist enjoys his most successful period in the late 1950's when he has eleven Top 10 *Billboard* hits including "Blueberry Hill" and "Ain't That a Shame." He becomes one of the ten original inductees into the Rock and Roll Hall of Fame in 1986.
1949 ~ Representative William Dawson, from Tennessee, is the first Black to chair a U.S. congressional committee.

1949 ~ Edward R. Dudley becomes the first Black to be appointed Ambassador of the United States when he is chosen to serve that role in Liberia.

1949 ~ Ray Charles records "Confession Blues," which becomes his first national hit, reaching #2 on the *Billboard* R&B chart. His unique soul style combines R&B, gospel and jazz, resulting in #1 hits such as "I Can't Stop Loving You," "Georgia on My Mind" and "Hit the Road Jack." On their list of the "100 Greatest Artists of All Time" *Rolling Stone* ranks Ray Charles as #10.

1949 ~ Jesse B. Blayton Sr. launches the first Black-owned and operated radio station when WERD hits the airwaves in Atlanta on October 3rd.

1949 ~ Jane Hinton and Alfreda Johnson Webb share the honors of becoming the first Black female veterinarians in the U.S.

1949 ~ After honing his skills on Beale Street in Memphis, B.B. King makes his first recordings for RPM Records. He goes on to become one of the most legendary blues guitarists ever with hits including "Lucille" and "The Thrill Is Gone." King is inducted into the Rock and Roll Hall of Fame in 1987.

1950 ~ Juanita Hall becomes the first Black to win a Tony Award, receiving the accolade for her portrayal of Bloody Mary in the original Broadway production of Rodgers and Hammerstein's *South Pacific*.

1950 ~ Gwendolyn Brooks becomes the first Black to win a Pulitzer Prize, achieving the award for her book of poetry *Annie Allen*.

1950 ~ Ralph Bunche becomes the first Black to win the Nobel Peace Prize, achieving the honor for his work as a U.N. mediator in the Arab-Israeli peace settlement.

1950 ~ Nat King Cole becomes the first Black to have a #1 hit on the *Billboard* singles chart when Mona Lisa hits #1 on July 15th.

1950 ~ Edith S. Sampson becomes the first Black U.S. delegate to the United Nations.

1950 ~ Hazel Scott becomes the first Black woman to host her own TV series. *The Hazel Scott Show* is a variety show which premieres on the now-defunct DuMont network on July 3rd. The jazz singer, who was born in Trinidad, enjoys a resurgence in popularity after the 2019 Grammys when Alicia Keys gives her a shout-out while replicating her signature move of playing two pianos at the same time.

1951 ~ After spending most of her adult life in France, Josephine Baker returns to the United States for just the second time in the past

30 years. She immediately immerses herself in the civil rights movement, a cause for which she would staunchly advocate for the rest of her life.

1951 ~ Enter Ike Turner. His group, the Kings of Rhythm, records the song "Rocket 88" at Sun Records in Memphis, Tennessee. That record is in the discussion as to what qualifies as the "first rock and roll record." Of that song, music historian Nick Tosches writes "[it] was possessed of a sound and a fury the sheer, utter newness of which set it apart from what had come before."

1951 ~ Willie Dixon signs with Chess Records and goes to work as a singer, songwriter, producer and session musician. His songwriting is particularly significant in connecting the dots between the blues and rock & roll with tunes including "Hoochie Coochie Man," "Little Red Rooster," and "Spoonful." He influences a list of artists too vast to mention.

1951 ~ Howlin' Wolf, under the direction of Ike Turner, makes his first recordings for Chess Records. The guitarist and singer goes on to become one of the most renown Chicago blues artists. *Rolling Stone* ranks him at #54 on its list of the greatest musical artists of all time, and his most noteworthy recordings include "Spoonful" and "Smokestack Lightnin'."

1952 ~ Cora Brown becomes the first Black U.S. state senator, having been elected to that position in Michigan.

1952 ~ Alice Coachman becomes the first Black (male or female) to obtain an endorsement deal, when Coca-Cola reaches out to her. Her selling power emanates from the fact she had won the Olympic gold medal in the high jump in London in 1948.

1954 ~ Benjamin O. Davis Jr., formerly of the Tuskegee Airmen, becomes the first Black U.S. Army general.

1954 ~ The Supreme Court delivers its verdict in the Brown v. Board of Education case ending racial segregation in schools and essentially reversing the Plessy v. Ferguson "separate but equal" doctrine which had been in place since 1896.

1954 ~ Dorothy Dandridge becomes the first Black actress to be nominated for an Academy Award after starring in the movie *Carmen Jones*, a Hollywood musical with an all-Black cast. She is also the first Black woman to be featured on a *Life* magazine cover in 1955 and she wins a Golden Glove for the musical *Porgy and Bess* in 1960.

1955 ~ Emmett Till, a 14-year-old Black boy, is kidnapped and murdered in Mississippi. The failure to bring justice to any of the White perpetrators is seen as a catalyst for the next phase of the civil rights movement.

1955 ~ Marian Anderson becomes the first Black singer to perform with the New York Metropolitan Opera.

1955 ~ Sammy Davis Jr. becomes the first Black to have a #1 album on the *Billboard* chart when *Starring Sammy Davis Jr.* secures the top spot. Davis is actually just the second person to have a #1 album as *Billboard* did not start charting albums until 1955. Who did Davis unseat as the reigning #1? The answer, probably someone you've never heard of, would be Crazy Otto, a German piano player!

1955 ~ First Claudette Colvin, then Rosa Parks, refuse to surrender their seats to Whites on a Montgomery bus. Their arrests lead to the Montgomery Bus Boycott.

1955 ~ Arthur Mitchell joins the New York City Ballet becoming the first Black male dancer in a major ballet company.

1955 ~ August Martin becomes the first Black pilot of a U.S. airline when he flies for the cargo airline Seaboard & Western Airlines.

1955 ~ "Just let me hear some of that rock and roll music!" Chuck Berry's first single "Maybellene" is released on Chess Records and reaches #5 on the *Billboard* singles chart. Demonstrating the tune's staying power, it currently ranks as #18 on *Rolling Stone*'s list of "The 500 Greatest Songs of All Time."

1956 ~ James Brown cuts his first record. After joining the Fabulous Flames upon his release from jail in 1953, James and the Flames' first single is a tune written by Brown called "Please, Please, Please." The Godfather of Soul goes on to score seventeen #1 hits on the *Billboard* charts and rack up 94 records in the *Billboard* Hot 100.

1956 ~ Charles Gittens becomes the first Black U.S. Secret Service agent.

1956 ~ Nat King Cole becomes the first Black to host a nationwide TV variety show. The eponymous program is called *The Nat King Cole Show* and runs on NBC.

1956 ~ Little Richard breaks out during this year as his first two releases "Tutti Frutti" and "Long Tall Sally" become crossover hits in both the U.S. and U.K. He is known for his ability to appeal to a biracial audience and "Good Golly, Miss Molly," he does go on to become one of the ten original inductees into the Rock and Roll Hall of Fame.

1957 ~ The National Guard oversees the "Little Rock 9" integration of Central High School in Little Rock, Arkansas.

1957 ~ Sam Cooke's R&B/pop crossover hit "You Send Me" launches a prolifically successful career in which he would land 29 singles in the Top 40, also including "Wonderful World," "Chain Gang" and "Twistin' the Night Away." His career is tragically cut short when he is shot to death by a Los Angeles hotel manager under questionable circumstances in 1964.

1958 ~ Tommy Edwards becomes the first Black to reach #1 on the *Billboard* Hot 100 with the song "It's All in the Game." This accolade is to some degree a game of semantics. Prior to August 4, 1958 this musical sales list had been published under the moniker of the "*Billboard* Singles Chart," and as noted earlier, Nat King Cole had reached #1 in that list with "Mona Lisa" in 1950.

1958 ~ Betty Shabazz marries Malcolm X and becomes an active participant in the crusade for civil rights. After joining the nation of Islam in 1956, the couple mutually leaves in 1964 and she witnesses his assassination the following year.

1959 ~ Ella Fitzgerald becomes the first Black female to win a Grammy Award and the girl actually wins two – one for Best Jazz Performance (*soloist for Ella Fitzgerald Sings the Duke Ellington Songbook*) and the second for Best Female Pop Vocal Performance (*Ella Fitzgerald Sings the Irving Berlin Songbook)*. The legendary Ella goes on to win 14 Grammys throughout her career and she receives the Lifetime Achievement Award in 1967.

1959 ~ Count Basie becomes the first Black man to win a Grammy Award and, like Ella above, he also wins two, winning for Best Group Jazz Performance and Best Performance by a Dance Band (for the album *Basie*).

1959 ~ Louis Lomax becomes the first Black television journalist. One of his first projects is collaborating with fellow journalist Mike Wallace on a 5-part documentary about the Nation of Islam and its leaders. This is the first time that many Whites are exposed to the Nation and its leaders Elijah Muhammad and Malcolm X.

1959 ~ The saga begins which will anoint Motown Records as "The Sound of Young America." With an $800 loan from family and friends, Berry Gordy Jr. founds Tamla Records which evolves into

Motown by 1960. During its first decade, the Motown label charts 79 Top 10 songs in the *Billboard* Hot 100. Creating Black music with incredible crossover appeal is the genius behind the sound's success. Marquee artists include Stevie Wonder, the Temptations, the Four Tops, Marvin Gaye, Diana Ross & the Supremes, and the Jackson 5.

1960 ~ Edith S. Sampson becomes the first Black delegate to the North Atlantic Treaty Organization (NATO).

1960 ~ The Shirelles become the first Black female artist(s) to score a #1 hit with "Will You Still Love Me Tomorrow."

1960 ~ Ike & Tina Turner release their first single called "A Fool in Love." Performing as the Ike & Tina Turner Revue, the group is backed by the Kings of Rhythm band, which Ike had formed in 1951, and a chorus of female background vocalists billed as the Ikettes. "Proud Mary" earns them a Grammy in 1972 and that song is joined by "River Deep – Mountain High," in the Grammy Hall of Fame. They are ranked as the #2 duo of all-time by *Rolling Stone* and inducted into the Rock and Roll Hall of Fame in 1991.

1960 ~ Four Black college students at North Carolina A & T initiate the "Sit-In Movement" when they take seats at an F.W. Woolworth's lunch counter and remain throughout the day despite not being served as per Woolworth's "Whites-only" policy. This event sparks the founding of the Student Nonviolent Coordinating Committee (SNCC) which initiates a nationwide strategy of nonviolent sit-ins, at a wide variety of establishments, to facilitate the civil rights movement.

1960 ~ Harry Belafonte becomes the first Black to win an Emmy. On June 20th the singer/actor takes home the award for his TV special *Tonight with Harry Belafonte*.

1961 ~ Dick Gregory is discovered in a small Chicago club by Hugh Hefner. Hef gives Gregory a one-night stand at the Playboy Club which turns into a 6-week run launching the comedian's career.

1961 ~ In May of that year the Congress of Racial Equality (CORE) follows up the sit-in movement by setting up the "Freedom Ride," a bus tour from Washington to New Orleans with 13 participants, seven Black & six White. Their oppression during the ride prompts Attorney General Robert Kennedy to intervene, helping to assure segregation in interstate travel.

1961 ~ Aretha Franklin hits the *Billboard* Hot 100 for the first time with a song called "Won't Be Long." It will be a long time before that chart run would end as Franklin places 73 songs in the Hot 100 throughout her illustrious career. Her signing with Atlantic Records in 1966 initiates her greatest wave of popularity featuring hits such as "Respect" and "(You Make Me Feel Like) A Natural Woman." In *Rolling Stone*'s "100 Greatest Singers of All Time," she is ranked #1 and in the "100 Greatest Artists of All Time" she comes in at #9.

1961 ~ Nathan Boya becomes the first Black daredevil to go over Niagara Falls. Taking the plunge in a metal ball he calls the "Plunge-O-Sphere," he survives the fall and goes on to land multiple TV appearances.

1962 ~ A Supreme Court decision forces the integration of the University of Mississippi (Ole Miss). In September of 1962 the enforcement of the decision requires President Kennedy to send in 31,000 National Guard troops to overcome the Mississippi governor's attempt to block the enforcement of the Supreme Court decision.

1963 ~ Martin Luther King Jr. is the first Black to be named *Time* magazine's Man of the Year.

1963 ~ Walter Harris becomes the first Black chess master in the country.

1963 ~ Diahann Carroll becomes the first Black nominated for an Emmy Award. Her performance in the "A Horse Has a Big Head, Let Him Worry" episode of *The Naked City* earns her a nomination for Outstanding Performance by an Actress in a Lead Role.

1963 ~ In Birmingham, Alabama, four young Black girls are killed when a KKK bomb explodes at the 16th Street Baptist Church. The church bombing is the third in 11 days, after the federal government had ordered the integration of Alabama's school system.

1963 ~ Ronnie Spector and the Ronettes release "Be My Baby." In 2017, *Billboard* names the song #1 on their list of the "100 Greatest Girl Group Songs of All Time."

1963 ~ On August 28, 1963, some 250,000 people – both Black and White – participate in the March on Washington for Jobs and Freedom. The march culminates with Martin Luther King Jr.'s "I Have a Dream" speech delivered from the steps of the Lincoln Memorial. "Free at last! Free at last! Thank God Almighty, we are free at last!"

1963 ~ Cicely Tyson becomes the first Black with a recurring role in a TV drama playing Jane Foster, the secretary for a New York City social worker played by George C. Scott. While critically acclaimed, *East Side/West Side* becomes controversial for openly dealing with unsavory inner-city issues such as rape and prostitution. Despite a massive letter-writing campaign by supporters, the show is canceled after one season.

1964 ~ David Harris becomes the first Black pilot for a major commercial airline, flying for American Airlines.

1964 ~ The movie *One Potato, Two Potato* written by Orville H. Hampton becomes the first major American film featuring an interracial marriage.

1964 ~ In July Congress passes the Civil Rights Act which gives the federal government more power to protect citizens against discrimination on the basis of race, religion, sex or national origin.

1964 ~ Civil rights organizations urge White students from the North to travel to Mississippi for what is billed as a "Freedom Summer" where they help register Black voters and build schools for Black children. While there are some significant successes, the Klan kidnaps and murders three participants initiating arrests and a trial that lasts through 1967 with sporadic results. The slayings become known as the "Mississippi Burning" murders.

1965 ~ Morrie Turner becomes the first Black to create a nationally syndicated newspaper cartoon which is called *Wee Pals*.

1965 ~ Micki Grant becomes the first Black cast member of a daytime soap opera, playing Peggy Noland Harris on *Another World*.

1965 ~ Jennifer Jackson becomes the first Black *Playboy* "Playmate" centerfold appearing in the March issue.

1965 ~ Benjamin Oliver Davis Jr. becomes the first Black U.S. Air Force General.

1965 ~ Patricia Roberts Harris becomes the first Black woman Ambassador of the United States serving in that capacity to the country of Luxembourg.

1965 ~ Frank Street Jr. becomes the first Black to win a national chess championship when he takes the U.S. Amateur title.

1965 ~ On February 7th, Malcolm X is shot to death while speaking in Harlem. The assassination is motivated by a rift between Malcolm X and Elijah Muhammad, the leader of the Nation of Islam.

1965 ~ On March 7th "Bloody Sunday" occurs in Selma, Alabama. Shortly after the beginning of a planned protest march from Selma to the state capital in Montgomery, 600 marchers get as far as the Edmund Pettus Bridge just outside Selma when they are attacked by state troopers wielding whips, nightsticks and tear gas. The brutal scene is captured on television, enraging many Americans and drawing attention to the civil rights movement. On March 21st, after a U.S. district court orders Alabama to permit the Selma-Montgomery march, some 2,000 marchers set out on the three-day journey, this time protected by U.S. Army troops and Alabama National Guard forces under federal control. "No tide of racism can stop us," King proclaims from the steps of the state capitol building, addressing the nearly 50,000 supporters – Black and White – who meet the marchers in Montgomery.

1965 ~ In August, Congress passes the Voting Rights Act calling for federal legislation to ensure protection of the voting rights of Blacks.

1965 ~ Bill Cosby becomes the first Black actor to have a leading role in a television series, co-starring with Robert Culp in *I Spy*. Cosby wins three Emmy Awards for his role in the spy drama which runs on NBC from 1965 to 1968.

1966 ~ Edward Brooke becomes the first post-Reconstruction Black to be elected to the U.S. Senate, as a Republican in Massachusetts.

1966 ~ Robert C. Weaver becomes the first Black U.S. Cabinet secretary, serving in that capacity for the Department of Housing and Urban Development.

1966 ~ The Black Panther Party is founded in Oakland by Huey P. Newton and Bobby Seale. From its inception, the party endeavors to use armed patrols to monitor police activity.

1967 ~ In the case of Loving v. the State of Virginia, the Supreme Court ends the 303-year-old law that had made interracial marriages illegal in some parts of the country.

1967 ~ Carl B. Stokes becomes the first Black elected mayor of a large U.S. city, Cleveland, Ohio.

1967 ~ Thurgood Marshall becomes the first Black to be appointed as a justice to the U.S. Supreme Court.

1967 ~ Jimi Hendrix releases his first album, *Are You Experienced* by the Jimi Hendrix Experience. Although his career spans just four years with four studio albums to his credit, he is in the discussion as to who was the greatest guitarist of all time. His performances at the Monterey Pop Festival and Woodstock remain legendary. Hendrix dies of drug-related causes on September 18, 1970.

1967 ~ Robert Henry Lawrence Jr. becomes the first Black selected for astronaut training.

1967 ~ Sammy Davis Jr. and Nancy Sinatra share TV's first interracial kiss with a quick peck on the lips at the end of a skit in Sinatra's *Movin' with Nancy* variety special.

1968 ~ The ante would be upped the following year when William Shatner and Nichelle Nichols shared TV's first full-fledged interracial kiss on a network TV drama in *Star Trek*'s "Plato's Stepchildren" episode. After their minds are telekinetically controlled by aliens, Captain Kirk and Lt. Uhura enjoy a passionate kiss.

1968 ~ The Fair Housing Act of 1968, meant as a follow-up to the Civil Rights Act of 1964, marks the last great legislative achievement of the civil rights era.

1968 ~ Shirley Chisholm becomes the first Black woman elected to the U.S. House of Representatives, coming from the State of New York.

1968 ~ The Studio Museum in Harlem becomes the first fine-arts museum devoted solely to Black artists.

1968 ~ Nancy Hicks Maynard becomes the first Black woman reporter for *The New York Times*.

1968 ~ Diahann Carroll becomes the first Black woman to have the lead role in a weekly TV series (in which she does not play a domestic). She plays a widow raising her young son, while working as a nurse, on the NBC series *Julia* which ran from 1968 to 1971.

1968 ~ On April 4th, Martin Luther King Jr. is shot and killed on the balcony of a motel in Memphis, Tennessee. His assassin, James Earl Ray, would be arrested by Scotland Yard on June 8th at London's Heathrow Airport.

1969 ~ *The Bill Cosby Show* debuts as the first eponymous Black TV sitcom. This was the show in which Bill Cosby starred as a phys ed teacher (as opposed to *The Cosby Show* which ran from 1984-1992).

1969 ~ The Falcon from Marvel Comics' "Captain America" #117 becomes the first Black superhero.

1969 ~ Gordon Parks becomes the first Black director of a major Hollywood film, *The Learning Tree*. Future films he would direct include *Shaft* in 1971.

1969 ~ Arthur Mitchell becomes the founder of a classical training school and ballet company, the Arthur Mitchell Dance Theatre of Harlem.

1969 ~ At the age of 75, Moms Mabley becomes the oldest person to ever score a Top 40 hit when her cover version of "Abraham, Martin and John" goes to #35 on the *Billboard* chart.

1969 ~ Linda Martell becomes the first Black woman to appear on the stage of the Grand Old Opry.

1969 ~ Trumpeter W.C. Handy becomes the first Black performer to have his image grace a U.S. postage stamp.

1970 ~ Gail Fisher becomes the first Black woman to win an Emmy, securing the award for Best Supporting Actress for her role as Peggy Fair in the CBS TV series *Mannix* which runs from 1968-1975.

1970 ~ Cheryl Brown becomes the first Black contestant in the Miss America pageant, representing the State of Iowa.

1970 ~ Lionel Hampton becomes the first Black to perform at a Super Bowl halftime show.

1971 ~ Gail Fisher becomes the first Black of either gender to win a Golden Globe Award, again for her role in *Mannix*.

1971 ~ Charley Pride becomes the first Black to win the Country Music Association Artist of the Year award. To date, he is the only Black to have won this award.

1971 ~ Darine Stern becomes the first Black *Playboy* cover girl, appearing on the October issue.

1972 ~ *Time* magazine features a cover story proclaiming Flip Wilson to be "TV's First Black Superstar."

1972 ~ Sammy Davis Jr. and Carroll O'Connor combine for the first interracial male kiss on network TV. Appearing as himself, Davis surprises Archie by sneaking a kiss during a photo op in the "Sammy's Visit" episode of *All in the Family*.

1972 ~ Redd Foxx brings his comedy act to the small screen when *Sanford and Son* debuts on NBC.

1972 ~ Democrat Shirley Chisholm, a member of the House of Representatives from New York, becomes the first Black woman to become a major party presidential candidate. Her campaign slogan is "Unbought and Unbossed," and she receives the fourth most votes at the Democratic National Convention.

1972 ~ Isaac Hayes becomes the first Black to win an Academy Award for something other than acting. His "Theme from *Shaft*" takes the Oscar for Best Original Song. The soundtrack from *Shaft* is also nominated for Best Original Score.

1972 ~ *Fat Albert and the Cosby Kids* proves that Bill Cosby truly can do it all as he creates, produces, hosts and stars in the first animated series with an all-Black cast. The show, based upon Cosby's childhood, runs from 1972-1984.

1973 ~ Yaphet Kotto becomes the first Black Bond villain and Gloria Hendry becomes the first Black Bond girlfriend in the classic James Bond film *Live and Let Die*.

1973 ~ Reggae rocks onto the scene. In what music historian Roger Steffens describes as "an incredible one-two punch that knocked out America for Jamaican music," this year sees the release of Jimmy Cliff's *The Harder They Come* and Bob Marley and the Wailers' *Catch a Fire*. For the record, *The Harder They Come* is a soundtrack album which includes other artists in addition to Cliff.

1973 ~ Doris A. Davis becomes the first Black woman mayor of a major U.S. city, Compton, California.

1973 ~ DJ Kool Herc uses two turntables and a microphone to create the musical sound which earns him the nickname "Father of Hip-Hop." Believe it or not, it all starts at an August back-to-school party on Sedgwick Avenue in the Bronx. As the "Father of…" moniker would imply, Herc becomes a major influence for future artists such as Afrika Bambaataa and Grandmaster Flash.

1974 ~ Beverly Johnson becomes the first Black model to appear on the cover of *Vogue* magazine.

1974 ~ Stevie Wonder becomes the first Black to win the Grammy Award for Best Album. His *Innervisions* takes this first award and he will also take home the trophy two more times in the next three years. Wonder's *Fulfillingness' First Finale* captures the prize in 1975, and *Songs in the Key of Life* wins in 1977.

1974 ~ Richard Pryor wins the first of three consecutive Grammy Awards for Best Comedy Album.

1975 ~ Richard Pryor becomes the first Black to host SNL.

1975 ~ Adam Wade becomes the first Black host of a network TV game show, *Musical Chairs* on CBS.

1975 ~ Daniel James Jr. becomes the military's first four-star general, achieving that rank in the Air Force.

1975 ~ Barbara Jordan (Texas congresswoman) and Addie L. Wyatt (labor movement) become the first Black women named as *Time* magazine's Person of the Year.

1975 ~ After "Movin' on up to the East Side," *The Jeffersons* TV series continues to break ground by featuring TV's first interracial couple. Roxie Roker plays the Black wife in the Willis couple who are the neighbors of the Jeffersons. Add-on fun fact: Roxie Roker was also the mother of musician Lenny Kravitz.

1977 ~ Patricia Roberts Harris becomes the first Black woman member of the U.S. Cabinet, serving as Secretary of Housing and Urban Development.

1977 ~ Azie Taylor Morton becomes the first Black woman to have her signature appear on U.S. currency while serving as the Treasurer of the United States.

1978 ~ The University of California v. Bakke Supreme Court decision rules that institutions of higher education could rightfully use race as a criterion in admissions decisions in order to ensure diversity.

1978 ~ Prince releases his first album *For You*. Of his 39 albums, 1984's *Purple Rain* would be the most iconic, topping the *Billboard* charts for 24 weeks while selling 25 million copies. By the time of his death in 2016, Prince had lit up the *Billboard* charts with 47 hits in the Hot 100, and 19 tunes in the Top 10, five of them reaching #1.

1978 ~ Max Robinson becomes the first Black network news anchor when he begins serving as Frank Reynold's co-anchor on *ABC World News Tonight*.

1979 ~ The Sugar Hill Gang releases "Rapper's Delight," a tune which is widely credited with bringing rap music to a broader crossover audience. The song cracks the *Billboard* Top 40 in America and hits the Top 10 in the U.K. and Canada.

1979 ~ Al Freeman Jr. becomes the first Black to win a Daytime Emmy Award for Lead Actor in a Soap Opera. He is recognized for his portrayal of Ed Hall in ABC's *One Life to Live*.

1979 ~ On February 10th, Cicely Tyson becomes the first Black female to host *Saturday Night Live*.

1980 ~ Robert L. and Sheila Johnson launch the first Black TV network, BET (Black Entertainment Television). Things go well. They go on to become the first Black American billionaire couple.

1980 ~ Eddie Murphy makes his *Saturday Night Live* debut initiating a four-year run as a regular cast member.

1982 ~ Roscoe Robinson Jr. becomes the first Black U.S. Army four-star General.

1982 ~ Michael Jackson releases *Thriller*, one of the most successful and influential albums of all time. It tops the *Billboard* charts for 37 consecutive weeks, sells 66 million copies and produces seven Top 10 hits. When Jackson moonwalks through "Billie Jean" on the 1983 *Motown 25* special, MTV, which had previously not played Black artists' videos, finally caves and opens up its playlist to Jackson as well as other Blacks.

1983 ~ Vanessa Williams becomes the first Black to win the Miss America pageant. When it comes to light that nude photos of her are about to be published in *Penthouse* magazine, Williams resigns and is replaced by her runner-up Suzette Charles from New Jersey who is also Black.

1983 ~ Guion Bluford becomes the first Black U.S. astronaut in space when he flies on the Challenger mission STS-8.

1983 ~ Robert C. and Nancy Hicks Maynard become the first Black owners of a big city newspaper when they acquire the *Oakland Tribune*.

1983 ~ Debbie Allen becomes the first Black woman to win a Golden Globe Award, honored for her role on the NBC series *Fame*.

1984 ~ Jesse Jackson seeks the Democratic nomination for the presidency and finishes in a respectable 3rd place in the primaries, behind only Walter Mondale and Gary Hart. In the process he becomes the first Black to win U.S. presidential primaries and caucuses, doing so in Virginia, South Carolina, Mississippi, Louisiana and the District of Columbia.

1985 ~ Donnie Cochran becomes the first Black member of the U.S. Navy's Blue Angels. He also becomes the first Black to command the precision flying team.

1985 ~ Sherian Cadoria becomes the first Black woman U.S. Army general.

1986 ~ On January 20th, Martin Luther King Jr. Day is celebrated as a national holiday for the first time.

1986 ~ Chuck Berry, James Brown, Ray Charles, Sam Cooke, Fats Domino and Little Richard become the first Black musicians inducted into the Rock and Roll Hall of Fame. Five of the original ten inductees are Black.

1986 ~ Oprah Winfrey launches her syndicated talk show, initiating her rise to fame as one of the most iconic Black women of her era.

1987 ~ Aretha Franklin becomes the first Black woman, as well as the first woman, inducted into the Rock and Roll Hall of Fame.

1987 ~ Jennifer Jones becomes the first Black Radio City Music Hall Rockette. (Note: This is not the Jennifer Jones who enjoyed a successful five-decade career as an actress.)

1987 ~ Teddy Seymour becomes the first Black man to sail around the world solo.

1988 ~ Jesse Jackson again competes for the presidency and garners 24% of the Democratic primary vote. He wins seven states and finishes second only to Democratic nominee Michael Dukakis.

1989 ~ Just one year after co-starring in the hit film *Coming to America*, comedian Arsenio Hall breaks late-night barriers by becoming the first Black late-night talk show host. *The Arsenio Hall Show* would become a breakout success and run until 1994.

1989 ~ Colin Powell is appointed Chairman of the Joint Chiefs of Staff, the first Black to hold that position.

1989 ~ Barbara Clementine Harris becomes the first Black woman, as well as the first woman, to be ordained as a bishop in the Episcopal Church.

1989 ~ Ron Brown becomes the first Black Chairman of the Democratic National Committee.

1990 ~ Douglas Wilder becomes the first elected Black governor in the U.S., assuming that office in the State of Virginia.

1990 ~ Chris Rock makes his *Saturday Night Live* debut initiating a three-year run as a regular cast member.

1990 ~ The Wayans family brings their sketch-variety show *In Living Color* to the Fox network. It would run through1994 and feature Paul Mooney.

1990 ~ Barack Obama becomes the first Black elected president of the *Harvard Law Review*.

1990 ~ Carole Gist becomes the first Black Miss USA, representing Michigan. (Note: Not to be confused with the Miss America title that Vanessa Williams had won as noted above.)

1990 ~ Renee Tenison becomes the first Black *Playboy* "Playmate of the Year."

1992 ~ Mae Jemison becomes the first Black woman astronaut when she flies on the Space Shuttle Endeavour.

1992 ~ Carol Mosely Braun becomes the first Black woman elected to the U.S. Senate, representing Illinois.

1992 ~ Whitney Houston achieves her breakthrough with the release of the original soundtrack album of *The Bodyguard*. The album sells 45 million copies and becomes the all-time best-selling soundtrack ever, topping the charts for 20 weeks and taking home that year's Grammy for Album of the Year. The single "I Will Always Love You" hits #1 for 14 weeks.

1992 ~ Carole Simpson becomes the first Black woman to moderate a Presidential debate, the second one between Clinton and Bush.

1992 ~ Bruce W. Smith becomes the first Black to direct a full-length animated film, *Bébé's Kids*.

1992 ~ Four days of riots break out in Los Angeles after the acquittal of the four LAPD officers who had severely beaten Rodney King during a March 1991 arrest.

1993 ~ Angela Bassett scores an Oscar nomination for Best Actress for her portrayal of Tina Turner in the biopic *What's Love Got to Do with It*. This highlights a four-decade career in which she also plays iconic Black women such as Rosa Jackson, Coretta Scott King, Katherine Jackson and Betty Shabazz.

1993 ~ Toni Morrison becomes the first Black to win the Nobel Prize for Literature, acknowledging her work on the *Beloved* trilogy.

1993 ~ Rita Dove becomes the first Black woman to be named Poet Laureate of the United States, as well as the youngest person named to that position.

1993 ~ Joycelyn Elders becomes the first Black appointed Surgeon General of the United States.

1993 ~ Charley Pride becomes the first Black to be inducted as a member of the Grand Ole Opry. He is currently joined by two other Blacks in that organization, DeFord Bailey and Darius Rucker.

1994 ~ Darnell Martin becomes the first Black woman director of a major film, Columbia Pictures' *I Like It Like That*.

1995 ~ Jesse Jackson Jr. wins election to the United States House of Representatives from Illinois.

1995 ~ Hal Jackson becomes the first Black inductee to the National Radio Hall of Fame. As a disc jockey and radio personality, Jackson is noted for numerous breakthroughs in the field of radio broadcasting.

1995 ~ Chelsi Smith, representing the state of Texas, becomes the third Black USA, then the first Black Miss Universe. She goes on to make TV appearances on the shows *Martin* and *Due South*, as well as the documentary *The History of the Bathing Suit*. We'll let you make the determination as to whether or not that documentary falls into the category of "Must See TV."

1995 ~ The Million Man March draws hundreds of thousands of Black men to Washington, D.C. The rally's stated purpose is to instill a sense of solidarity and of personal responsibility to improve the participants' own condition.

1996 ~ J. Paul Reason becomes the first Black U.S. Navy four-star admiral.

1997 ~ The Million Woman March in Philadelphia echoes the initiative of 1995's Million Man March.

1997 ~ Beyoncé goes on record. As one-third of the girl group Destiny's Child, Beyoncé releases her first major label recording with the song "Killing Time" from the soundtrack to the film *Men in Black*. In 2003, she goes solo embarking upon an accolade-laden career. She sells 125 million records and is the first artist whose first six albums all debut at #1. Here are some of her award totals, all of which are highs for any singer, male or female. Beyoncé has won 31 BET Awards, 28 Grammys, 26 MTV Video Music Awards and 24 NAACP Image Awards. Certainly some Texas talent at its best.

1997 ~ The Kings of Comedy tour hits the road breaking the record for the highest grossing comedy tour ever. This show features Steve Harvey, Bernie Mac, D.L. Hughley and Cedric the Entertainer. A grand slam of comedic talent if there ever was one.

1999 ~ Franklin Raines becomes the first Black CEO of a Fortune 500 company, Fannie Mae.

1999 ~ Lauryn Hill's killer album *The Miseducation of Lauryn Hill* becomes the first hip-hop record to win the Grammy Award for Album of the Year.

1999 ~ Shirley Ann Jackson becomes the first Black woman university president at Rensselaer Polytechnic Institute.

2000 ~ Charley Pride becomes first Black inducted into the Country Music Hall of Fame. The only other Black currently in the CMHOF is DeFord Bailey.

2001 ~ George W. Bush appoints Colin Powell as the first Black Secretary of State of the United States.

2001 ~ Condoleezza Rice becomes the first Black woman to serve as U.S. National Security Advisor.

2001 ~ Robert L. Johnson and his wife Sheila, founders of Black Entertainment Television (BET), become the first Black billionaires.

2002 ~ Halle Berry becomes the first Black woman to win an Academy Award for Best Actress, achieving the award for her appearance in the film *Monster Ball*.

2002 ~ Whoopi Goldberg becomes one of just sixteen people in entertainment history to win an EGAT Award, the term bestowed upon those who have won an Emmy, Grammy, Academy and Tony Award.

2002 ~ Vernice Armour becomes the first Black woman combat pilot in the U.S. Armed Services while serving in the Marine Corps.

2003 ~ York, a slave who accompanied Lewis and Clark, becomes the first Black to appear on a circulating coin when the three men are depicted on the Mississippi coin in the U.S. State Quarter Collection.

2003 ~ Dave Chappelle debuts *Chappelle's Show,* beginning its three-year run on Comedy Central.

2005 ~ Condoleezza Rice becomes the first Black woman to serve as U.S. Secretary of State.

2005 ~ Jeanine Menze becomes the first Black woman to serve as a U.S. Coast Guard aviator.

2005 ~ Rosa Parks becomes the first Black woman, as well as the first woman period, to lie in state at the U.S. Capitol.

2006 ~ Walter E. Gaskin becomes the first Black to command a U.S. Marine Corps division.

2006 ~ Sophia Danenberg is the first Black of either gender to reach the peak of Mount Everest.

2007 ~ Barbara Hillary becomes the first Black woman to reach the North Pole.

2008 ~ Shawna Rochelle Kimbrell becomes the first Black woman combat pilot in the U.S. Air Force.

2009 ~ Eric Holder becomes the first Black U.S. Attorney General.

2009 ~ Susan Rice becomes the first Black woman to serve as U.S. Ambassador to the U.N.

2009 ~ Duke Ellington becomes the first Black to appear by himself on a circulating U.S. coin. His image is seen on the District of Columbia coin in the U.S. State Quarter Collection. (Note: The Booker T. Washington 1946 half dollar was a memorial coin not in general circulation and the 2003 Mississippi State quarter depicted York with Lewis and Clark.)

2009 ~ Alysa Stanton becomes the first Black woman rabbi.

2009 ~ Darius Rucker becomes the first Black to win the Country Music Association New Artist of the Year award.

2009 ~ Ursula Burns becomes the first Black woman to serve as CEO of a Fortune 500 company, the Xerox Corporation.

2009 ~ Barack Obama becomes the first Black President of the United States.

2012 ~ Monika Washington Stoker becomes the first Black woman to command a U.S. Navy missile destroyer.

2012 ~ Barack Obama becomes the first Black to be re-elected President of the United States.

2013 ~ Tim Scott becomes the first Black U.S. Senator from the former Confederacy since Reconstruction, serving South Carolina after being appointed by then-Governor Nikki Haley.

2013 ~ Cheryl Boone Isaacs becomes the first Black president of the Academy of Motion Picture Arts and Sciences.

2013 ~ Jeh Johnson becomes the first Black United States Secretary of Homeland Security.

2013 ~ In July 2013, the phrase "Black Lives Matter" is used for the first time. It appears on social media after the acquittal of George Zimmerman in his murder trial for the death of Black teenager Trayvon Martin who had been killed in February, 2012.

2014 ~ Michelle J. Howard becomes the first Black woman four-star admiral in the U.S. Navy.

2014 ~ Tim Scott becomes the first Black U.S. Senator to be elected in the South since Reconstruction, continuing in the position to which he had been appointed by Nikki Haley in 2013.

2015 ~ Loretta Lynch becomes the first Black woman to serve as Attorney General of the United States.

2015 ~ Lester Holt becomes the first Black sole anchor of a network evening newscast on the *NBC Nightly News*.

2016 ~ Channing Dungey is the first Black of either gender to become president of a major broadcast TV network, the Warner Bros. Television Group.

2017 ~ Writer, producer and actress Lena Waithe becomes the first Black woman to win an Emmy for comedy writing. The award comes for the Netflix series *Master of None*. In addition to playing Denise on the popular series, Waithe also writes the much-acclaimed coming-out "Thanksgiving" episode.

2017 ~ Donald Glover becomes the first Black man to win an Emmy for directing a comedy series. The award is bestowed for his work on the FX series *Atlanta*.

2017 ~ Appearing in the *Billboard* Hot 100 for the 74th time, Nicki Minaj passes Aretha Franklin to become the most charted female singer of all time.

2018 ~ Sterling K. Brown becomes the first Black man to win a Golden Globe for Best Actor in a TV Drama for his role as Randall in NBC's *This Is Us*.

2018 ~ Rapper Kendrick Lamar wins the Pulitzer Prize for his album *Damn*. Every previous winner had come from one of two genres, either classical or jazz. Lamar is lauded for "capturing the complexity of modern African-American life."

2019 ~ Elijah Cummings, Representative from Maryland, becomes the first Black elected official to lie in state at the U.S. Capitol.

2019 ~ Childish Gambino's "This Is America" becomes the first rap song to win Grammys for Song of the Year and Record of the Year.

2020 ~ The murder of George Floyd galvanizes the Black Lives Matter movement.

2020 ~ Charles Q. Brown Jr. becomes the first Black to be appointed Chief of Staff of the Air Force and the first Black to lead any branch of the U.S. Armed Forces.

2020 ~ John Lewis, Representative from Georgia, becomes the second Black elected official to lie in state at the U.S. Capitol.

2021 ~ Raphael Warnock becomes the first Black Democrat elected to the Senate in a former Confederate state, representing Georgia.

2021 ~ Kamala Harris becomes the first Black vice president of the United States.

2021 ~ Lloyd Austin becomes the first Black United States Secretary of Defense.

2021 ~ On June 17th President Joe Biden signs the Juneteenth National Independence Day Act officially establishing Juneteenth as a national holiday.

2021 ~ Zaila Avant-garde, a 14-year-old girl from Harvey, Louisiana becomes the first Black to win the Scripps National Spelling Bee.

FOOTNOTES

CHAPTER 1

[1] "Funny Dave Chappelle quotes." funnycomedianquotes.com. http://funnycomedianquotes.com/funny-dave-chappelle-jokes-and-quotes.html, accessed June 21, 2021.

[2] "Redd Foxx Quotes." AZ Quotes. https://www.azquotes.com/author/5084-Redd_Foxx, accessed June 22, 2020.

[3] "Chris Rock Quotes." Wealthygorilla.com. https://wealthygorilla.com/chris-rock-quotes/, accessed July 5, 2020.

[4] Ibid.

[5] "Born a Crime." Barnes and Noble. https://www.barnesandnoble.com/readouts/born-a-crime-stories-from-a-south-african-childhood/, accessed Dec, 30, 2020.

[6] "Eddie Murphy Quotes and Sayings." inspiringquotes.us. https://www.inspiringquotes.us/author/2227-eddie-murphy, accessed July 3, 2020.

CHAPTER 2

[1] King, Martin L., Jr. "I Have a Dream Speech." March on Washington, Lincoln Memorial, Washington, D. C., Aug. 28, 1963.

[2] *The Tonight Show Starring Johnny Carson*, produced by Art Stark, season 7, episode 1361, NBC, aired Feb. 8, 1968. https://www.youtube.com/watch?v=kGuVQa38o3o&t=35s.

[3] "*The Playful Side of Dr. Martin Luther King Jr."* https://www.oprah.com/own-master-class/the-playful-side-of-dr-martin-luther-king-jr., accessed July 22, 2020.

[4] *The Late Show with Stephen Colbert*, produced by Christopher A. Licht, season 4, episode 538, CBS. https://www.youtube.com/watch?v=tfJRoZWq2VU, accessed July 22, 2020.

CHAPTER 3

[1] "Here's Why Dave Chappelle Walked Away From $50 Million." TheThings. https://www.thethings.com/heres-why-dave-chappelle-walked-away-from-50-million/, accessed June 22, 2020.

[2] "*Dave Chappelle is making $60 million for his Netflix comedy specials."* Business Insider. https://www.businessinsider.com/dave-chappelle-salary-netflix-comedy-specials-deal-2016-11, accessed July 22, 2020.

[3] "Funny Dave Chappelle quotes." funnycomedianquotes.com. http://funnycomedianquotes.com/funny-dave-chappelle-jokes-and-quotes.html, accessed June 21, 2020.

[4] *Comedy Central's 100 Greatest Standups of All Time."* ranker.com. https://www.ranker.com/list/comedy-central_s-100-greatest-standups-of-all-time-v1/celebrity-insider, accessed June 22, 2020.

[5] Ibid.

[6] Ibid.

[7] Ibid.

[8] Ibid.

[9] "Redd Foxx – I Love Mexicans." SongMe. https://songme.ru/song/4165544-i-love-mexicans-by-redd-foxx, accessed June 21, 2020.

[10] "Redd Foxx Quotes." AZ Quotes. https://www.azquotes.com/author/5084-Redd_Foxx, accessed June 22, 2020.

[11] "On Location: Redd Foxx." HBO special, (1 Apr. 1978), Director Marty Callner, https://www.youtube.com/watch?v=qVs8yr-1ZIY&t=18s, accessed June 22, 2020.

[12] Ibid.

[13] "Redd Foxx Quotes." AZ Quotes. https://www.azquotes.com/author/5084-Redd_Foxx, accessed June 22, 2020.

[14] Ibid.

[15] Ibid.

[16] "On Location: Redd Foxx." HBO special, (1 Apr. 1978), Director Marty Callner. https://www.youtube.com/watch?v=qVs8yr-1ZIY&t=18s, accessed June 22, 2020.

[17]"Sneezes – Redd Foxx." YouTube, uploaded by Drip Fox, 1 Apr. 2011, https://www.youtube.com/watch?v=cgy2asi4UT0, accessed June 20, 2020.
[18]"*TV Guide*'s 50 Best Shows of All Time." *TV Guide,* 13 May 2002. https://www.imdb.com/list/ls000996988/, accessed June 29, 2020.
[19]"Bill Cosby Quotes and Sayings." inspiringquotes.us. https://www.inspiringquotes.us/author/2741-bill-cosby/, accessed June 30, 2020.
[20]Ibid.
[21]Ibid.
[22]Ibid.
[23]Ibid.
[24]"Bill Cosby quotes." BrainyQuote. https://www.quotes.net/mquote/27845, accessed July 2, 2020.
[25]"*Saturday Night Live*: 145 Cast Members Ranked. Rolling Stone. https://www.rollingstone.com/tv/tv-lists/saturday-night-live-all-145-cast-members-ranked-146340/, accessed July 2, 2020.
[26]"Eddie Murphy Delirious." Famous Quotes and Sayings. https://www.quotes.net/mquote/27845, accessed July 3, 2020.
[27]"Eddie Murphy Quotes and Sayings." inspiringquotes.us. https://www.inspiringquotes.us/author/2227-eddie-murphy, accessed July 3, 2020.
[28]Ibid.
[29]"Chris Rock just made a groundbreaking $40 million deal for 2 Netflix specials." Business Insider. https://www.businessinsider.com/chris-rock-netflix-deal-stand-up-specials-2016-10, accessed July 5, 2020.
[30]"Magazine Names Chris Rock As Funniest Man." AP News. https://apnews.com/article/d6225a782f18e3bd0d968845d4898e55, accessed July 5, 2020.
[31] "Rock breaks UK comedy gig record." BBC. http://news.bbc.co.uk/2/hi/entertainment/7416498.stm, accessed July 5, 2020.
[32]"*Biographies Comedians*." Biography Online. https://www.biographyonline.net/comics.html, accessed July 6, 2020.
[33]*Late Night with David Letterman*, produced by David Letterman, season 16, episode 3333, CBS. https://www.youtube.com/watch?v=mFNCLtV03Jw, accessed July 6, 2020.
[34]"Chris Rock Argues President Obama is White in Message to Voters." The Hollywood Reporter. https://www.hollywoodreporter.com/tv/tv-news/chris-rock-argues-president-obama-386240/, accessed July 6, 2020.
[35]"Funny Chris Rock Quotes." funnycomedianquotes.com. http://funnycomedianquotes.com/funny-chris-rock-jokes-and-quotes.html?, accessed July 5, 2020.
[36]Ibid.
[37]Ibid.
[38]"*Comedy Central's 100 Greatest Standups of All Time*." ranker.com. https://www.ranker.com/list/comedy-central_s-100-greatest-standups-of-all-time-v1/celebrity-insider, accessed July 7, 2020.
[39] 50 Best Stand-Up Comics of All Time." RollingStone. https://www.rollingstone.com/culture/culture-lists/50-best-stand-up-comics-of-all-time-126359/, accessed July 8, 2020.
[40]"Richard Pryor." iComedyTV. https://www.icomedytv.com/famous-comedian/term/653, accessed July 8, 2020.
[41]"1940-2005: Richard Pryor." Newsweek. https://www.newsweek.com/1940-2005-richard-pryor-114071, accessed July 9, 2020.
[42]"1971: On Stage On This Date." Lobero Theatre. https://www.lobero.org/2020/07/1971-richard-pryor/, accessed July 8, 2020.
[43]"Richard Pryor." hobbyDB. https://www.hobbydb.com/marketplaces/hobbydb/subjects/richard-pryor-actor, accessed July 8, 2020.
[44]"60 Controversial Richard Pryor Jokes to Make You Think." everydaypower.com. https://everydaypower.com/richard-pryor-quotes/, accessed July 8, 2020.
[45]Ibid.
[46]Ibid.
[47]"Funny Richard Pryor Quotes." funnycomedians.com. http://funnycomedianquotes.com/funny-richard-pryor-jokes-and-quotes.html?, accessed Aug. 3, 2020.

[48] "Richard Pryor's Quotes and Sayings." inspiringquotes.us. https://www.inspiringquotes.us/author/2506-richard-pryor, accessed Aug, 2. 2020.
[49] "51 Richard Pryor Quotes from the Iconic Stand-Up Comedian." kidadl.com. https://kidadl.com/articles/richard-pryor-quotes-from-the-iconic-stand-up-comedian, accessed Aug, 2, 2020.
[50] "Funny Richard Pryor Quotes." funnycomedians.com. http://funnycomedianquotes.com/funny-richard-pryor-jokes-and-quotes.html?, accessed Aug. 3, 2020.
[51] "Paul Mooney Quotes." BrainyQuote. https://www.brainyquote.com/quotes/paul_mooney_607278, Aug. 2, 2020.

CHAPTER 4
[1] "Josephine Baker: Story of Awakening," directed by Ilana Navaro. PBS Documentary 2018.
[2] "40 Fascinating Facts About the Fabulous Josephine Baker." History Collection. historycollection.com,https://historycollection.com/40-fascinating-facts-about-the-fabulous-josephine-baker/29/, accessed Oct. 26, 2020.
[3] "Interesting Facts About Josephine Baker." Orlandoshakes. https://www.orlandoshakes.org/2021/02/01/interesting-facts-about-josephine-baker/, accessed Oct. 24, 2020.
[4] "Josephine Baker: Story of Awakening," directed by Ilana Navaro. PBS Documentary 2018.
[5] "Josephine Baker Quotes." BrainyQuotes. https://www.brainyquote.com/quotes/josephine_baker_537596#, accessed Sep. 19, 2020.
[6] "Chicago's Little Esther, Now Petted by Royalty, Wins Over Jim Crowism." *The Chicago Defender*, September 14, 1929.
[7] Ibid.
[8] "Brazilian Navy Band Played For Lil' Esther." *The Baltimore Afro-American*, August 22, 1931.
[9] "Big Midnight Crowd Enjoys NAACP Benefit." *The Baltimore Afro-American*, July 28, 1934.
[10] "Helen Kane Suit Charging Theft Of 'Boop' Is Lost: Justice McGoldrick Rules Singer Didn't Prove She Invented Syncopated Bleat." *New York Herald Tribune*, May 6, 1934.
[11] "Gladys Bentley: Drag King of Harlem Renaissance." PBS American Masters. https://www.pbs.org/wnet/americanmasters/meet-gladys-bentley-drag-king-of-the-harlem-renaissance/18075/, accessed Sep. 18, 2020.
[12] Wilson, James (2010). *Bulldaggers, Pansies, and Chocolate Babies*, p. 172, ISBN 978-0472117253.
[13] "Women's History Month – 'Hattie McDaniel' – Groundbreaker !!." MySpiritDC. https://myspiritdc.com/1599921/womens-history-month-hattie-mcdaniel-groundbreaker/, accessed Sep.16, 2020.
[14] Jackson, Carlton. *Hattie: The Life of Hattie McDaniel*. Madison Books, 1990. p. 52.
[15] "Nichelle Nichols on how Dr. MLK, Jr. dissuaded her from quitting Star Trek." Emmy TV Legends.org. https://www.youtube.com/watch?v=pSq_UIuxba8, accessed Jan. 18, 2021.
[16] "The Comedy Central Roast of William Shatner." YouTube, uploaded by The Comedy Central Roast Collection, accessed Jan. 18, 2020.

CHAPTER 5
[1] "The Last Black Unicorn-Mascots and Bar Mitzvahs." BookRags. http://www.bookrags.com/studyguide-the-last-black-unicorn/chapanal001.html#gsc.tab=0, accessed Oct. 29. 2020.
[2] Ibid.
[3] Ibid.
+Ibid.
[5] Ibid.
[6] Ibid.
[7] Ibid.
[8] "42 Tiffany Haddish Quotes to Brighten Your Day." WealthyGorilla. https://wealthygorilla.com/tiffany-haddish-quotes/, accessed Nov. 1, 2020.
[9] *Saturday Night Live*, produced by Lorne Michaels, season 6, episode 892. NBC, 11 Nov. 2017. https://www.youtube.com/watch?v=cXfSL1XOIdM&t=4s, accessed Nov. 1, 2020.

[10] "The Misadventures of Awkward Black Girl." Paperzz. https://paperzz.com/doc/7655147/the-misadventures-of-awkward-black-girl, accessed Jan.5, 2021.
[11] *Late Night with Seth Meyers*, produced by Seth Meyers and Mike Shoemaker, season 4, episode 482, NBC, 1 Feb. 2017. https://www.youtube.com/watch?v=elg1BF_hfII
[12] "Author Amber Ruffin." Archive. https://archive.bookfrom.net/amber-ruffin/page,6,574770-youll_never_believe_what_happened_to_lacey.html, accessed Feb. 27, 2021.
[13] "You Can't Touch My Hair." Google Books. https://books.google.com/books?id=mcm-CwAAQBAJ&pg=PA80&lpg=PA80&dq=phoebe+robinson+you+can%27t+touch+my+hair+Jennifer-Lawrence-falling-up-the-stairs-at-the-2013-Oscars, accessed Oct. 9, 2020.
[14] "You Can't Touch My Hair." Google Books. https://www.google.com/books/edition/You_Can_t_Touch_My_Hair/Utv4DAAAQBAJ?hl=en&gbpv=1&dq=phoebe+robinson+you+can%27t+touch+my+hair+Your+Parents+Might+Say+They+Didn%E2%80%99t, accessed on Oct. 7, 2020.
[15] "You Can't Touch My Hair." Google Books. https://books.google.com/books?id=mcm-CwAAQBAJ&pg=PA80&lpg=PA80&dq=phoebe+robinson+you+can%27t+touch+my+hair+Jennifer-Lawrence-falling-up-the-stairs-at-the-2013-Oscars, accessed Oct. 9, 2020.
[16] "YCTMH by My Free Kindle." Issuu. https://issuu.com/myfreekindle/docs/yctmh, accessed Oct. 10, 2020.
[17] "Phoebe Robinson Quotes." Goodreads. https://www.goodreads.com/quotes/search?page=39&q=oprah, accessed Oct. 9, 2020.
[18] "You Can't Touch My Hair." Google Books. https://books.google.com/books?id=Utv4DAAAQBAJ&pg=PA173&lpg=PA173&dq=phoebe+robinson+you+can%27t+touch+my+hair+Look,+I+love+me+some+Val+Kilmer.+Anytime+I+watch+Batman+Forever,+there%E2%80%99s+light+precipitation+going+on+in+my+vagina+walls, accessed Oct. 7, 2020.
[19] "You Can't Touch My Hair." Google Books. https://books.google.com/books?id=Utv4DAAAQBAJ&pg=PA197&lpg=PA197&dq=phoebe+robinson+you+can%27t+touch+my+hair+OK,+wow.+So+you%E2%80%99re+a+lesbian.+You%E2%80%99re+in+an+interracial+relationship.+You%E2%80%99re+sleeping+with+the+hired+help, accessed Oct. 7, 2020.
[20] "You Can't Touch My Hair." Google Books. https://www.google.com/books/edition/You_Can_t_Touch_My_Hair/mcm-CwAAQBAJ?hl=en&gbpv=1&dq=phoebe+robinson+you+can%27t+touch+my+hair+Even+if+my+hair+catches+on+fire,+do+not+come+to+my+rescue%3B+just+let+me+do+a+Michael+Jackson+spin+move+to+put+the+blaze+out, accessed Oct. 7, 2020.

CHAPTER 6

[1] "Black History Month Profiles: Claudette Colvin." DiversityInc. https://www.diversityinc.com/black-history-month-profiles-claudette-colvin-civil-rights-activist, accessed Dec. 4, 2020.
[2] "In Newly Found Audio, A Forgotten Civil Rights Leader Says Coming Out 'Was An Absolute Necessity.'" NPR. https://www.npr.org/2019/01/06/682598649/in-newly-found-audio-a-forgotten-civil-rights-leader-says-coming-out-was-an-absolute-necessity, accessed Dec. 5, 2020.
[3] "Bayard Rustin." JacksonFreePress. https://www.jacksonfreepress.com/news/2015/jan/19/bayard-rustin/, accessed Dec. 15, 2020.
[4] "Pioneering Politician, Advocate Shirley Chisholm Dies." Washington Post. https://www.washingtonpost.com/archive/local/2005/01/04/pioneering-politician-advocate-shirley-chisholm-dies/, accessed Feb. 19, 2021.
[5] "Shirley Chisholm." Washington Post. https://www.washingtonpost.com/archive/opinions/2005/01/05/shirley-chisholm/, accessed Feb. 19, 2021.
[6] "Funniest Barack Quotes of All-Time." Liveabout. https://www.liveabout.com/funniest-barack-obama-quotes-of-all-time-4078438/, accessed Dec. 4, 2020.
[7] Ibid.
[8] Ibid.
[9] Ibid.
[10] Ibid.
[11] Ibid.

[12] Ibid.
[13] Ibid.
[14] Ibid.
[15] Ibid.
[16] "The Funniest Lines in Barack Obama's White House Correspondents' Dinner Speech." Washington Post. https://www.washingtonpost.com/news/reliable-source/wp/2015/04/25/the-funniest-lines-in-president-obamas-white-house-correspondents-dinner-speech/, accessed Dec. 4, 2020.
[17] "Funniest Barack Quotes of All-Time." Liveabout. https://www.liveabout.com/funniest-barack-obama-quotes-of-all-time-4078438/, accessed Dec. 4, 2020.
[18] Ibid.
[19] Ibid.
[20] "The Funniest Lines in Barack Obama's White House Correspondents' Dinner Speech." Washington Post. https://www.washingtonpost.com/news/reliable-source/wp/2015/04/25/the-funniest-lines-in-president-obamas-white-house-correspondents-dinner-speech/, accessed Dec. 4, 2020.

CHAPTER 7

[1] "I Might Need Security." directed by Chuck Vinson, HBO special, 2002. https://www.google.com/search?q=jamie+foxx+i+need+security&sxsrf=AOaemvIeKv9Dhgx-Puqjdkxsnb9TnGnq4w%3A1638498420561&source, accessed Dec. 29, 2020.
[2] Ibid.
[3] "I'm a Grown Little Man," directed by Shannon Hartman, Netflix special, 2009. https://www.youtube.com/watch?v=xZM9TfZzXLY, accessed Dec. 29, 2020.
[4] Ibid.
[5] Ibid.
[6] Ibid.
[7] "You So Crazy," directed by Thomas Schlamme, HBO special, 1994. https://www.youtube.com/watch?v=h3MjtFdfaqE&t=2053s, accessed Feb. 9, 2021.
[8] "Tracy Morgan on TNT pre-game show." YouTube, uploaded by ph1llydiehard, Jan. 27, 2011. https://www.youtube.com/watch?v=bBIh04-I-iQ, accessed Dec. 29, 2020.
[9] "Born a Crime." Barnes and Noble. https://www.barnesandnoble.com/readouts/born-a-crime-stories-from-a-south-african-childhood/, accessed Dec, 30, 2020.
[10] Ibid.
[11] Ibid.
[12] Ibid.
[13] Ibid.
[14] Ibid.
[15] "The Awkward Thoughts of W. Kamau Bell." Audio Book Store. https://www.audible.com/ep/freetrial?source_code=GO1DH13310082090OS&device=d&cvosrc=ppc.goo gle.audible.com&cvo_campaign=13262341865&cvo_crid=524073073864&Matchtype=p&gclid=Cj 0KCQiAnaeNBhCUARIsABEee8WrNAOPDO5OiLhJ7sri2eKFMRNWyj4Mse9bi51AuPPhvJQCBxqu WUwaAnAcEALw_wcB&gclsrc=aw.ds
[16] Ibid.
[17] Ibid.
[18] Ibid.
[19] Ibid.
[20] Ibid.
[21] Ibid.
[22] "When Is It Okay for White People to Say "Nigger"?. YouTube, uploaded by Kill Rock Stars, Jan. 11 2017, https://www.youtube.com/watch?v=gJkbsmouvJY, accessed Dec. 29, 2020.
[23] "The Awkward Thoughts of W. Kamau Bell." Audio Book Store. https://www.audible.com/ep/freetrial?source_code=GO1DH13310082090OS&device=d&cvosrc=ppc.goo gle.audible.com&cvo_campaign=13262341865&cvo_crid=524073073864&Matchtype=p&gclid=Cj 0KCQiAnaeNBhCUARIsABEee8WrNAOPDO5OiLhJ7sri2eKFMRNWyj4Mse9bi51AuPPhvJQCBxqu WUwaAnAcEALw_wcB&gclsrc=aw.ds, accessed Oct. 13, 2020.

[24]Ibid.
[25]"Semi-Prominent Negro." The Laugh Button. https://thelaughbutton.com/semi-prominent-negro-w-kamau-b, accessed Oct.13, 2020.

CHAPTER 8

[1]"Unforgiveable Blackness: The Rise and Fall of Jack Johnson." PBS. https://www.pbs.org/video/unforgivable-blackness-rise-and-fall-jack-johnson, accessed Mar. 5, 2021.
[2]"Unforgiveable Blackness: The Rise and Fall of Jack Johnson – Speeding Ticket." PBS. https://www.tpt.org/unforgivable-blackness-the-rise-and-fall-of-jack-johnson/video/speeding-tickets-jceubw/, accessed Mar. 5, 2021.
[3]"Dr. John Baxter Taylor Jr., The First African American Olympic Gold Medalist. WingedFist. http://www.wingedfist.org/John_Baxter_Taylor_Jr.htmlell-required-listening, accessed Mar.18, 2021.
[4]"Negro Runner Dead; John B. Taylor, Quarter Miler, Victim of Typhoid Pneumonia." The New York Times. Dec. 3, 1908.
[5]"On the Shoulders of Giants." Amazon. https://www.amazon.com/Shoulders-Giants-Kareem-Abdul-Jabbar/dp/B07HXPN37N, accessed May 17, 2021.
[6]"The 88 Best Satchel Paige Quotes." SportsFeelGoodStories. https://www.sportsfeelgoodstories.com/the-88-best-satchel-paige-quotes/, accessed Apr. 8, 2021.
[7]"Satchell Paige Quotes." BrainyQuote. https://www.brainyquote.com/authors/satchel-paige-quotes/, accessed Apr. 7, 2021.
[8]Ibid.
[9]"Top 30 Quotes of Satchell Paige." inspiringquotes.us. https://www.inspiringquotes.us/author/8247-satchel-paige, accessed April 7, 2021.
[10]"Satchell Paige Quotes." BrainyQuote. https://www.brainyquote.com/authors/satchel-paige-quotes/, accessed April 7, 2021.
[11]"Top 30 Quotes of Satchell Paige." inspiringquotes.us. https://www.inspiringquotes.us/author/8247-satchel-paige, accessed April 7, 2021.
[12]"30 of Muhammad Ali's Best Quotes." USA Today. https://www.usatoday.com/story/sports/boxing/2016/06/03/muhammad-ali-best-quotes-boxing/85370850/, accessed Oct. 11, 2020.
[13]"Muhammad Ali Quotes." QuoteFancy. https://quotefancy.com/quote/869627/Muhammad-Ali-I-m-so-fast-I-could-hit-you-before-God-gets-the-news, accessed Oct. 12, 2020.
[14]"30 of Muhammad Ali's Best Quotes." USA Today. https://www.usatoday.com/story/sports/boxing/2016/06/03/muhammad-ali-best-quotes-boxing/85370850/, accessed Oct. 11, 2020.
[15]Ibid.
[16]Ibid.
[17]"Muhammad Ali Quotes." BrainyQuote. https://www.brainyquote.com/quotes/muhammad_ali_167371, accessed Oct. 11, 2020
[18]"30 of Muhammad Ali's Best Quotes." USA Today. https://www.usatoday.com/story/sports/boxing/2016/06/03/muhammad-ali-best-quotes-boxing/85370850/, accessed Oct. 11, 2020.

CHAPTER 9

[1]"Pigmeat Markham." DeadFrogComedyDB. https://www.dead-frog.com/comedians/comic/pigmeat-markham, accessed May 30, 2021.
[2]Fox, Ted, Showtime at the Apollo, Ce Capo, p 94. ISBN 9780030605338.
[3]"Pigmeat Markham." DeadFrogComedyDB. https://www.dead-frog.com/comedians/comic/pigmeat-markham, accessed May 30, 2021.
[4]"Slappy White Quotes." AZ Quotes. https://www.azquotes.com/author/42243-Slappy_White, accessed Apr. 26, 2021.
[5]Ibid.
[6]"I Found Me A White Man You Find Yourself One!." YouTube, uploaded by ReelBlack, June 4, 2019. https://www.youtube.com/watch?v=XEEdgtKkYlA&t=1238s, accessed Apr. 26, 2021.
[7]Ibid.

[8] Ibid.
[9] Ibid.
[10] "Bonus round stars: 9 celebrities who found their greatest fame on game shows." The A.V. Club. https://www.avclub.com/bonus-round-stars-9-celebrities-who-found-their-greate-1798269752, accessed Mar. 9, 2021.
[11] "Black Laughter / Black Protest." Rutgers University Library. https://rucore.libraries.rutgers.edu/rutgers-lib/24723/PDF/1/play/, accessed Nov. 27.
[12] "Nipsey Russell, A Comic with a Gift for Verse, Dies at 80." *The New York Times.* Oct. 4, 2005.
[13] "Time Magazine Cover: Flip Wilson – Jan 31, 1972." Time Magazine. http://content.time.com/time/covers/0,16641,19720131,00.html, accessed Sep. 19, 2020.
[14] Flip Wilson. The Devil Made Me Buy This Dress. Little David Records. Feb, 1970.
[15] Flip Wilson. The Devil Made Me Buy This Dress. Little David Records. Feb, 1970.
[16] "Top 18 Quotes of Flip Wilson."inspiringquotes.us. https://www.inspiringquotes.us/author/4261-flip-wilson, accessed Sep. 21, 2020.
[17] "Flip Wilson Quotes." BrainyQuote. https://www.brainyquote.com/authors/flip-wilson-quotes, accessed Sep. 21, 2020.
[18] "Top 18 Quotes of Flip Wilson." inspiringquotes.us. https://www.inspiringquotes.us/author/4261-flip-wilson, accessed Sep. 21, 2020.
[19] "Rolling Stone 50 Best Stand-Up Comics of All Time." Rolling Stone. https://www.rollingstone.com/culture/culture-lists/50-best-stand-up-comics-of-all-time-126359/, accessed Oct. 24, 2020.
[20] "120+ Dick Gregory Quotes From a Multifaceted Civil Rights Activist." ComicBookAndBeyond. https://comicbookandbeyond.com/dick-gregory-quotes/, accessed Oct. 25, 2020.
[21] "Dick Gregory Quotes." BrainyQuote. https://www.brainyquote.com/quotes/dick_gregory_472457l, accessed Oct. 24, 2020.
[22] "Top 30 Quotes of Dick Gregor." inspiringquotes.us. https://www.inspiringquotes.us/author/6029-dick-gregory, accessed Oct. 24, 2020.
[23] Ibid.
[24] Ibid.
[25] Ibid.

CHAPTER 10

[1] "African American Odyssey: A Quest for Full Citizenship." Library of Congress. https://www.loc.gov/exhibits/african-american-odyssey/learn-more.html, accessed Jan, 28, 2021.
[2] "Africa, Soviet Imperialism & the Retreat of American Power." Commentary.org. https://www.commentary.org/articles/bayard-rustin-2/africa-soviet-imperialism-the-retreat-of-american-power/, accessed Jan. 27, 2021.
[3] "A Half Century of Jewish Emigration from the Former Soviet Union." daviscenter.fas.harvard. https://daviscenter.fas.harvard.edu/sites/default/files/files/2021-04/Tolts%20M.%20A%20Half%20Century%20of%20Jewish%20Emigration%20from%20the%20Former%20Soviet%20Union%20-%20Haarvard4%20_0.pdf, accessed Jan 28, 2021.
[4] "Opal Lee Walked Hundreds of Miles to Help Make Juneteenth a U.S. Holiday." CBC. https://www.cbc.ca/radio/thecurrent/the-current-for-july-2-2021-1.6085982/opal-lee-walked-hundreds-of-miles-to-help-make-juneteenth-a-u-s-holiday-at-94-she-s-not-done-fighting-yet-1.6085985, accessed Feb. 19, 2021.
[5] "About – The Real Opal Lee." The Real Opal Lee. https://www.opalswalk2dc.com/aboutl, accessed Feb 19, 2021.
[6] "The Wiz." Origin Theatrical. https://www.origintheatrical.com.au/article/1e6c33ab-89b0-40c2-bf02-26715d0f6a54.html, accessed Feb 19, 2020.
[7] "Motown 25: Yesterday, Today, Forever," produced by Suzanne de Passe, NBC, 1983.

CHAPTER 11

[1] "Dr. Comic: Sociologist with Ph.D. left classroom to tell jokes." Ebony Magazine, April 1992, https://books.google.com/books?id=xdQDAAAAMBAJ&pg=PA70&lpg=PA70&dq=bertrice+berry+line+white+fat+don%27t+look+like+mama+cass, accessed Aug. 9, 2020

[2] Dance, Daryl Cumber, Honey, Hush! : An Anthology of African American Women's Humor. WW Norton & Co. 1998. p. 81.

[3] Dance, Daryl Cumber, Honey, Hush! : An Anthology of African American Women's Humor. WW Norton & Co. 1998. p. 267-268. [4]"Pipe Laying Dan." YouTube, uploaded by Steve D. https://www.youtube.com/watch?v=5KeuY1KebpI, accessed on July 16, 2020

[5]"Lawanda Page Quotes." LibQuotes. https://libquotes.com/lawanda-page/quote/lbz0j3d, accessed July 15, 2020.

[6]"Pipe Laying Dan." YouTube, uploaded by Steve D. https://www.youtube.com/watch?v=5KeuY1KebpI. accessed July 16, 2020

[7]Ibid.

[8]Ibid.

[9]"Whoopi Goldberg on Moms Mabley." Showbiz. https://www.showbiz411.com/2013/04/22/whoopi-goldberg-on-moms-mabley-she-was-clearly-out-and-didnt-give-a-hoot, accessed July 15, 2020.

[10]"Moms Mabley: She Finally Makes the Movies." Ebony. Johnson Publishing Company. April 1974. p. 88.

[11]"Moms Mabley Quotes." AZ Quotes. https://www.azquotes.com/author/26561-Moms_Mabley, accessed July 15, 2020.

[12]Ibid.

[13]"Moms Mabley 'Men & Marriage' on Ed Sullivan Show." YouTube, uploaded by Ed Sullivan Show Aug. 29, 2020, accessed July 15, 2020.

[14]"Moms Mabley interview." YouTube, uploaded by Reelin In The Years 66. https://www.youtube.com/watch?v=1T45-hBsHSA, accessed July 15, 2020.

CHAPTER 12

[1]"Cathay Williams Story." BuffaloSoldier. https://www.buffalosoldier.net/CathayWilliamsFemaleBuffaloSoldierWithDocuments.htm, accessed Aug, 26, 2020.

[2]Ibid.

[3]Ibid.

[4]Ibid.

[5]Ibid.

[6]"No Mail, Low Morale." Army University Press. https://www.armyupress.army.mil/Journals/Military-Review/English-Edition-Archives/Jan-Feb-2019/Warrington-Mail/, accessed Mar. 28, 2021.

[7]Terkel, Studs. American Dreams: Lost and Found. Patheon Books, p. 359-360.

[8]"Eleanor Roosevelt's Flight With the First Black Aviators." NPR. https://www.npr.org/sections/pictureshow/2011/03/25/134769323/black_aviators, accessed Mar. 28, 2021.

CHAPTER 13

[1]"Williams, Bert." Discography of American Historical Recordings. https://adp.library.ucsb.edu/index.php/mastertalent/detail/103803/Williams_Bert, accessed Nov. 29, 2020.

[2]"Ziegfeld and Vaudeville." Travalanche. https://travsd.wordpress.com/2010/03/21/ziegfeld-and-vaudeville/, accessed Nov. 29, 2020.

[3]"65 Live Philosophy Quotes." Pinterest. https://www.pinterest.com/pin/648448046337873831/, accessed Nov. 29, 2020

[4]"Lost Sounds: Blacks and the Birth of the Recording Industry." Google Books. https://books.google.com/books?id=lf7NTiZVvy0C&pg=PA124&lpg=PA124&dq=tim+brooks+williams+had+become+a+star&source, accessed Nov. 30, 2021.

[5]"Bert Williams 1874-1922." Blackface!. https://black-face.com/Bert-Williams.html, accessed Nov. 28, 2020.

[6]"Bert Williams Quotes and Sayings." inspiringquotes.us. https://www.bhttps//www.inspiringquotes.us/author/9195-bert-williams, accessed Nov. 30, 2020.

[7]"Bert Williams Quotes." BrainyQuote. https://www.brainyquote.com/authors/bert-williams-quotes, accessed Nov. 29, 2020.

[8]Ibid.

[9]"Image Speak." Media Diversified. https://mediadiversified.org/2013/10/04/photo-gallery-black-actors-on-stage-and-screen/image-speak/, accessed Nov. 28, 2020.
[10]"The Tutt Brothers: Pioneering Black Impressarios." American Vaudeville. https://vaudeville.sites.arizona.edu/node/72, accessed Apr. 2, 2021.
[11]Ibid.
[12]"Jelly Roll Queen." YouTube, uploaded by Althazarr. https://www.youtube.com/watch?v=_iW692OyOMI
[13]"Butterbeans and Susie." The Audio DB. https://www.theaudiodb.com/artist/140592, accessed Apr. 3, 2021.
[14]Ibid.
[15]Ibid.
[16]"This is the Actor that Divided Black America." History Collection. https://historycollection.com/this-is-the-actor-that-divided-black-america-and-heres-why/, accessed Mar. 20, 2021.
[17]"Why Jack Johnson Would Be King Today." CyberBoxingZone. http://www.cyberboxingzone.com/boxing/casey/MC_JJohnson.html, accessed Mar. 20, 2021.
[18]"Ali's Phantom Punch Mystery Explained." PBS. https://www.pbs.org/wgbh/roadshow/stories/articles/2021/5/24/ali-phantom-punch-controversy-explained, accessed Mar. 20, 2021.
[19]"William 'Willie' Best." BlackThen. https://blackthen.com/william-willie-best-african-american-actor-sleep-n-eat-who-appeared-in-comedy-roles/, accessed Mar. 22, 2021.
[20]"Willie Best 1913-1962." Blackface!. https://black-face.com/Willie-Best.html, accessed Mar. 22, 2021.

CHAPTER 14

[1]"Cotton Mather and the Boston Smallpox Epidemic of 1721-1722." Jama Network. https://jamanetwork.com/journals/jama/article-abstract/374575, accessed Mar. 24, 2021.
[2]"The 100 Best Bostonians of All-Time." Boston Magazine. https://www.bostonmagazine.com/news/2016/01/05/100-best-bostonians/, accessed Mar. 24, 2021.
[3]"Proceed Great Chief with Mercy on My Side." LCPS. https://www.lcps.org/cms/lib4/VA01000195/Centricity/Domain/1665/14%20-%20Revolutionary%20War%20Notes%20Part%201%20Filled%20In.pdf, accessed Mar. 27, 2021.
[4]"Bass Reeves: The Real Lone Ranger." BlackAmericaWeb. https://blackamericaweb.com/2021/02/04/bass-reeves-the-lone-ranger/, accessed Mar. 28, 2021.
[5]"Bill Pickett Quotes." LibQuotes. https://libquotes.com/bill-pickett, accessed Sep. 17, 2020.
[6]"Madam C. J. Walker born." OUPblog. https://blog.oup.com/2011/12/madam-cj-walker/#:~:text=Walker%20born-,Madam%20C.%20J.,was%20promoted%20to%20the%20washtub.&text=Walker%20was%20born%20on%20a%20Louisiana%20plantation%20in%201867%20as%20Sarah%20Breedlove, accessed Apr. 5, 2021.
[7]"Bessie Coleman." PBS American Experience. https://www.pbs.org/wgbh/americanexperience/features/flygirls-bessie-coleman/, accessed Aug. 19, 2020.
[8]"Top 5 Lessons from Bessie Coleman's Legacy." Medium.com. https://medium.com/faa/top-5-lessons-from-bessie-colemans-legacy-f12e0576e2f3, accessed Aug. 19, 2020.
[9]"Scottsboro: An American Tragedy / Transcript." PBS American Experience, http://www.shoppbs.pbs.org/wgbh/amex/scottsboro/filmmore/pt.html, accessed Aug 25, 2020.
[10]Ibid.
[11]Ibid.
[12]Ibid
[13]Ibid.

CHAPTER 15

[1]"The Original Kings of Comedy." YouTube, uploaded by Audiore. https://www.youtube.com/watch?v=bT_UP2iFtr0, accessed Sep. 23, 2020.
[2]Ibid.
[3]Ibid.
[4]Ibid.

[5] Ibid.
[6] Ibid.
[7] "Steve Harvey Quotes and Jokes." FunnyComedianQuotes. http://funnycomedianquotes.com/funny-steve-harvey-jokes-and-quotes.html, accessed Sep. 24, 2020.
[8] "The Original Kings of Comedy." YouTube, uploaded by Audiore. https://www.youtube.com/watch?v=bT_UP2iFtr0, accessed Sep. 23, 2020.
[9] Ibid.
[10] Ibid.
[11] Ibid.
[12] "Whoopi Goldberg: Direct from Broadway." YouTube, uploaded by Random Tubes, https://www.youtube.com/watch?v=rnWreiWF2nQ&t=5s, accessed Oct. 11, 2021.
[13] Ibid.
[14] Ibid.
[15] "Paul Mooney as Self, Negrodamus." IMDb. https://www.imdb.com/title/tt0353049/characters/nm0600763, accessed Oct. 30, 2020.
[16] "Paul Mooney Quotes." BrainyQuote. https://www.brainyquote.com/authors/paul-mooney-quotes, accessed Oct. 30, 2020.
[17] Ibid.
[18] "Paul Mooney Quotes and Sayings." inspiringquotes.us. https://www.inspiringquotes.us/author/8526-paul-mooney, accessed Oct. 30, 2020, accessed Oct. 30, 2020.
[19] "Paul Mooney 'The Godfather of Comedy' Dives into the Racial Divide." The Washington Post. https://www.washingtonpost.com/blogs/therootdc/post/paul-mooney-the-godfather-of-comedy-know-your-history--jesus-was-black-so-was-cleopatra/2012/07/12/gJQAFwSEgW_blog.html, accessed Oct. 29, 2020.
[20] "Paul Mooney-1-900-Blame-A-Nigger." https://songme.ru/song/5868982-1-900-blame-a-nigger-by-paul-mooney.
[21] "Nigger Raisins by Paul Mooney." Premium Live Music. https://www.livexlive.com/song/paul-mooney/nigger-raisins, accessed Oct. 30, 2020.
[22] Dance, Daryl Cumber, Honey, Hush! : An Anthology of African American Women's Humor. WW Norton & Co. 1998. p. 336.

ABOUT THE AUTHORS

We have a rather unique back story, most of which is set in upstate New York. We met on the first day of high school, brought together by the merger of two neighboring school districts. We ended up dating for all four years of high school, then went to different colleges and, as fate would have it, we ended up not seeing each other again for literally 40 years.

Tim's mom passed away a few years ago and Deb heard about it through the grapevine in Virginia Beach where she was teaching. She sent him a sympathy card, he wrote back, one thing led to another and Tim ended up coming down to Virginia Beach at the end of that school year to pick Deb up and bring her back home to New York.

The thing Deb remembers most from that courtship period when she was in Virginia, but longing to be back in New York, was that every day at school when she went to her mailbox, there was an envelope from Tim. And each one contained an original letter Deb had written to him 40 years ago. He had saved every one. His go-to line regarding that part of the story is to say, "Yeah, it took me a long time to play those cards!" Sometimes the best things in life are worth waiting for.

We got engaged on Deb's mother's birthday (December 4) and we got married on Tim's mother's birthday (June 12). Because we both have Native American ancestry, we had the ceremony performed at the Ganondagan Historic Site by the Native American leader there, as well as a former student of Tim's.

So how did we get into this writing gig? Well, as fate would have it, we happen to live right next door to the newspaper office in our town. After hearing some of our stories, the publisher of the paper, Chris Carosa, suggested we write about our background and share it with the community. So we started by telling the personal story of our relationship, and we haven't stopped writing since. Currently our weekly feature comprises the entire back page of the *Mendon-Honeoye Falls-Lima Sentinel* and we have now upped our production to include two more columns within the paper. Contributing to the community is a passion of ours.

We write about an eclectic variety of topics including entertainment, sports, travel, history and human interest. Chris Carosa, who we mentioned above, had been encouraging us to write a book since we first began writing for the paper. That first book came to fruition with the publication of *The Beatles, The Bible & Manson: Reflecting Back with 50 Years of Perspective* during the summer of 2019.

We followed up in 2020 with *Tit For Tat Exchanges ~ Tim & Deb's Greatest Hits* and in 2021 with *What's in a Name? ~ Your Geography Hall of Fame*, both of which we described in the "Acknowledgements" component in the beginning of this book. And at this point we hope you've just finished *Blacks Facts ~ An Ultimate Primer of the Historical and the Hysterical* and have enjoyed it so much you'll be interested in checking out the rest of our work.

Made in the USA
Middletown, DE
24 January 2022